SECOND EDITION

THE STUDENT LEADERSHIP CHALLENGE

Five Practices for Becoming an Exemplary Leader

James Kouzes and Barry Posner

Published by The Leadership Challenge®
A Wiley Brand
One Montgomery Street, Suite 1200, San Francisco, CA 94104-4594

www.leadershipchallenge.com

Cover design: Adrian Morgan

For additional copies or bulk purchases of this book or to learn more about The Leadership Challenge®, please contact us toll free at 1-866-888-5159 or by email at leadership@wiley.com.

Wiley also publishes its books in a variety of electronic formats and by print-on-demand. Some material included with standard print versions of this book may not be included in e-books or in print-on-demand. If the version of this book that you purchased references media such as a CD or DVD that was not included in your purchase, you may download this material at http://booksupport.wiley.com. For more information about Wiley products, visit www.wiley.com.

Library of Congress Cataloging-in-Publication Data has been applied for and is on file with the Library of Congress.

ISBN 978-1-118-39007-8 (paper); ISBN 978-1-118-60253-9 (ebk.); ISBN 978-1-118-60255-3 (ebk.)

Printed in the United States of America

PB Printing 10 9 8 7 6 5

Contents

Preface: Making Extraordinary Things Happen with Others xi

1 Introduction: When People Are at Their Best as Leaders 3

The Five Practices of Exemplary Leadership

PRACTICE 1: MODEL THE WAY

2 Commitment #1: Clarify Values 22

Find Your Voice

Affirm Shared Values

3 Commitment #2: Set the Example 40

Live the Shared Values

Teach Others to Model the Values

PRACTICE 2: INSPIRE A SHARED VISION

4 Commitment #3: Envision the Future 66

Imagine the Possibilities
Find a Common Purpose

5 Commitment #4: Enlist Others 89

Appeal to Common Ideals
Animate the Vision

PRACTICE 3: CHALLENGE THE PROCESS

6 Commitment #5: Search for Opportunities 114

Seize the Initiative
Exercise Outsight

7 Commitment #6: Experiment and Take Risks 136

Generate Small Wins
Learn from Experience

PRACTICE 4: ENABLE OTHERS TO ACT

8 Commitment #7: Foster Collaboration 164

Create a Climate of Trust
Facilitate Relationships

9 Commitment #8: Strengthen Others 186

Enhance Self-Determination

Coach for Competence and Confidence

PRACTICE 5: ENCOURAGE THE HEART

10 Commitment #9: Recognize Contributions 212

Expect the Best

Personalize Recognition

11 Commitment #10: Celebrate the Values and the Victories 234

Create a Spirit of Community

Get Personally Involved

12 A Call to Action for Young Leaders 257

Your Continuing Leadership Journey

Acknowledgments 269

About the Authors 273

Index 277

THE STUDENT LEADERSHIP PRACTICES INVENTORY® SELF ONLINE

If you purchased a new copy of this book, you will find a unique single-use access code for the Student Leadership Practices Inventory Self Online assessment in the back of it. Go to slpiself.studentleadershipchallenge.com and enter your code to take the inventory. If you purchased a used copy, or rented or borrowed a copy of this book, the code may already have been used, in which case you can purchase a new code at www.studentlpi.com/assess.

The Student Leadership Practices Inventory (Student LPI®) is the cornerstone of The Five Practices of Exemplary Leadership® model. Created by leadership educators James M. Kouzes and Barry Z. Posner, this powerful leadership development model approaches leadership as a measurable, learnable, and teachable set of behaviors, because everyone can be a leader—whether in a designated leadership role or not. The Student LPI offers you a method for accurately assessing your leadership skills based on The Five Practices of Exemplary Leadership, by measuring the frequency with which you engage in 30 behaviors that research shows lead to the best leadership outcomes.

Preface: Making Extraordinary Things Happen with Others

Leaders get people moving. They energize and mobilize. They take people to places they have never been before. The leadership challenge never goes away. In uncertain and turbulent times, accepting that challenge is the only antidote to chaos, stagnation, and disintegration. Times change, problems change, technologies change, and people change. Leadership endures.

Change is the province of leaders. It is the work of leaders to inspire people to do things differently, to struggle against uncertain odds, and to persevere toward a distant yet compelling image of a better future. Without leadership there would not be the extraordinary efforts necessary to solve existing problems and realize unimagined opportunities. We have today, at best, only faint clues of what the future may hold, but we are confident that without leadership the possibilities will neither be envisioned nor attained. This is as true for leaders in business and industry as it is true for you while you're still in school or preparing for your career.

THE STUDENT LEADERSHIP CHALLENGE

The Student Leadership Challenge is about how young leaders, people just like you, mobilize others to want to make extraordinary things happen. It's about the practices they use day to day. Leaders use these practices to transform values into actions, visions into realities, obstacles into innovations, separateness into solidarity, and risks into rewards. It's about leadership that creates the place in which people turn challenging opportunities into remarkable successes.

The publication of this second edition of *The Student Leadership Challenge* marks six years since the book was first published. We've continued over that time to research, consult, teach, and write about what young leaders do and how anyone, regardless of age, can learn to be a better leader. We're honored by the reception we've received in the education marketplace. While we and other authors regularly contribute new works, we are blessed that students, educators, and practitioners continue to find that *The Student Leadership Challenge* is still useful to them, both conceptually and practically, and that it stands the test of time.

We persist in asking today the same basic question we asked when we started our journey into understanding exemplary leadership: What did you do when you were at your personal best as a leader? One of the most typical and profound realizations from this reflection is, as one student explained: "Growing up, I assumed leaders had certain traits and qualities that I didn't seem to have. I thought there were 'natural' leaders who were born to lead. I thought leadership was the description of what these people did. When you asked me to describe my personal-best leadership experience, I found to my surprise, that I had those leadership abilities myself." Another student told us that "writing down and thinking through my personal-best experience really helped me identify my skills and areas for improvement." Still another student said that she learned "that anybody can be a leader. I had never considered myself a leader, but when I was needed to step up and deal with a situation, I was able to find the leader within me."

We've talked to thousands of young men and women, representing many educational institutions and youth organizations from many different places around the world. Their stories, and the behaviors and actions they've described, combined with those of thousands of other leaders, reveal The Five Practices of Exemplary Leadership® framework, which you can use to become a better, more effective leader. When leaders do their best, they Model the Way, Inspire a Shared Vision, Challenge the Process, Enable Others to Act, and Encourage the Heart. These are The Five Practices we have discovered by studying thousands of leaders, your age and older, around the world. And these are the practices we describe in great detail in this book.

The Student Leadership Challenge is evidence-based. The Five Practices are derived from research, and are illustrated with examples from real student leaders doing real things. With the second edition of this book, we update the research—both our own findings and those from other scholars around the globe. We report new stories, cases, examples, and illustrations of exactly what young people like you do when they are at their leadership best. Also, with this new edition we get the chance to be clearer about what is still important, throw out what's not, and add what we have learned that is new about young leaders. We get the chance to make concepts easier to understand so you can focus on applying what works. We get the chance to help you answer the call to be the best leader you can be.

The more we research and the more we write about leadership, the more confident we become that leadership is within the grasp of everyone and that opportunities for leadership are everywhere. No matter what your past experience is as a leader, we know that you have the capacity to lead if you choose to. Leadership is not about a position or title, as many young leaders presume. It is about a role you chose to take throughout your life—a role with the goal to make extraordinary things happen on a regular basis.

Of course, with each edition, we also get to address a new generation of emerging leaders. This motivates us to collect new stories, examine new research findings, and talk with people who have recently demonstrated extraordinary leadership. It encourages us to perform a litmus test of the relevance of our results: Does this model of leadership still make sense? If we started out all over again, would we find new leadership practices? Would we eliminate any of the practices? In this regard, we are aided by the ongoing empirical data provided by the online version of the Leadership Practices Inventory (LPI) and Student Leadership Practices Inventory (Student LPI). These inventories, which assess The Five Practices, provide several hundred thousand responses annually, and keep us on guard and on target in identifying the behaviors that make a difference.

Also, with this new edition, we get a chance to speak again with those of you who might have read the earlier edition of *The Student Leadership Challenge* or our classic work, *The Leadership Challenge*. If you're reading this book for the first time, welcome. If you are returning to it again, welcome back. We are thrilled you have chosen to explore your potential to lead. We know that you can, we know that your leadership matters, and we know that building your leadership capacity will shape our world for years to come.

In reading this new edition we hope you get a deep understanding of The Five Practices and what they look like in action today. In using The Five Practices in your life, we hope you continue to grow, to develop yourself as a leader, and to make a difference. You are in a stage of life where those opportunities to make a difference are all around you: in your schools, youth groups, clubs and organizations, athletics, classes, and your community. As you take advantage of these opportunities to learn and lead, others will begin to take note and look to you to help them figure out how they can develop themselves as leaders. You don't just owe it to yourself to become the best leader you can possibly be. You have a responsibility to others as well. You may not yet know it, but people all around you need you to do your best and be your best.

A GUIDE FOR STUDENT LEADERS

How do you get other people to want to follow you? How do you get other people, by free will and free choice, to move forward together on a common purpose? How do you get people energized to work hard together to get something done that everyone can feel proud of? These are the important questions we address in *The Student Leadership Challenge*. Think of this book as a guide to take along on your leadership journey. Think of it as a manual you can consult when you want advice and guidance on how to get extraordinary things done. Think of it as a place to go when you're not really sure what to do as a leader.

In Chapter 1 we introduce our leadership framework by sharing a Personal Best Leadership Experience—a case study about how one leader acted on her values and pursued a path of commitment and action to make a difference for the environmental future of her country. We provide an overview of The Five Practices of Exemplary Leadership, summarizing the findings about what leaders do when they are at their best, and show how these actions make a difference.

The ten chapters that follow describe the Ten Commitments of Leadership—the essential behaviors—that leaders use to get extraordinary things done. We also explain the fundamental principles that support each of The Five Practices. A great thing about accepting and adopting this framework of leadership is that it isn't difficult to understand, doesn't cost any money or require anybody else's permission. It simply requires a commitment from you and ongoing practice to make them habits in your life.

In Chapter 12, we offer a call to action to accept personal responsibility to be a role model for leadership and to make these leadership practices part of your daily life, in all aspects of your life. The first place to look for leadership is within you. Accepting the leadership challenge requires practice, reflection, humility, and making the most of every opportunity to make a difference. In the end, we conclude: Leadership is not an affair of the head. Leadership is an affair of the heart. You'll see what we mean by that and how that applies to you in the final chapter.

We recommend that you first read Chapter 1, but after that there is no right order to proceeding through the rest of this book. Go wherever your interests are. We wrote *The Student Leadership Challenge* to support you in your leadership development. Just remember that each practice is essential. Although you might skip around in the book, you can't skip doing any of these fundamentals of leadership.

Finally, technology allows us to offer you insights beyond those in this book. On our website, http://www.studentleadershipchallenge.com, you can find out more about how you can work on The Five Practices with tried-and-true tools in addition to new ones. You can also learn what others are doing in schools and youth organizations as well as more about our research.

The domain of leaders is the future. The leader's unique legacy is the creation of valued organizations and groups that survive over time. The most significant contribution leaders make is the long-term development of people so they can adapt, change, prosper, and grow. This includes groups you can lead now as well as those you will find yourself leading throughout your life: community organizations, clubs, religious congregations, and even your own family.

We hope this book contributes to the success you have working with others, to the creation of new ideas and enterprises, to the renewal of healthy schools and prosperous communities, and to greater respect and understanding in the world. We also fervently hope that it enriches your life.

Leadership is important in every sector, every school, every community, every organization, and in every country. It is important right now, wherever you are in your life, no matter what stage or what level of experience you have in school or your community. More exemplary leaders are needed right now, and more than ever leaders who can unite us and ignite us. There is so much extraordinary work that needs to be done, and so many opportunities ahead.

Leadership development is fundamentally self-development. Meeting the leadership challenge is a personal—and a daily—challenge for everyone. We know that if you have the will and the way to lead, you can. You have to supply the will. We'll do our best to keep supplying the way.

James M. Kouzes
Orinda, California
Barry Z. Posner
Berkeley, California

THE STUDENT LEADERSHIP CHALLENGE

Leadership defined:

Leadership is the art of mobilizing others to want to struggle for shared aspirations.

1

Introduction: When People Are at Their Best as Leaders

You don't have to be a superstar or an overachiever to lead; you just need to care about something and do something about it. It doesn't have to be big, just do something. Every great change starts small. You just need to take that first step, not because you necessarily have the authority or responsibility, but because you care.

—Elliese Judge, Panama City, Panama

This was the thinking that got Elliese Judge going. When she was nineteen, she helped start a nonprofit organization called Arvita that continues to focus on improving environmental awareness through organic recycling and sustainable reforestation.[1]

Elliese was born in Australia and moved with her family to Panama when she was fourteen. When she got a part-time job at a Panama City bank she wanted to recycle some of the papers in the office. "While I was working there," Elliese told us, "I realized how inconvenient it was to recycle and how nobody seemed to think it was important. There was no truck or pick-up; you had to take everything to the landfill yourself and nobody wanted to be bothered."

When Elliese went to the landfill she met some of the people in the community who were living right next to it. The whole neighborhood smelled terrible and this bothered her deeply. She realized that her family and others like it were producing a great deal of waste that was being dumped directly next to these people. That didn't feel right. Her new perspective on the whole cycle of waste in the country deepened her belief that this was a significant issue, a problem that needed to be addressed. So she decided to do something about it, first at the bank, then in her own home, and from there the idea started to grow, bit by bit.

As Elliese talked about it more with her friends, she found there were others who shared her passion. When she met Milko Dilgado while camping with friends at an Ecological Music Festival, they quickly discovered they were both passionate about the environment and eager to do something to make a difference in protecting and restoring it. So they began a very simple organic recycling project in Elliese's backyard: a simple worm farm they started from scratch with a pound of worms. From that modest beginning their vision for a more eco-friendly Panama began to take form. As they looked more deeply into all the organic waste being produced they discovered that it could be used to regenerate growth in deforested areas. They saw a connection between the issues of bad waste management and the rampant deforestation throughout Panama that their project could address. They kept asking themselves: "Once we recycle all this organic waste, turning it into fertilizer, can't we find a way to put it to good use?"

Elliese and Milko started visiting restaurants, sharing with them the negative impacts that restaurant waste had on people and the environment, and explaining the positive impacts it could have in reforestation. They believed that by showing people a different picture of how things might work to help Panama, they could influence restaurant owners, employees, and customers to act in more responsible ways towards the environment. The idea was that through Arvita, restaurants would be able to play a part in restoring Panama's forests by separating their organic waste and donating it to the foundation's recycling effort. Arvita would take the restaurants' organic waste and turn it into compost, fertilizers, and raw material for their worm farm. The products would then be used to support the planting of native trees and bringing animals back to deforested areas. "Our vision," explains Elliese, "is that every restaurant in Panama will be eco-friendly, do organic recycling, and support sustainable reforestation."

Starting Arvita was not without challenges. Environmental awareness and consciousness were relatively low in Panama. There were few young people driving change of any sort in Panama to serve as role models, and Elliese and her colleagues encountered skepticism about whether people their age could have a significant impact on environmental issues. But Elliese and Milko recognized that each time they connected with a restaurant, explaining the degrading effects of their waste on the environment and the positive change possible from recycling organic waste, the direct connection made a difference, and so they continued promoting environmental awareness restaurant by restaurant.

Elliese's story speaks to a fundamental question: When does leadership begin? The answer is that leaders seize the moment. Elliese saw an opportunity and took it, first in the bank where she had a part-time job, and then with Milko with the backyard worm farm. Those fairly small opportunities transformed into something much greater. Elliese and Milko didn't wait for someone to appoint either of them as "the" leader. They recognized an issue, had a passion for it, found others with a similar vision, and just got started. Then they kept going. Although leadership, just like any other skill in life, can be learned and strengthened through coaching and practice, you don't have to wait for that support and preparation to happen before you start to lead. In fact, no amount of coaching or practice can make much of a difference if you don't care about doing or making something better than it currently is.

Everyone has the capacity to lead whether or not they are in a formal position of authority or even part of an organized group.[2] That's what we mean when we say leadership is everyone's business. It is not about being a president, captain, director, editor, CEO, general, or prime minister. It's not about celebrity, wealth, or even age. It's not about your family background or the neighborhood you come from. It's about knowing your values and those of the people around you and taking the steps, however small, to make what you do every day demonstrate that you live by those values.

As we continue to learn from Elliese's leadership experience, it is clear that leadership is about transforming values and goals into action. The operational side of bringing an effort like Arvita to life was brand-new territory for Elliese and Milko. They started with lots of passion and plans but turning them into a reality seemed overwhelming. "We didn't know where to start," Elliese said. "We had tons of energy and ideas, but making it happen seemed overwhelming." Elliese told us about several things she and Milko did that helped them get going. For example, they knew enough to realize that there was much they didn't know, and so they took the time to visit farms in the area that were doing sustainable agriculture, asked a lot of questions, and learned from the farmers themselves. They knew that they couldn't get everyone to change right away, or to care about the environment like they did, so they took a one-step-at-a-time approach. To start, they found one restaurant that was willing to experiment with their recycling program. Armed with that success, they lobbied more to join. They found an arborist who agreed to help them design a reforestation plan for half his usual fee because he was so taken with the foundation's plans and the determination he saw in Elliese and Milko to have those plans succeed. They produced a documentary film to promote

Arvita and environmental awareness; in the process they interviewed political figures and other environmental entrepreneurs in Panama, thereby starting a network of support for the foundation. All the while they worked hard to get more young people interested in working with them as volunteers.

In addition, they each took the time at the beginning to write out their personal reasons for wanting to build the foundation. Elliese said: "That helped a lot because we now understand what motivates and challenges us individually and collectively and we can keep that in our minds as we go about our business." They also made it a point to provide encouragement to everyone involved in the foundation and its various projects, because they realize how important such support is in helping everyone to keep going as they struggle to reach their aspirations. What's more, Elliese told us, she and Milko appreciate that there isn't a single leader in their organization; everyone takes the lead in different ways. For example, Milko is the one who generally gets out to the environmental fairs around Panama to talk about Arvita. He is not necessarily the one you'd think should do that, Elliese says, because she is, by her own admission, "the talker." Milko is rather shy and reserved and has a stutter. But when they go to the fairs, he's the one who is most passionate in speaking and getting people excited about what they are trying to do. "He takes this risk," Elliese points out, "and I let him know how much I appreciate it. We all tell one other that when we do things that move us forward. We're a team."

Early in their partnership, Elliese and Milko realized the value of acknowledging how others contribute to the success of their organization. They understood how recognizing the part that Arvita volunteers and business partners play strengthens relationships and builds a positive reputation for their organization and the values it espouses. For example, Elliese makes it a goal in every interaction to treat with respect the people they work with. She told us about how she once gave someone a great big "thank you" even though that person had ignored her for forty-five minutes before attending to her business. Elliese observes that "people will almost always help you if you make them feel respected, valued, and part of something. I showed that person my gratitude for her time and let her see how her actions were not just helping me, but helping our country."

Elliese and Milko's experience shows something we have seen over and over: leadership begins when you find something you care about. It doesn't necessarily require an organization, a budget, a hierarchy, a position, or a title. "The most important thing," Elliese says, "is to believe in yourself and not be afraid to take a risk. If you believe in something passionately chances are there are others who do as well. Go for it, even if it fails you'll know you tried and you'll learn something. Nothing wrong with that!"

Of course there are challenges, but leaders like Elliese and Milko face them one at a time and make progress in their unique way. Leadership potential is lost when people are convinced that there is just one straight path and one certain type of person that is destined for success. You don't need to be perfect to start anything; you simply need passion, initiative, and the desire to make a difference.

THE FIVE PRACTICES OF EXEMPLARY LEADERSHIP

In undertaking the establishment of their nonprofit organization, Elliese seized an opportunity to make a difference. And although her story is exceptional, it is not unique. We've been conducting original research all over the globe for more than thirty years, and we've discovered that such achievements are actually commonplace. When we ask young leaders to tell us about their Personal-Best

Leadership Experiences—experiences that they believe are their individual standards of excellence—there are thousands of success stories just like this one.[3] We've found them everywhere, and it proves that leadership knows no ethnic or cultural borders, no racial or religious bounds, no differences between young and old. Leaders reside in every city and every country, in every function and every organization. Exemplary leadership can be found everywhere we look.

After analyzing these leadership experiences, we discovered, and continue to find, that regardless of the times or setting, people who guide others along new journeys follow surprisingly similar paths. Though each experience was unique in its individual expression, there were clearly identifiable behaviors and actions that made a difference. When getting extraordinary things done with others, leaders engage in what we call The Five Practices of Exemplary Leadership:

- Model the Way
- Inspire a Shared Vision
- Challenge the Process
- Enable Others to Act
- Encourage the Heart

These practices are not the private property of the people we studied. Nor do they belong to a few select shining stars. Leadership is not about personality or popularity and it's not about age; it's about behavior. The Five Practices are available to anyone who accepts the leadership challenge. This includes you! The leadership challenge is the challenge of taking people to places they have never been before, and doing something that has never been done before. It is the challenge of moving beyond the ordinary to the extraordinary, regardless of your setting, environment, or circumstances.

The Five Practices have passed the test of time, even though the *context* of leadership has changed dramatically while we have been doing our research. Technological advances, shifts in the world's economies, and social changes all influence the context in which you will lead. We also know that such changes will continue at a rapid pace. And yet, while the leadership environment has changed, the *content* of leadership has not changed much at all. Our research tells us that the fundamental behaviors, actions, and practices of effective leaders have remained essentially the same and are as relevant today as they were when we first began our study of exemplary leadership.

When you explore The Five Practices of Exemplary Leadership in depth in Chapters 2 through 11, you'll find examples from the real-life experiences of people like Elliese and Milko who have accepted the leadership challenge. But first, let's begin with a brief overview of each of The Five Practices.

Model the Way

Titles are granted, but it's your behavior that earns you respect. This sentiment was shared across all the cases we collected. Exemplary leaders know that if they want to gain commitment and achieve the highest standards, they must be models of the behavior they expect of others.

To effectively Model the Way you must first be clear about your own guiding principles. You must *clarify values by finding your voice.* When you understand who you are and what your values are, then you can give voice to those values. Finding your voice encourages others to do the same, paving the way for understanding. But *your* values aren't the only values that matter. In every team, organization, and community, there are others who also feel strongly about matters of principle. As a leader, you also must help identify and *affirm the shared values* of the group. Leaders' actions are far more important than their words when others want to determine how serious leaders really are about what they say. Words and actions must be consistent. Exemplary leaders *set the example by aligning actions with shared values*. Through their daily actions they demonstrate their deep commitment to their beliefs and to the groups they are part of. One of the best ways to prove that something is important is by doing it yourself and setting an example, by "walking the talk."

Inspire a Shared Vision

People describe their personal-best leadership experiences as times when they imagined an exciting, better future for themselves and others. They had visions and dreams of what *could* be. They had absolute and total personal belief in those dreams, and they were confident in their abilities to find a way to make extraordinary things happen. Every organization, every social movement, every big event begins with a dream. The dream, or vision, is the force that creates the future.

Leaders *envision the future by imagining exciting and ennobling possibilities*. You need to make something happen, to change the way things are, to create something new and exciting. In some ways, this means having a real sense of the past and also a clear vision of what the results should look like before starting any project regardless of size and scope, much as an architect draws a blueprint or an engineer builds a model. But you can't command commitment to a new future, as exciting as it may seem to you; you have to inspire it. You have to *enlist others in a common vision by appealing to shared aspirations*. You can do this by talking to others and, even more important, listening to them to understand what motivates them. You enlist others by helping them feel they are part of something that matters, something that will make a difference, and something that you all believe is important to accomplish together. When you express your enthusiasm and excitement for the vision, you ignite a similar passion in others.

Challenge the Process

Challenge is the spark for greatness. Every single personal-best leadership case involved a change from the status quo. Not one person claimed to have achieved a personal best by keeping things the same. The challenge might have been launching an innovative new event, tackling a problem in a different way, rethinking a service their group provides, creating a successful campaign to get students to join an environmental program, starting up a brand-new student group or team, achieving a revolutionary turnaround of a university policy, or getting a new event under way with the intent that it become a new school tradition. It could also be dealing with daily obstacles and challenges, such as finding ways to solve a group conflict or attack a major class project.

Leaders are willing to step out into the unknown. But leaders aren't the only creators or originators of new ideas, projects, services, or processes. In fact, it's more likely that they're not. Innovation comes more from listening than from telling. You must constantly be looking outside of yourself and your group for new and innovative ways to do things. You need to *search for opportunities by seizing the initiative and by looking outward for innovative ways to improve.* Because innovation and change involve *experimenting and taking risks*, your major contributions as a leader will be to encourage experimentation and idea generation, to recognize and support the best of those ideas, and to be willing to challenge the system.

Mistakes and failures will be inevitable, but proceed anyway. One way of dealing with the potential risks and failures of experimentation is *by constantly generating small wins and learning from experience.* There's a strong correlation between the actions of leaders and the process of learning: the best leaders are the simply the best learners.[4] Leaders are constantly learning from their errors and failures and helping the groups they are part of to do the same. Life is the leader's laboratory, and exemplary leaders use it to conduct as many experiments as possible.

Enable Others to Act

A grand dream doesn't come true through the actions of a single person. It requires a team effort. It requires solid trust and strong relationships. It requires deep competence and cool confidence. It requires group collaboration[5] and individual accountability. No leader ever got anything extraordinary done by working solo. True leadership is a team effort.

Leaders *foster collaboration by building trust and facilitating relationships*. They believe in the potential of others and the power of collaboration. They act on those beliefs by bringing people together and trusting that old truth that "together we achieve more." Leaders do what it takes to give people the confidence and competence they need to face the challenges ahead, to support each other and move together toward success. They engage all those who must make the project work—and in some way, all who must live with the results. People don't perform at their best nor do they stick around for very long if you make them feel unimportant, weak, or alienated. By promoting the development of personal power and ownership, and by giving your power away, you make others stronger and more capable. When you *strengthen others by increasing self-determination and developing competence* they are more likely to give it their all and exceed their own expectations. By focusing on serving the needs of others, and not your own, you build people's trust in you as a leader. And the more people trust their leaders, and each other, the more they take risks, make changes, and keep organizations, projects, teams, and movements alive. When people are trusted and have more choice in how they do their work, more authority, and more information, they're much more likely to use their energies to produce extraordinary results. Through that relationship, leaders turn others into leaders themselves.

Encourage the Heart

Achieving great change is a long and bumpy road. People become exhausted, frustrated, disillusioned and are often tempted to give up or disengage. They may ask themselves, "Is all this work really worth it?" Genuine acts of caring give people the heart to keep going.

Leaders *recognize contributions by showing appreciation for individual excellence.* It can be one to one or with many people. It can come from dramatic gestures or simple actions. It's part of your responsibility as a leader to show appreciation for people's contributions and to create a place where people can *celebrate the values and victories by creating a spirit of community.* Recognition and celebration aren't necessarily about fun and games, though there is a lot of fun and there are a lot of games when people encourage the hearts of others. Neither are they necessarily about formal awards. Ceremonies designed to create the "official" recognition can be effective, but only if they are perceived as sincere. Encouragement is valuable and important because it connects what people have done with the successes the group has to celebrate. Make sure that people appreciate how their behavior is connected with their values and the values of the group. Celebrations and rituals, when done sincerely and from the heart (as opposed to doing them just because you have to or because they have always been done), give a group a strong sense of identity and team spirit that can carry it through tough times.

The Ten Commitments of Exemplary Leadership

The Five Practices of Exemplary Leadership are the core leadership competencies that emerged from analyzing thousands of personal-best

The Five Practices and Ten Commitments of Exemplary Leadership

Model the Way

1. Clarify values by finding your voice and affirming shared values.
2. Set the example by aligning actions with shared values.

Inspire a Shared Vision

3. Envision the future by imagining exciting and ennobling possibilities.
4. Enlist others in a common vision by appealing to shared aspirations.

Challenge the Process

5. Search for opportunities by seizing the initiative and by looking outward for innovative ways to improve.
6. Experiment and take risks by constantly generating small wins and learning from experience.

Enable Others to Act

7. Foster collaboration by building trust and facilitating relationships.
8. Strengthen others by increasing self-determination and developing competence.

Encourage the Heart

9. Recognize contributions by showing appreciation for individual excellence.
10. Celebrate the values and victories by creating a spirit of community.

leadership cases. When leaders are doing their best they Model the Way, Inspire a Shared Vision, Challenge the Process, Enable Others to Act, and Encourage the Heart.

Embedded in The Five Practices are behaviors that can serve as the basis for learning to lead. We call these The Ten Commitments of Exemplary Leadership. They focus on actions you need to apply to yourself and that you need to take with others.

These ten commitments serve as the guide for explaining, understanding, appreciating, and learning how leaders get extraordinary things done with others, and we discuss each of them in depth in Chapters 2 through 11. But, what's the evidence that these practices, commitments, and behaviors really matter? Do they truly make a difference in how we lead others to create change? The research we've done makes the case that they do.

The Five Practices Make a Difference

The truth is that exemplary leader behavior makes a profoundly positive difference in people's commitment and the way they do their work. In getting a higher level of commitment and performance, student leaders who more frequently use The Five Practices of Exemplary Leadership are considerably more effective than those who don't.

In other words, the way young leaders behave is what explains how hard people work and how engaged they feel in the work they are doing. Our research tells us that the more you use The Five Practices of Exemplary Leadership, the more likely it is that you'll have a positive influence on others and on their efforts and commitment to their group, team, campus, or cause. That's what all the data adds up to. If you want to have a significant impact on people, on organizations, and on communities, you need to invest in learning the behaviors that enable you to become the very best leader you can be.

Here's something else we found from the constituents of student leaders: the more frequently they reported that student leaders were engaging in The Five Practices the more they reported being satisfied with that person's leadership and proud to tell others that they were working with this leader. In addition, they were more likely to feel appreciated and valued, to agree that their efforts were making a difference, and to feel that they were highly productive. And, by the way, the leaders benefited significantly because their constituents (typically their peers) viewed them as more effective as a direct function of their use of The Five Practices. Constituents who indicated that the leadership skills of their student leader were not very developed compared with peers indicated that the use of The Five Practices by these student leaders was nearly 35–50 percent lower than reported about more effective student leaders. Our research also revealed something else that's extremely important: the effective use of The Five Practices is not affected by gender, ethnicity, age, or year in school.[6]

To sum it all up: what matters as a leader is how you behave.

You Make a Difference

It's very clear that engaging in The Five Practices of Exemplary Leadership makes a significant difference—no matter who you are or what you are leading. How you behave as a leader matters, and it matters a lot. It makes a difference. You make a difference. We believe it is the right, and even the responsibility, of all young people to look into their hearts, determine what they believe in, and by acting on that belief make the world a better place. In the chapters that follow, we'll provide you the ideas, tool, and techniques that will serve you well on any leadership journey.

NOTES

1. Unless otherwise noted, all stories and quotations are from student leaders around the world who shared with us, in their own words, their personal-best leadership experiences, their most admired leaders, and the lessons they have learned about leadership. Their stories are used with their permission. Many will have moved on, and the organizations in which some of their personal-best experiences occurred may no longer exist by the time you read this, but the details on their roles, organizations, and experiences were accurate at the time of this writing.
2. When we use the term *group* we mean any collective organization a student is a member of or is leading: an athletic team, a club or common-interest group, any specialized activity or project, an academic team, or even a class group. We also use the word *leaders* to refer to students we have studied, not just students in formal leadership positions but students who have taken the challenge and worked with others to make extraordinary things happen in groups to which they belong.
3. Visit http://www.studentleadershipchallenge.com for continuing updates on personal-best leadership stories from young leaders around the world. For detailed information on our research methodology, the theory and evidence behind The Five Practices of Exemplary Leadership, our research methodology, our personal-best questionnaire, the psychometric properties of our Leadership Practices Inventory (LPI) and reports on our analysis of our data, please see the research section of our website: http://www.leadershipchallenge.com/WileyCDA/Section/id-131060.html.
4. J. M. Kouzes and B. Z. Posner, *The Truth About Leadership: The No-Fads, Heart-of-the-Matter Facts You Need to Know* (San Francisco: Jossey-Bass, 2010).
5. Throughout this book we use *cooperate* and *collaborate* synonymously. Their dictionary definitions are very similar. In *Merriam-Webster's Collegiate Dictionary*, Tenth Edition (2001), the first definition of *cooperate* is "To act or work with another or others: act together" (p. 254). The first definition of *collaborate* is "To work jointly with others or together esp. in an intellectual endeavor" (p. 224).
6. B. Z. Posner, "The Impact of Gender, Ethnicity, School Setting, and Experience on Student Leadership: Does It Really Matter?" Paper presented

at the Western Academy of Management, Santa Fe, NM, March, 2013. See also B. Z. Posner, "Effectively Measuring Student Leadership," *Administrative Sciences* 2, no. 4 (2012): 221–234, doi:10.3390/admsci2040221; and B. Z. Posner, "What Does the Research Show About Student Leadership?" Paper presented at The Leadership Challenge Forum, San Diego, CA, August, 2010.

PRACTICE 1

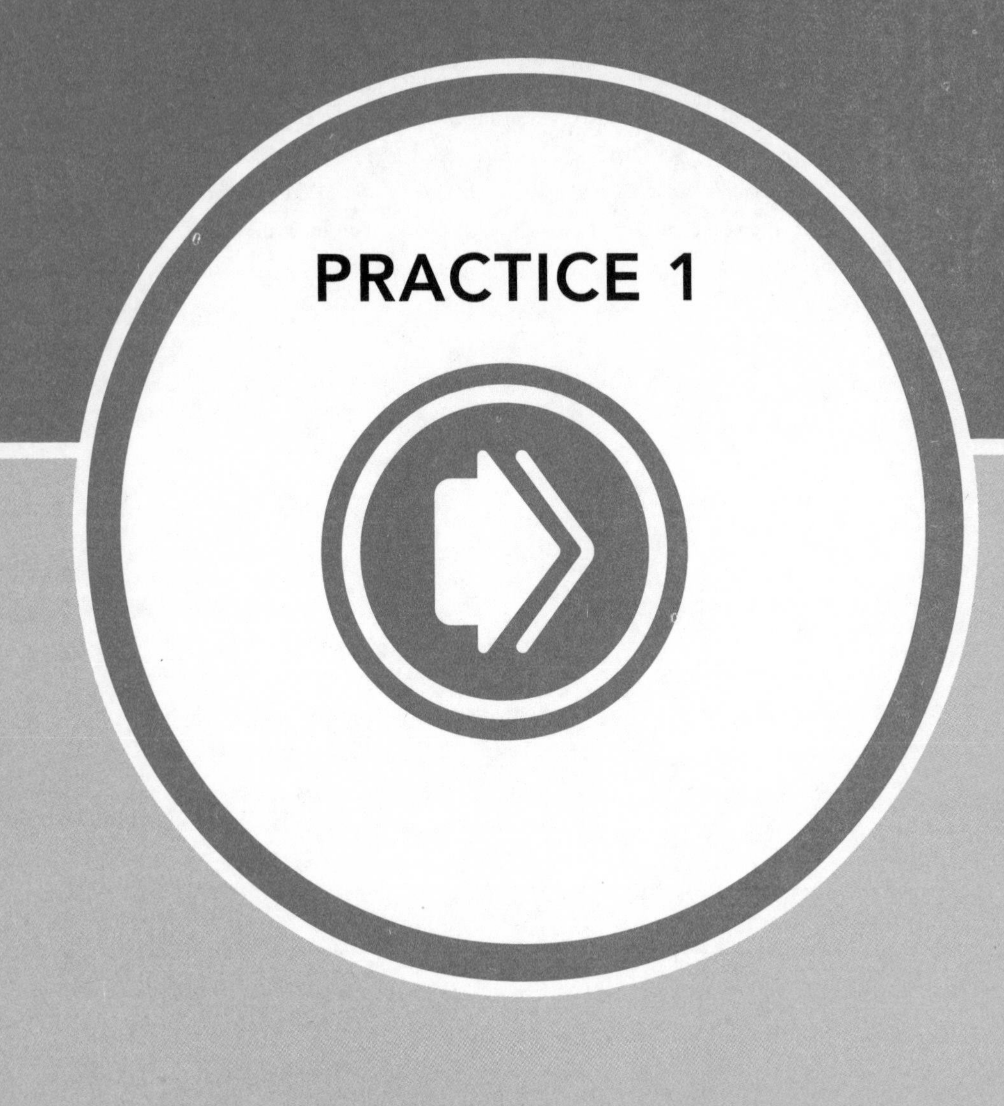

Model the Way

The first step you must take along the path to becoming an exemplary leader is inward. It's a step toward discovering who you are and what you believe in. We refer to that process as *clarifying values by finding your voice*. You must discover the principles that guide your decisions and actions. And you must find a way to express a leadership philosophy in your own words, not in someone else's.

But as a leader you don't just speak for yourself. You also speak for the groups, teams, and organizations to which you belong, and even for your communities. Leadership is a dialogue, not a monologue. Therefore, you must reach out to others. You must understand and appreciate their values and find a way to confirm and support the values you all share. As a leader you need to build unity, not force it. You must give people reasons to care, not simply orders to follow.

Leaders stand up for their beliefs. They practice what they preach. They show others by their actions that they live by the values they claim. They also ensure that others stand by the values that have been agreed upon. It is consistency between words and actions that builds credibility.

In the next two chapters, we take a look at how you as a leader must:

- **Clarify Values by finding your voice and affirming shared values.**
- **Set the Example by aligning actions with shared values.**

2

Commitment #1: Clarify Values

"Hi, I'm your new leader."

Imagine that someone approaches you with this proclamation. What is the first question you want to ask this person? We've posed this scenario to thousands of people, and the most common thing they say they want to know is "Who are you?" More than likely this is one of the questions you'd most want to ask someone who's your new leader. If it is, then doesn't it make sense that "Who are you?" is the first question you should be able to answer for yourself? Finding that answer is where every leadership journey begins.

When Grant Hillestad joined an organization called Students Stay Leaders Forever (STLF), he soon found himself on a "Pay It Forward Tour," one of STLF's community service road trips that go from city to city doing different service projects. Students travel on a chartered bus to visit cities large and small to learn about a variety of social issues; the idea is that in the process they will discover more about themselves, their own community, and the world. This experience was transformative for Grant.

Although he had been active in Boy Scouts, became an Eagle Scout, was involved with Student Council, and was in the National Honor Society, Grant felt he was doing these things for all the wrong reasons. He had pursued these activities to be "cool," acting more like a follower than a leader. His first "Pay It Forward Tour" changed all that. "That trip showed me that I didn't need to try to fit in," he told us, "that it's just so much more important to be yourself. If you can trust in yourself, listen to and believe in yourself, you can be a leader and make a difference. That was huge. It really changed who I was as a person."

When Grant started college he was eager to start an STLF chapter there to help expose students to that kind of experience, but he realized it wasn't going to be easy. He didn't know anyone very well, STLF wasn't established in the area high schools, and he had no experience in creating a student organization. What he did have was a strong belief in the value of the program and a strong belief in himself. He started by talking openly and honestly with others about the value he saw in STLF, and not long after he was able to gain enough support to have the organization recognized on his campus.

That was a positive first step but getting students to actually join a road trip was another challenge. The first one was going to happen over spring break, plus it would be a lot of hard work and cost the students money. Grant told us, "Friends would say things like, 'You want me to *pay* to go and *work* during spring break. Are you nuts?'"

> I knew what they were feeling; they wanted to do what everyone else was doing for spring break and many were nervous about the trip and all the unknowns. I just kept telling people how much my trips had meant to me, what we accomplished, and what I learned about myself and people in communities different from my own.

Grant discovered that others needed the time to figure out how the trip would mesh with their own values; then they could each take the first step and make the sacrifices required to participate in STLF. Once they did, the road trip was a big success. It began as an experience for twenty-seven strangers and finished as an adventure for twenty-seven best friends. The students discovered individually and collectively the deep value of going into new places, facing very challenging situations, and working together to get something done to help others. Grant said that they also learned a lot about themselves.

> I see the leadership potential in so many students and there's something holding them back; they're afraid and don't want to stick out. And it is scary. When you are your own self, not knowing whether you'll be accepted or not, that's when you're the most vulnerable, but that's also when you can connect to the most people. You've got to take a chance to show your values. You can't be afraid to stand up for what you believe in. If you do, then others may stand up as well, and that's how you discover what you care about as a group.

The personal-best leadership cases we've collected are, at their core, the stories of people like Grant who were clear about their personal values and understood how this clarity gave them the courage to navigate difficult situations and make tough choices. People expect their leaders to speak out on matters of values and conscience, to be clear about what matters to them. But to speak out you have to know what to speak about. To stand up for your beliefs, you have to know the beliefs you stand for. To walk the talk, you have to have a talk to walk. To do what you say, you have to know what you want to say. To earn and sustain personal credibility, you must first be able to clearly articulate deeply held beliefs.

Model the Way is the first of The Five Practices of Exemplary Leadership we discuss in this book, and one of the commitments you have to make in order to effectively Model the Way is to Clarify Values. In beginning your leadership journey it's essential that you:

- **Find your voice**
- **Affirm shared values**

To become a credible leader you first have to fully comprehend the deeply held beliefs—the values, standards, ethics, and ideals—that drive you. You have to freely and honestly choose the principles you will use to guide your decisions and actions. Then you have to genuinely express yourself. By *genuinely* we mean that you communicate in a way that truly portrays who you are as a person and as a leader. You have to authentically communicate your beliefs in ways that clearly represent who you are so that people can know you—the real you, not some portrayal of who you think you should be.

However, leaders aren't just speaking for themselves when they talk about the values that should guide decisions and actions. When leaders passionately express a commitment to learning or innovation or service or some other value, those leaders aren't just saying, "*I* believe in this." They're also making a commitment for an entire group. They're saying, "*We all* believe in this." Therefore, leaders must not only be clear about their own personal guiding principles, but they must also make sure that there's agreement on a set of shared values among everyone they lead. And they must hold others accountable to those values and standards.

FIND YOUR VOICE

How do you want to be known as a person? How do you want to be thought of as a leader? What would you say if someone asked you those questions? Are you prepared right now to answer them? If you aren't, you should be. And if you are, you need to think about them every single day.

Before you can become a credible leader—one who connects "what you say" with "what you do"—you first have to find your voice. If you can't find your voice, you'll end up sounding like someone else is talking for you. We've all known people who "fake it," who try to sound like someone else, or try to convince you of something they don't really mean. When that happens, there is a disconnect; there's that little inner voice that tells you not to completely buy into what is being said. If the words you speak are not your words but someone else's, you won't be consistent, in the long term, in what you say and what you do. You won't have the credibility or trustworthiness to successfully lead others.

To find your voice, you have to explore your inner self. You have to discover what you care about, what defines you, and what makes you who you are. You can only be authentic when you lead according to the principles that matter most to you. Otherwise you're just putting on an act. Consider Angel Accosta. Angel works for an organization called College for Every Student (CFES), a nonprofit organization that raises the academic aspirations and performance of low-income kids so that they can prepare for, gain access to, and succeed in college.

Angel is the fifth of six children raised by a single mother from the Dominican Republic who worked multiple jobs and saved enough to bring her whole family to the United States in pursuit of the American Dream. "I was the first one in my family to graduate from high school, let alone go to college," Angel told us. "And it wasn't easy."

> I had always loved to read, but I was part of the hip-hop culture and intellectual pursuits were laughed at. My friends made fun of me if I talked about the books I was reading. There was a lot of pressure to just stay down.

Angel also faced a lot of pressure from his family. They were so excited about his potential that they thought they knew what path he should take. When Angel decided to major in Anthropology, there were some long and hard conversations, but in the end Angel's family supported him and he kept going. "My family's values have always been 'never say never,'" Angel said, "and I found my way. So now I am helping my nieces find theirs. It's tough, but I've been there and

I know what they are facing. When I tell them my story they seem to listen a little more. They believe me."

To be most effective, leaders must learn to find the voice that represents who they are. When you have clarified your values and found your voice, you will also find the inner confidence necessary to express ideas, choose a direction, make tough decisions, act with determination, support others, and be able to take charge of your life—rather than copying others.

Let Your Values Guide You

Values influence every aspect of your life: your moral judgments; your responses to others; your commitments to your family, friends, school, and community; and your personal goals. Values set the boundaries for the hundreds of decisions and choices you make every day, consciously and subconsciously. And believe us: you make hundreds of decisions every day. Usually people don't seriously consider choices that are outside their value system. It just doesn't feel right to them. But sometimes a "whatever" attitude kicks in and they make poor choices. The question is, can you recognize when that attitude is kicking in? Can you stop yourself from giving in to it and instead listen to the voice in your head that knows "this doesn't feel right"? We believe the best chances of this happening are when your internal voice is loud and clear.

Values constitute your personal "bottom line." They serve as guides to the actions you take. They inform the priorities you set and the decisions you make. They tell you when to say yes and when to say no. They also help you explain the choices you make and why you made them. If you believe, for instance, that diversity makes things better, then you should know what to do if people with differing views keep getting cut off when they offer up fresh ideas. If you value working together over individual achievement, then you'll know what to do when your teammate goes for the shot and ignores the better pass. If you value independence and initiative over conformity and obedience, you'll be more likely to challenge what a good friend or someone of authority says if you think it's wrong. All of the most critical decisions a leader makes involve values.

As Angel's experience illustrates, values are guides. They supply you with a compass by which to navigate the course of your daily life. Clarity of values is essential to knowing which way is north, south, east, and west. The clearer you are about your values, the easier it is for you and for everyone else in your group to stay on the chosen path and commit to it. This kind of guidance is especially needed in difficult and uncertain times. When there are daily challenges that can throw you off course, it's crucial that you have some signs that tell you where you are.

Say It in Your Own Words

People can only speak the truth when speaking in their own true voice. The guidance from leadership books—including this one—is not a substitute for who and what you are. Once you have the words you want to say, you must also give voice to those words. You must be able to express yourself so that everyone knows that it's you who's speaking.

There is a lot of scientific data to support our assertions about each of The Five Practices of Exemplary Leadership. But keep in mind that leadership is also an art. And just as with any other art form—whether it's painting, playing music, dancing, acting, or writing—leadership is a means of personal expression. To become a credible leader you have to learn to express yourself in ways that are uniquely your own. Take it from Taylor Putz.

Taylor was still in high school when he learned the importance of finding his voice. Although he felt too young to lead anything, he saw the need and necessity to address a concern in his community. Driven by issues of heavy drinking in his family and the fact that he was seeing more and more of his classmates abusing alcohol, he decided that he needed to stand up to address the problem of underage drinking. Taylor's mission was particularly challenging when he found himself talking to adults about this problem. Given the community's history and culture around alcohol, many people didn't think underage drinking was much of a concern, and Taylor wasn't sure what kind of reception he would get. Nevertheless, he mobilized other students around him by talking about the issue and why he thought it was so important.

With traditional celebratory events like prom and graduation coming up, Taylor knew it was a particularly risky time of the year for underage drinking. As he talked more and more about how he became aware of the risks involved and felt the potential for disaster, other students began to listen and share their personal stories and experiences too. Taylor found that many around him had similar perspectives and beliefs about protecting life from the very real threat of underage drinking. This helped them develop a unified voice that his group used to mobilize others in the community to talk about the issue to the city council. As a result, the city council agreed to sponsor a campaign to provide a drug-free environment and use a little-referenced city sign ordinance to reduce prominent alcohol advertising from area businesses by 25 percent.

Taylor's experience shows the importance of being clear in your convictions and expressing your stance in your unique way. Taylor was able to bring others along who had similar concerns about the drinking issue, but he wouldn't have been able to do that without being sure and articulate about where he stood. Drinking can be a taboo topic, one that many people may want to address but feel inhibited by their culture. It takes a strong will to stand up to peers, particularly in a time of traditional celebrations. It takes a solid foundation of belief to stand up to a community that has ignored an issue for years.

One of Taylor's biggest challenges, as he spoke out, was making sure he voiced a position that others not only shared but also supported. By becoming very clear about what he was trying to accomplish, others joined him. Standing together, the members of his "coalition" gained a greater sense of confidence because they together became very clear and eloquent in their unified voice. Taylor and his peers had at first been somewhat intimidated by the group of adults and local politicians they were dealing with. Their unified voice made it easier to bring the issue out in the open and to approach those powers that be. Their unified voice helped them see themselves as more than "a bunch of students." Instead they were a group of citizens standing up for something important to them individually and as a group, and doing something that mattered.

Taylor's actions spoke volumes about how he and others in the community needed to take ownership of things they believed in and valued. Like Taylor, you cannot lead through someone else's values or someone else's words. You cannot lead out of someone else's experience. You can only lead out of your own. Unless it's your style, your manner, your words, it's not you—it's just an act. People don't get truly engaged with you because of your title or your position. They follow *you*. If you're not the real deal, can you really expect others to want to follow? To be a leader, you've got to awaken to the fact that you don't have to copy someone else, you don't have to read a script written by someone else, and you don't have to wear someone else's style. Instead, you are free to choose what you want to express and the way you want to express it. In fact, you have a responsibility to others to express yourself in an authentic manner, in a way they would immediately recognize as yours.

Clarify Values to Spark Commitment

Personal values drive commitment. Clear personal values are the route to motivation and productivity. How can this be? How can it be that people who are very clear about their own values are more likely to stick around and work harder than those who know what the group stands for but are not clear about their own beliefs? Think about it. Have you ever had the feeling that "This place is not for me"? Have you ever walked into a place, immediately gotten the sense that "I don't belong here," and just walked right out? Or, have you ever just known that you belong, that you can be yourself, that "This is the right place for me"? Of course you have. Everyone has had those experiences.

It's the same way in any group you're in or job you might have. There comes a point when you recognize it is or isn't a good fit with your values and beliefs. Even if you didn't know the specific values of the organization, you see how the group behaves and performs. You won't stick around a place (or a project, or a class) for very long when you feel in your heart and in your soul that you don't belong. It's one big reason why people join groups and then don't stay for very long. Commitment is based upon alignment with personal values and who you are and what you are about. People who are clearest about personal values are better prepared to make choices based on principle—including deciding whether the principles of the organization fit with their own!

AFFIRM SHARED VALUES

Leadership is not simply about your own values. It's also about the values of those you are hoping to lead. Just as your own values drive your commitment to the organization, club, or team, other members' personal values drive their own commitment. People will be significantly more engaged in a place where they believe they can stay true to their beliefs. While clarifying your own values is essential, understanding the values of others and building alignment around values that everyone can share is equally critical.

Bethany Fristad was a college freshman when she first felt there was something important inside of her pushing to come out. In high school she hadn't been very involved, didn't feel much sense of purpose, and didn't have any direction in life. Halfway through her first year in college something began to change. As she made friends at her new school and around the small town community, she started to recognize that she could serve a greater purpose. She began to bring together a small group of people who helped her establish a nonprofit organization focused on helping underprivileged children. It was called "Firefleyes" to symbolize its ability to ignite the fire in peoples' hearts and eyes. Bethany set out to recruit an even larger group of students at her college who had an interest in helping disadvantaged children.

Firefleyes members believe that underserved children can flourish if they have an environment where they can find their own "voices" through music, sports, arts, books, and crafts. The group promoted this belief by collecting enough resources to travel to Sierra Leone and start the first of what Bethany calls "Creation Nation," which are essentially playrooms where children explore their creative sides with all sorts of arts, crafts, and music.

By giving voice to her convictions, Bethany found many supportive and willing participants who shared her beliefs about how to help children do well and saw the value in what she wanted to do. Had she not been clear on what she was trying to accomplish and why, particularly in such a new and large endeavor, others could have easily cast aside her ideas as impractical. Yet Bethany persisted and appealed to the ideas she believed others shared about the need to help those less fortunate. She knew that the people she spoke with understood the value of creativity in helping children find their own dreams. She said that, ultimately, it was relatively simple to help fellow students see how they could transform their own values into specific actions that would benefit others as well.

Shared values are the pillars of productive and genuine working relationships. Credible leaders, like Bethany, honor the uniqueness and individuality of all the members of the group, but they also stress their common values. Leaders build on agreement. They don't try to get everyone to be in agreement on everything. This goal is unrealistic, and trying to get everyone to agree or to make everyone happy can negate the very advantages of diversity. But to take the first step, and then a second, and then a third, people must have some common core of understanding. After all, if there's no agreement about values, then what exactly are the leader and everyone else going to model? If disagreements over fundamental values continue, the results will be intense conflict, false expectations, and diminished capacity.[1] Leaders ensure that everyone is aligned through the process of affirming shared values—holding one another accountable to what "we" value. Once people are clear about the leader's values, about their own values, and about shared values, they know what's expected of them and how they can count on others.

Give People Reasons to Care

Important as it is that leaders communicate the principles for which they stand, the values leaders live by must be consistent with the desires and needs of those who follow them. Leaders who promote values that aren't representative of the group won't be able to get people to act as one. There has to be a shared understanding of what's expected. Leaders need to build agreement on a common cause and a common set of principles. They must be able to maintain a community of shared values. In this way a leader's promise is really an organization's promise, regardless of whether the organization is a team of two, an intramural softball team of ten, a fraternity of one hundred, a campus of seven thousand, a company of twenty thousand, or a town of two hundred thousand. Unless there's agreement about which promises are to be kept, the organization, its members, and its leaders risk losing credibility.

Recognition of shared values provides people with a common language. Tremendous energy is generated when individual, group, and organizational values are in sync. Commitment, enthusiasm, and drive are intensified. People have reasons for caring about what they are doing. When individuals truly care about what they are doing, they are more effective and satisfied. They stay committed to the group, are more engaged in what's going on, and are likely to actively participate more. They experience less frustration with the task or the group.

Remember Grant Hillestad's story at the beginning of this chapter of starting up an STLF chapter at his college? In arranging their first road trip, Grant said that the group's planning for each city had been assigned to different people in order for them to learn and grow from the experience. Even though they were nervous that not enough preparations had been made in some locations, they had to let it play out because the organization valued learning by doing so deeply. "We were really worried that we'd get to a certain city and nothing would be ready," Grant said. "If that happened the whole trip might be remembered for that aspect of the event. It really took a lot for us to say, 'No, our mission is to "reveal" leadership through service. We have to trust that it will work out and that each of us will learn how to make it work out, not just a select few.'"

Grant's experience is an example of how people become more committed when they can find alignment between their values and those of the group. The quality and accuracy of communication within the group, along with the integrity of the decision-making process, increase when people feel part of a team with the same values. Confidence in one another grows; stress and worry are reduced. People work harder and are more creative because they become fully engaged in what they are doing. We know that when there is solid understanding of the alignment between an individual's values and those of the group, there is much greater productivity and success for everyone involved.

Exemplary leaders spend time with their group talking about values. Too many school groups spend very little time doing this. It tends to take place as a single occurrence, at the beginning of the school year or when a group is first formed or new members brought in. Frequent and continuing conversations reminding people why they care about what they are doing renew commitment and help people feel that they are on the same team. When people are clear about the leader's values, about their own values, and about shared values, they know what's expected of them. This understanding increases their ability to make choices, enables them to better handle difficult situations, and enhances understanding and appreciation of the choices made by others.

Frequent and ongoing conversations with your group reinforce what is important to the group and to the individuals who make it up. Think about a time when you joined an organization as a new member. Did anyone talk to you about what the group stood for? Did you ask the question, "What is important to this group?" If you did, was the answer clear? If you didn't, how do you know what the group was all about? The group's values will guide everything they do and therefore it is very important to spend time, regularly, talking about those values. We know this can be initially challenging for any leader.

Consider the experience of Kara Koser when she was a student at a major urban university. As a resident assistant, Kara was trying to figure out how she could best meet the needs of her diverse resident population. With so many individuals, she wasn't sure what activity she could ever do that would be of interest to the entire floor. She realized that she first had to listen inward, to herself, and then take the time to listen to others. What it took, she learned, was patience. Kara slowly understood that it takes time for people to become comfortable sharing. Just as Taylor Putz discovered when he first started working on his community's underage drinking situation, some people find it intimidating to share what is important to them. Kara took the approach she called "leading out front and leading from the back." What this meant to her was really listening to what others were thinking and talking about, and hearing what was important to them. "The difference in this type of leading was subtle," Kara said, "but both approaches were important because they were done with the interests of the group, in my case, my floor residents, in mind."

Kara didn't give up trying to have conversations with her residents about what they needed and wanted. The more they talked, the more they and other residents became comfortable sharing their ideas and visions. Kara worked to regularly create an environment where people could freely and easily contribute. She encouraged her residents knowing that if she could be respectful of the values of others while at the same time not letting her own voice be dimmed, the light would shine on the best solution for all. These conversations allowed the residents to develop a greater sense of community and discover their shared values as they got to know each other better, and subsequently, how they wanted to spend their time together.

Forge Unity, Don't Force It

When leaders spend the time and energy required to establish shared values, those who follow them are more positive. They make personal choices more easily and feel a significantly stronger sense of personal effectiveness.

By encouraging ongoing discussion about the common values of the group, leaders avoid the pitfall of people wasting time and energy trying to figure out what they are supposed to do. When people are unsure about their roles they tend to lose focus or draw the group off topic; they may stop participating or leave the group altogether. The energy that goes into dealing with incompatible values, through arguments or misunderstandings, takes its toll on both the effectiveness of the leader and the activity level of the group. "What are our basic principles?" and "What do we believe in?" are far from simple questions. Even with commonly identified values, there may be little agreement on the meaning of values statements. One study reported 185 different behavioral expectations about the value of integrity alone.[2] The lesson here is that leaders must encourage ongoing discussions about values. Even if there are many interpretations of a particular value, talking about them can lead to a common understanding and deeper commitment.

Shared values emerge from a process, not a pronouncement. Leaders can't impose their values on the group's members; they must actively involve people in the process of creating a set of shared values. These values are the result of listening, appreciating, building consensus, and resolving conflicts. For people to truly share values, they must participate in the process. In creating opportunities for ongoing conversations about shared values, it's important that people get to reflect on and discuss how their personal beliefs and behaviors align with and are influenced by what the group stands for.

In addition, for values to be truly shared, they must be more than catchphrases or advertising slogans. They must be well understood and broadly endorsed beliefs about what's important to the people who hold them. People must be able to talk about the values freely and have common interpretations of how those values will be put into practice. They must know what their values will look like in action and how their efforts directly contribute to the larger success of the group.

Having everyone on the same page when it comes to values has many benefits. It ensures consistency in what the group says and what they do. The result is high individual credibility and an excellent reputation for the group, further preparing people to discuss values and expectations when recruiting, selecting, and orienting new members. Whenever new members join your group, whether at the beginning of a term or in the middle of the year, knowing what the group stands for and talking about it openly helps everyone make more informed decisions about their engagement with the group. Having everyone aligned about shared values builds commitment and community, and that is precisely what leaders ultimately hope to do in pursuit of a common vision.

TAKE ACTION: CLARIFY VALUES

The very first step on the journey to exemplary leadership is clarifying your values—discovering those fundamental beliefs that will guide your decisions and actions along the path to success and significance. That journey involves an exploration of your inner self, where your true voice resides. It's essential that you take yourself on this voyage because it's the only route to being a credible leader and because your personal values drive your commitment to the organization and to the cause. You can't do what you say if you don't know what you believe. And you can't do what you say if you don't believe in what you're saying.

Although clarity of personal values is essential for all leaders, that by itself isn't good enough. Leaders don't just speak for themselves; they speak for their groups and followers as well. There must be agreement on the shared values that everyone will commit to upholding. These give people reasons for caring about what they do, making a significant and positive difference in work attitudes and performance. A common understanding of shared values emerges from a process, not a pronouncement; unity comes about through conversation and debate, followed by understanding and commitment. Leaders must hold themselves and others accountable to a set of shared values, which is a topic explored more fully in the next chapter.

Model the Way begins with *clarifying values by finding your voice and affirming shared values*. There are some things you can do to explore the commitment to Clarify Values:

- Answer the questions: What does leadership mean to me? How would I describe my view of leadership to others?
- State the values that guide your current decisions, priorities, and actions. Make certain that you know what you mean by each value you list.
- Find your own words for talking about what is important to you.
- Help others describe why they choose to be involved in the things they are and why they care about those things.
- Look for opportunities to talk about individual values with others on the team. Ask the group to look for the common values that are revealed in these discussions of individual values. Ask the team to affirm that these values remain central.
- Record the shared values of the group, team, club, or organization. Post them and make them visible to the group. Review them periodically as a reminder of what "we" stand for.
- Be clear about how you will communicate what the group stands for when someone new comes into the group. Make sure that others in the group are on the same page with you in how to make this happen.

NOTES

1. C. Daniels, "Developing Organizational Values in Others," in D. Crandall (ed.), *Leadership Lessons from West Point* (San Francisco: Jossey-Bass, 2007), 62–87.
2. R. A. Stevenson, "Clarifying Behavioral Expectations Associated with Espoused Organizational Values," PhD dissertation, Fielding Institute, 1995.

3

Commitment #2: Set the Example

Haley Rudd participated in a leadership camp the summer before her senior year in high school. One of her assignments was to think about how she could make a difference somewhere in her community. At first Haley was lost on what to do or where to begin. She had been talking with her camp-assigned peer mentor and was beginning to explore some options when she discovered the perfect opportunity. It was at an area hospital where she had been visiting her infant nephew who was put in the Neonatal Intensive Care Unit (NICU) for about ninety days after his birth.

On one of her visits to see her nephew, Haley met a social worker who showed her around and introduced her to a program called Molly's Closet, started by a mother in honor of her daughter Molly who had died at the hospital as an infant. Haley learned that NICU babies were so small that very few of the outfits the hospital had would fit them. Molly's Closet was founded to provide premature babies born there with the clothing and supplies they needed. As Haley learned more about the purpose of Molly's Closet and its challenges in operating there and at other area hospitals, she became more inspired and began to talk about the situation with her friends at school and with people in her neighborhood and at her church. She was surprised to learn how many people didn't have the resources to provide the necessities for preemie infants and their families. It was then that Haley knew she wanted to do something about outfitting those babies.

Haley pulled together a small group of students to conduct a drive to gather outfits and supplies for the NICU babies and their families. She had two concerns on her mind as she was putting the donation drive together: first, she worried that her group wouldn't be taken seriously because they were so young and, second, that because she had a relative in need, there might be a perception that she was doing this for her own family's benefit. To show she was serious about having her project benefit all the NICU babies, now and in the future, Haley spent time working after school with the hospital social worker to learn more about what the babies needed. She developed a formal relationship with Molly's Closet so that there would be a way to distribute whatever donations her group came up with. She also asked the social worker for feedback on her thoughts about how to have Molly's Closet reach even more families and sought guidance on how best to approach her peers at school and people in the community to influence them to get involved. Haley thought carefully about how she would describe her project: she would emphasize that it was an outgrowth of an established program. She practiced her "pitch" with the hospital social worker to feel more confident and convincing when asking for donations and support.

One of Haley's basic beliefs about being a leader is to focus on others. "What I have learned about leadership is that you look for what you can do to impact others rather than for your own benefit," she told us. So she made it a point when encouraging others to participate in the project to appeal to their responsibility to help those who are "part of our collective future" and to tap into similar experiences they might have had with loved ones. All the while, she tried to make it clear in word and deed how much she cared for all the NICU babies and their families. She knew it was vital to walk her talk and embody the concern she felt. She set the example of what she was asking of others to do by collecting clothing and supplies for the NICU families and sharing her experiences with people she was trying to recruit for the cause.

The result was that people wanted to be a part of Haley's NICU project because they really believed in the things they heard Haley say as well as what they saw her doing. For example, Haley visited classes and student clubs, describing what her nephew and other preemies were experiencing in the NICU and explaining that the hospital didn't have the resources to help them thrive. She talked about how great she felt when she was able to take a donation to the hospital and see the babies wearing more comfortable clothing. She let her classmates know that they too could help the babies by providing clothes that fit and make their time in the NICU more beneficial by supplying toys or colorful art. Others heard and saw her passion for helping others—in this particular case, others who couldn't help themselves.

Haley began a new group at school, starting small at first with classmates she knew, and then expanding it to involve more of her fellow students. Early on, the group tried to do some fundraising. What they found was that most people their age didn't like to give money without knowing details about what they were funding and why. So Haley led her group to find innovative ways to advocate for their cause and spur noncash donations. Haley had told her group many stories about how donated clothing and supplies had made a big difference in the early lives of the NICU babies and their families. She and her group then retold those stories as they spoke at school and around their community. She challenged the group to connect with other student organizations that could not only donate goods and services but also advocate on their behalf. Haley herself identified and personally visited potential supporters, including seemingly unlikely groups such as the 4-H and Future Farmers of America groups, thinking they would be powerful advocates because they were well known at school and in the surrounding rural community. By leading her group in this effort, working right alongside them in collecting baby clothing and also devoting time to generating interest and concern for the families in need, Haley found backing for Molly's Closet that had much more impact than simply asking people to donate money.

At one point it became frustrating, Haley told us, because she wasn't seeing the success she had hoped for. She expected everyone to match her passion and commitment to the cause. This was a critical juncture for her and she dealt with it by putting in sharper focus the message she was sharing as well as expanding the ways her fellow students could spread the message about the help they were providing. Her refined approach, she said, was to use stories of the families they already had helped to set the example and show that anyone could make a difference, even with the smallest of donations. In the process Haley learned that there were always going to be naysayers and obstacles, but it was how she addressed those comments and reactions by consistent action that changed how others viewed the impact they actually could make.

Leaders like Haley quickly realize and appreciate that what you do speaks more loudly than what you say. Some of the most observable actions leaders can take include how they spend their time, what they pay attention to, ask questions about, and the language and stories they use. Actions like these give you a chance to make visible and tangible your personal commitment to a shared way of being. Each affords you the chance to show where you stand on matters of principle. This may sound simple to do, but you should remember that sometimes the greatest distance you have to travel is the distance from your mouth to your feet.

Haley's story illustrates the second commitment of Model the Way—leaders Set the Example. They take every opportunity to show others, by their own example, that they're deeply committed to the values and aspirations they claim. No one will believe you're serious until they see you doing what you're asking of others. You either lead by example or you don't lead at all. That's what it means to be credible: *you do what you say you will do*. You don't ask others to do something that you wouldn't be willing to do yourself or haven't already done yourself. It's how you provide the evidence that you're personally committed. It's how you make your values known and shown.

From our research we have determined that *credibility is the foundation of leadership*. People want to follow leaders in whom they can believe; they want leaders who show that what they say will be backed up by actions. The model that leaders set is the visible manifestation of their values. This chapter on Setting the Example is all about practicing what you preach, putting your money where your mouth is, following through on commitments, keeping promises, walking the talk, and doing what you say you will do.

Being a credible leader means you have to live the values. You have to put into action what you and others stand for. You have to be the example for others to follow. And, because you're leading a group of people—not just leading yourself—you also have to make certain that the actions of your group are consistent with the shared values of the organization. An important part of any leader's job is to educate others on what the team or organization stands for, why those things matter, and how others can authentically serve these values. As the leader you teach, coach, and guide others to align their actions with the shared values because you're accountable for their actions, too, not just your own.

In order to Set the Example you need to understand and engage in these two essentials:

- Live the shared values
- Teach others to model the values

In practicing these essentials you become a role model for what the group or organization promises, and you create a culture in which everyone commits to standing for these shared values.

LIVE THE SHARED VALUES

Leaders are their organizations' ambassadors of shared values. Their mission is to represent the values and standards to everyone around them, and it's their duty to serve the values to the best of their abilities.

As a leader, you are always having an influence. People watch your every action, even many people you are unaware of. They're trying to determine whether you're serious about what you say. You need to be conscious about the choices you make and the actions you take, because they send the messages that other people use to determine whether you're doing what you say.

Spend Your Time and Attention Wisely

How you spend your time is the single clearest indicator of what's important to you. Visibly spending time on what's important shows that you're putting your money where your mouth is. Whatever your values are, they have to show up consistently, during *all* your day-to-day activities if people are to believe those values are important to you. Take a look at how you spend your time each day. What's the connection between what you're doing each day and what you say are your key values?

Let's say one of your core values is teamwork. You're supposed to have a meeting with your capstone project team on Friday afternoon to go over how everyone's research is coming along, and one of your friends invites you to drive down that afternoon to the family's beach home for the weekend. Do you meet your obligations to your classmates because you are committed to being a good team player, or do you shine them on and go with your friends because you don't want to miss a weekend at the beach? What if your club decides to run a fundraising car wash? You know there will be plenty of people there and you have an important exam to study for. What choice do you make? These choices are not clear or easy, but ultimately, the things you spend your time on in your life are reflections of your priorities. Are your decisions based on how they reflect your values, or are they a sign that you're distracted or engaged in conflicting interests? This question applies to groups as well. Think about the meetings you attend. What do you spend most of the time discussing? Being present and consistently aligning your actions with your behaviors says more about what you value than any other message you share, whether it be on social media, in a text, or passed along through someone else. Your leadership behaviors and actions send signals to others about what's important to you and what's merely lip service.

When Michael Haenel was co-captain of his golf team, he promised to always be on time and be ready to get to work. He showed up for every practice, made every team meeting, adhered to a daily exercise routine. When it came to the golf team, these small actions paid big dividends in developing productive team chemistry. "This proved to my teammates that I was motivated to achieve a common goal," he said. "The sense of motivation was contagious and created a healthy team environment. The team was able to unite and strive to do our best."

You can make visible and tangible to others your personal commitment to your group and its values when you seize the kind of signal-sending opportunities that Michael did. Simple though they may appear, actions like just showing up are evidence of where you stand on matters of principle. Leaders like Michael are very mindful of the signals they send and how they send them whether through their actions or through their words.

Watch Your Language

Exemplary leaders understand the power of words. Words don't just give voice to a leader's own mindset and beliefs; they also evoke images of what people hope to create with others and how they expect people to behave. The tradition within fraternities and sororities of members referring to each other as "brother" or "sister" is a great example of this. It reinforces the sense of family and loyalty so valued in the fraternal system. Your words can have a powerful effect on how your constituents see themselves, those around them, and the events you all share, and you should choose what you say intentionally and carefully.

The University of North Carolina Women's Lacrosse team won the NCAA National Championship in 2013 in a dramatic triple overtime finish. It takes tremendous discipline as a team to reach the Final Four and mental discipline plays a big role. "At this level of competition, everyone is talented and prepared," Head Coach Jenny Levy had told the players. "At this point, it's what's between the ears that makes the difference."

The team took Coach Levy's counsel to heart and began to speak to each other about their destiny to win. A theme began and took hold: "road2one" became their mantra, an expression the women used before and after practices to help them feel their collective dream. Coach Levy explained: "Expressions like 'road2one' are what gain momentum in a team culture. 'Things' tend to fade, but expressions that bubble up and represent the core values of the team often catch fire. They made the slogan more their own by using the Twitter format #road2one on t-shirts and communications."

On the Final Four weekend, Mother Nature handed the team even bigger challenges. Their practice field was literally underwater from the previous week's rain, as was the game field. The women ended up practicing on an intramural field that was laid out differently from the one they would play on for the championship. The seniors, juniors, and coaching staff who had been to three Final Fours in a row knew this was the time to help the team stay focused and strong. "Be flexible" became the phrase they used to help the team feel confident that they weren't going to be distracted from their destiny with victory. Kara Cannazzaro, one of the team captains, had been on the teams that had made it to the Final Four the three previous years, but had always lost in the championship game. Leaders like Kara "don't dwell on those losses," Coach Levy told us, "but the memory is there, and if you let it color how you talk to your team, it can have impact. It was clear to me from Kara's language, that she had decided this was the year and this was the team to go all the way. Period."

The championship game went into three 3-minute overtime periods. Between periods, the team had a chance to huddle and receive coaching. After the first OT period the coaches reinforced the team's themes from the whole year: "Be in the moment" and "Win your individual battle on the field." After that, it was clear the coaches' job was done. They just stepped aside as Kara and her teammates chanted, "We got this! We got this! We're getting stronger! We are going to do this! This game is ours!" The women's upbeat, confident language tapped into the team's core belief that this championship was their ultimate destiny; it was a powerful way to say that they believed in each other and their combined ability to win the championship. After three tough overtime periods, they achieved their dream.

Leaders like Kara pay attention to the way they use language, and for good reason. Researchers have documented the power of language in shaping thoughts and actions. Just a few words from someone can make the difference in the beliefs that people articulate. At an east coast university there was a publicized incident of hate mail sent to an African American student. In a study at that institution researchers randomly stopped students walking across campus and asked them what they thought of the occurrence. Before the student could respond, a research partner impersonating another student would come up and answer with a response like "Well, he must have done something to deserve it." As you might expect, the first student's response was more often than not just like the student impersonator's. The researchers then stopped another student and asked the same question. This time the impersonator gave an alternative response, something like "There's no place for that kind of behavior on our campus." The response from the student being questioned again replicated the impersonator's.[1]

This classic study dramatically illustrates how potent language is in influencing people's responses to what's going on around them. Language helps to build the frame around people's views of the world, and it's essential for leaders to be mindful of their choice of words. If you want people to act like citizens of a village you have to talk about them that way, not as subordinates in a hierarchy. If you want people to appreciate the rich diversity in their organizations, you have to use language that's inclusive. If you want people to be innovative, you have to use words that spark exploration, discovery, and invention. "Watch your language" has come to take on a whole new meaning from when your teacher scolded you in school for the use of an inappropriate word. It's now about setting an example for others of how they need to think and act.

Ask Purposeful Questions

The questions you ask are also quite powerful in focusing attention. When leaders ask questions, they send others on mental journeys—"quests"—in search of answers. The questions that a leader asks send messages about the focus of the group, and they're indicators of what is of most concern to the leader. They're one more measure of how serious you are about the beliefs you claim. Questions direct attention to the values that should be attended to and how much energy should be devoted to them.

Questions develop people. They help keep people from being narrow-minded by broadening their perspectives and taking responsibility for their own viewpoints. Asking good questions also forces you to listen attentively to those around you and what they are saying. This action demonstrates your respect for their ideas and opinions. If you are genuinely interested in what other people have to say then you need to ask their opinion, especially before giving your own. Asking what others think encourages participation and commitment to whatever decision is ultimately determined and consequently increases support for that decision. Asking good questions reduces the risk that a decision might be undermined by either inadequate consideration or unexpected opposition.

Think about the questions you typically ask when you are working with others. How do these questions help to clarify and gain commitment to shared values? What would you like each person in your group to pay attention to each day? Be intentional and purposeful about the questions that you ask. Remember, you are always influencing. The questions you routinely ask model to the group similar questions they should be asking themselves in your absence. What information do you need from the group to show that people are living by shared values and making decisions that are consistent with their values? What questions should you ask if you want people to focus on integrity, or on trust, or community service, or safety, or personal responsibility? In Ask Purposeful Questions Daily, we've provided a few sample questions that you could intentionally ask every day to demonstrate the importance of shared values.

Ask Purposeful Questions Daily

- Teamwork: What did you do today to lend a hand to someone else in your group? What's one action you took in the last week as a result of a suggestion someone else made?
- Appreciation: What did you do today to express how grateful you were for something that someone else had done? What's one action you took in the last week to call attention to the good work done by one of your teammates?
- Learning: What's one mistake you made in the last week, and what did you learn from it? What's one action you took in the last week to help someone else benefit from your experience?
- Continuous improvement: What have you done in the past week to practice so that you can strengthen your talents? What's one action you took in the last week to build upon something you didn't previously know in some new way or application?

Whatever your shared values are—teamwork, appreciation, integrity, trust, safety, personal responsibility, or any number of others—the idea is to come up with a routine set of questions that will get people to reflect on the core values and what they have done each day to act on those values.

Seek Feedback

How can you know that you're doing what you say (which is the *behavioral* definition of credibility) if you never ask for feedback on how your behavior affects how others are doing? How can you really expect to match your words and your actions if you don't get information about how aligned they are? There's solid evidence that the best leaders are very aware of what's going on inside them as they are leading and are attuned to what's going on with others.[2] The best leaders are very self-aware, and they're very socially aware. Such leaders can tell whether they've done something that has enabled someone to perform at a higher level or whether they have diminished motivation. Leaders realize that although they may not always like the feedback they get, it is the only way they can really know how they are doing as a leader. Seeking feedback provides a powerful statement about the value of self-improvement and how everyone can be even better than they are today.

Self-reflection, the willingness to seek feedback, and the ability to then engage in new behaviors based on this information has been shown to be predictive of future success as a leader.[3] However, our own studies using the Leadership Practices Inventory (LPI)—our 360-degree feedback instrument for assessing the frequency to which people engage in The Five Practices of Exemplary Leadership—consistently show that the statement which receives the lowest rating, both from leaders and their constituents, is: "Asks for feedback on how his/her actions affect other people's performance."[4] In other words, the behavior that leaders and their groups consider to be the least frequently used is the behavior that most enables leaders to know how they're doing! You can't learn very much if you're unwilling to find out more about the impact of your behavior on the performance of those around you. It's your responsibility as a leader to keep asking others, "How am I doing?" If you don't ask, they're not likely to tell you. This can be hard for anyone to do because we are typically scared of what we might hear. Still, leaders must ask the question of others, frequently, about how they are doing.

It's not always easy to get feedback. It's not generally asked for, and most people aren't used to providing it. Skills are required to do both. You can increase the likelihood that people will accept honest feedback from you if you make it easier for people to give you feedback. To be most effective, good feedback needs to be specific and not general, focused on behavior rather than the individual (personality), solicited rather than imposed, timely rather than delayed, and descriptive rather than evaluative. You have to be sincere in your desire to improve yourself, and you have to demonstrate that you are open to knowing how others see you. You invite feedback; you don't demand it. For example, instead of asking, "How was that meeting?" you might say, "One thing I am trying to do as a leader is encourage others to contribute ideas. I tried to do that during our meeting today. How do you think it went? What could I have done differently?"

Of course, it's up to you to consider and act on the feedback. Consider checking with other people to determine the reliability of any feedback you receive. After all, few people see you in your totality. Sometimes feedback may be more about the sender than it is about the receiver. But remember this: If you don't do anything with the feedback you receive, people will stop giving it to you. They're likely to believe that you are arrogant enough to think that you are smarter than everyone else or that you just don't care about what anyone else has to say. Either of these outcomes seriously undermines your credibility and effectiveness as a leader.

All of this also applies when you are providing feedback to members of your group. The more frequently that feedback becomes part of the conversation, the easier it will be to hear and deal with it as constructive, especially when both sides share similar values and aspirations. Setting the right climate for feedback is critical. Remember there are always two sides to every story. Reviewing past behavior shouldn't be seen as an opportunity to fix the blame, but about staying curious about what happened and what it says about how you can move forward in line with your group's goals and values. Regularly asking for feedback should be a routine question of "what happened" with the intent to make sure that the focus is on "what can we learn" so that any problems that may have occurred are not repeated.

Often leaders fear the exposure and vulnerability that accompanies direct and honest feedback. Those giving the feedback can feel a bit exposed themselves and may even fear retribution or hurting someone's feelings or damaging a relationship. It's a risk, but the upside of learning and growth is far more beneficial than the downside of being nervous or embarrassed. Learning to be a better leader requires great self-awareness, and it requires making yourself vulnerable. Asking for feedback signals to others your openness to do what is right and makes it easier for others to be receptive to learning about how well they are modeling the way.

TEACH OTHERS TO MODEL THE VALUES

You're not the only role model in your group, team, or organization. Everyone should be setting the example. Everyone needs to match words and deeds, in all situations. One of your leadership responsibilities is to make sure that everyone keeps the promises the group has made. People are watching how you hold others accountable for living the group's shared values and how you deal with it when anyone moves off the chosen path. They're paying attention to what others say and do, and so should you. It's not just what *you* do that demonstrates consistency between word and deed. Every team member, partner, and colleague sends signals about what's valued. Therefore, you need to look for opportunities to teach not just by your example, but also by taking on the role of teacher and coach (we'll have more to say about this in Chapter 9 on Strengthening Others).

Kenzie Crane was responsible for the sorority recruitment program for a large university in the southern United States. In this capacity she guided nearly two dozen recruitment counselors, who worked to recruit new members for the sixteen different chapters. Their job was to recruit students and help them find the best fit in a sorority. Given that all of the recruitment counselors were already members of one of the sororities, it was sometimes challenging for them to be unbiased; thus, Kenzie not only had to model what it meant to be neutral but she also needed to hold others accountable for doing the same, and to teach them how to do that. One action she took each week was to get them all together and do role plays about how they would handle various questions in an unbiased fashion from the women being recruited. She also worked with them about changing the perception of sororities from simply social organizations to organizations focused on community engagement, intellectual enrichment, and personal growth. To make this shift credible, they would all have to be able to give examples of the positive experiences sororities offered for personal development. A top priority for Kenzie was making sure that the recruitment counselors knew how to talk about this. "This meant," she told us, "that I always and consistently used this perspective and fostered it in others, not just during the training and role-play sessions."

Exemplary leaders like Kenzie know that people learn lessons from how people handle the unplanned events on the schedule as well as the planned ones. They know that people learn from the stories that circulate on campus, in classes, in the dining halls, and in social media. In order to show others with what's expected and ensure that they hold themselves accountable, you need to confront critical incidents, tell stories, and find every opportunity to reinforce the behaviors you want repeated, just as Kenzie's frequent role plays helped prepare the recruiters for any circumstance, any attitude, or any questions they might encounter.

Confront Critical Incidents

You can't plan everything about your day. Even the most disciplined leaders can't stop the intrusion of the unexpected. Stuff happens. Critical incidents—chance occurrences, particularly at a time of stress and challenge—are a part of the life of every leader. They also offer significant moments of learning for leaders and group members. Critical incidents present opportunities for leaders to lead by example, to demonstrate appropriate norms of behavior.

In May 2013 a devastating tornado hit the town of Moore, Oklahoma. It came on fast and literally flattened most of the town, leaving death and widespread destruction in its path. Devin Murphy was a resident assistant at a nearby university when the tornado struck. Her first responsibility was to ensure the safety of her residents, but once the storm passed, she immediately reached out across campus to see how she could help. "When we realized the extent of the damage in nearby Moore," she said, "we wanted everyone to go into action." The university had already decided to help by opening student apartment housing to survivors of the storm. Many of the apartments were empty because most of the students had already left for the summer, but all of the units needed to be cleaned and readied for the families. Devin reached out to her friend Taylor Tyler in Student Life and together they hatched a plan. "We knew there were a lot of students still on campus and we knew they would want to help," Devin told us.

> This is a campus with a lot of students who study the arts. People in theater know how to pull together to get ready for a show, fine arts people know how to put in the long hours and do what it takes to get their projects done, music majors are used to long hours of rehearsal. This is not a group of people afraid of hard work. We are a campus with a "pull together, work hard, and get it done" attitude, so we looked for ways to tap into that.

Devin and Taylor created a Facebook page, where they asked for volunteers to help clean apartments. The call for volunteers produced enough people that in just twenty-four hours, they had sixty-nine apartments cleaned and ready for the exhausted citizens of Moore. "The support didn't stop there," Devin told us. Another student friend, Kelissa Sanders, was doing an internship at the state capital over the summer. She got connected with a popular barbeque restaurant chain there and persuaded them to donate food for a Memorial Day picnic for all the tornado survivors. Continuing to use social media, these leaders have been able to sustain support to the citizens of Moore as they rebuild their lives and in the process connect the needs of that community with the values of pulling together to get things done that they see on their campus.

Critical incidents are not always as dramatic as an F5 tornado. They are simply those events in the lives of leaders, and the groups they are a part of, that offer the chance to improvise while still staying true to the work the group is doing. Although you can't explicitly plan your response in advance, it's useful to keep in mind that the way you handle these incidents—how you link your actions and decisions to shared values—says a lot about what really matters to you. Critical incidents create important teachable moments. They offer leaders the occasion in real time to demonstrate what's valued and what's not.

During critical moments like these, leaders have to take action to put values out on the table and in front of others so that they can return to them as a common ground for working together. In the process, leaders make clear how their actions are compelled by shared values. In this way they set an example for what it means to take actions on the basis of values. By standing up for values, leaders show that having shared values requires a mutual commitment from everyone to align their words with their actions.

Tell Stories

Stories are another powerful tool for teaching people about what's important and what's not, what works and what doesn't, what is and what could be. Through stories leaders pass on lessons about shared values and encourage others to work together. This has been true throughout history and is true today for students as well as for people in the workforce.

Rana Korayem had just completed her undergraduate degree at the American University in Cairo, Egypt. Earning her degree had not been without its challenges, but she was feeling inspired and ready to begin the next phase of her life. She was aware that many women in her country would face great challenges in pursuing an education and she was compelled to try to inspire those she could reach. Rana found that opportunity in a public elementary school for girls.

In Egypt, the public schools serve the poorest young people in the society. The amount of education they get is limited, and many girls stop school at an early age to marry or care for the family. Rana was determined to help the girls see there were other choices and that they could achieve anything they set their minds to. "I came from a family of means," Rana told us, "and when I began to talk about my education, you could tell that they were not relating to me. They saw me as wealthy and therefore not like them. So I told them stories to show that I was not so different from them."

Rana shared stories with them about the risks she had taken to pursue her education and follow her dreams. As she told each story, the girls began to be drawn in, thinking about times they had been scared or lonesome, and recognized Rana as someone not unlike them. "I told them about going to the United States to study and leaving my family and my country for the very first time," she said. "I told them how homesick I was and how nervous to be in a totally new place, not knowing a soul." She talked about how frightening it was to reach out to new people and how she was determined to be brave and believe in herself. She shared with them the prejudice she faced at times, how frightening that was; she talked about how, by overcoming her fear and reaching out, she had learned so much and gained many new friends and rich experiences. She asked them about times they had been lonesome or scared and how they had found courage. "The stories were different for each of us," Rana said, "but the human emotion is the same and by sharing these stories we got closer."

Each week for several months, Rana visited the school and shared her stories with the young girls. "The theme was always the same," Rana said.

> The stories always had to do with how my education had shown me that the sky was the limit if you decided to learn and work hard. I wanted them to see their potential, that no matter what their circumstances, or gender, or how much money their family has, they could achieve anything they put their minds to if they were determined and willing to learn. I told them that my college education helped me feel strong, that as a woman I was strong and so were they.

Sharing stories is a powerful way for leaders to make values and visions come alive. The stories that Rana shared reinforced the values of self-reliance and independence that she holds dear and hoped to inspire in the young girls she chose to spend time with. Storytelling offers a bridge for people to connect their own experience with your message, and it provides an opportunity to lead through an example rather than to come across as lecturing or preaching.

Reinforce Through Systems and Processes

All exemplary leaders understand that you have to reinforce the key values that are important to building and sustaining the kind of group you all want. Think about how you recruit new group members, how you make certain selection decisions, when and how you share information, what kinds of training you provide, how you measure performance, how you provide rewards, and how you recognize someone when they do a great job. These all send signals about what you value and what you don't, and they must be aligned with the shared values and standards that you're trying to instill.

Team sports are full of great examples of this. Consider the stickers added to the helmets of football players to indicate the number of tackles, or the tradition for every member of the team to "suit up" in full uniform whether they will be "warming the bench" or in the game. All of these practices speak to the values of the team and give people a sense of group identity.

Or think about the way different organizations approach new-member recruitment and orientation. Sigma Phi Epsilon is one of the nation's largest fraternities and is committed to changing the negative perceptions of Greek life. Toward that end they created the Balanced Man Program, a concept of single-tiered membership and continuous development offering experiences that don't include some of the destructive traditions associated with Greek organizations, but focus instead on scholarship, leadership, professional development, and life skills. Members learn to live their best lives through unique, rewarding programming tailored to their unique needs and designed to prepare them for the journey of life ahead. The Balanced Man Program is a striking example of how student leaders can be more conscious of how they can use systems and processes within programs to reinforce their group's core values in a positive way. It speaks to the core values of the organization and its willingness to lead the way with positive change. "Being different is hard work, but our colleges and universities need the development-focused, SigEp style of fraternity, especially now," says SigEp's Executive Director Brian Warren.

As many fraternities draw the glare of the media spotlight for unacceptable behavior, educators and students alike have begun to question the role of Greek life on their campuses. SigEp not only stands out within the Greek world for aligning their recruiting, their programs, and all their activities with the values expressed in their simple mission, "Building Balanced Men"; the fraternity is also a striking example of ways to get student leaders to be more conscious of how they can use systems and processes to reinforce their group's core values in a positive way.

TAKE ACTION: SET THE EXAMPLE

One of the toughest parts about being a leader is that you're always onstage. People are always watching you, always talking about you, and always testing your credibility—whether you are aware of it or not. That is why it's essential to make use of all the tools you have available to set the example.

Leaders send signals in a variety of ways and in all kinds of settings, and followers read those signals as indicators of what's OK and what's not OK to do. How you spend your time is the single best indicator of what's important to you. Time is a precious asset, because once passed it can never be recovered. But if invested wisely, it can earn you great returns. The language you use and the questions you ask are other powerful ways that shape perceptions of what you value. You also need feedback in order to know if you're doing what you say.

But it's not just what *you* do that matters. You are also measured by how consistent your followers' actions are with the group's shared values, so you must teach others how to set an example. Critical incidents—those chance occurrences in the lives of all groups, teams, and organizations—offer significant teachable moments. They offer you the opportunity to pass along lessons in real time, not just in theory or in your group meetings. Often critical incidents become stories, and stories are among the most influential teaching tools you have. And remember that what gets reinforced gets done. You have to keep score in order for people to know how they're doing and to improve how they're doing it. You also have to reward the appropriate behavior if you expect it to get repeated.

The second commitment of Model the Way encourages leaders to *set the example by aligning actions with shared values*. Here are some things you can do to explore this commitment:

- Keep your commitments; follow through on your promises.
- Examine your past experiences to identify the values you use to make choices and decisions. Have there been times you did things that went against your values? Why do you think you make those choices? How does that action in your life influence who you are as a leader?
- Ask for feedback from others about what impact your actions have on them and make changes and adjustments based on the feedback you receive; otherwise people will stop bothering to provide it.
- Think about the way you will discuss with the group how all of you are living the values you agreed upon. Ask purposeful questions that keep people constantly focused on the values and priorities that are the most important.
- If you have examples of times or places where people or the group as a whole have strayed from your shared values, bring those instances up and talk about how you can get back to your values. Broadcast examples of exemplary behavior through memorable stories that illustrate how people are and should be behaving.
- When something happens that dramatically illustrates a shared value, especially something that isn't planned, make sure to call attention to it.
- Reinforce the behavior you want repeated in every way you can.

NOTES

1. F. A. Blanchard, T. Lilly, and L. A. Vaughn, "Reducing the Expression of Racial Prejudice," *Psychological Science* 2, no. 2 (1991): 101–105.

2. For in-depth examination of the importance of self-awareness and leadership effectiveness see the landmark book: D. Goleman, *Emotional Intelligence: Why It Can Matter More Than IQ* (New York: Bantam, 1995). See also D. Goleman, *Leadership: The Power of Emotional Intelligence—Selected Writings* (Northampton, MA, 2011); D. Goleman, *Social Intelligence: The New Science of Human Relationships* (New York: Bantam, 2006); D. Goleman, *Working with Emotional Intelligence* (New York: Bantam, 1998); and D. Goleman, A. McKee, and R. E. Boyatzis, *Primal Leadership: Realizing the Power of Emotional Intelligence* (Boston: Harvard Business School Press, 2002).
3. R.W. Eichinger, M. M. Lombardo, and D. Ulrich. *100 Things You Need to Know: Best Practices for Managers & HR* (Minneapolis, MN: Lominger, 2004), 492.
4. More information about the Leadership Practices Inventory, including its psychometric properties and use, can be found on the websites http://www.leadershipchallenge.com/WileyCDA/Section/id-131362.html and http://studentleadershipchallenge.com

PRACTICE 2

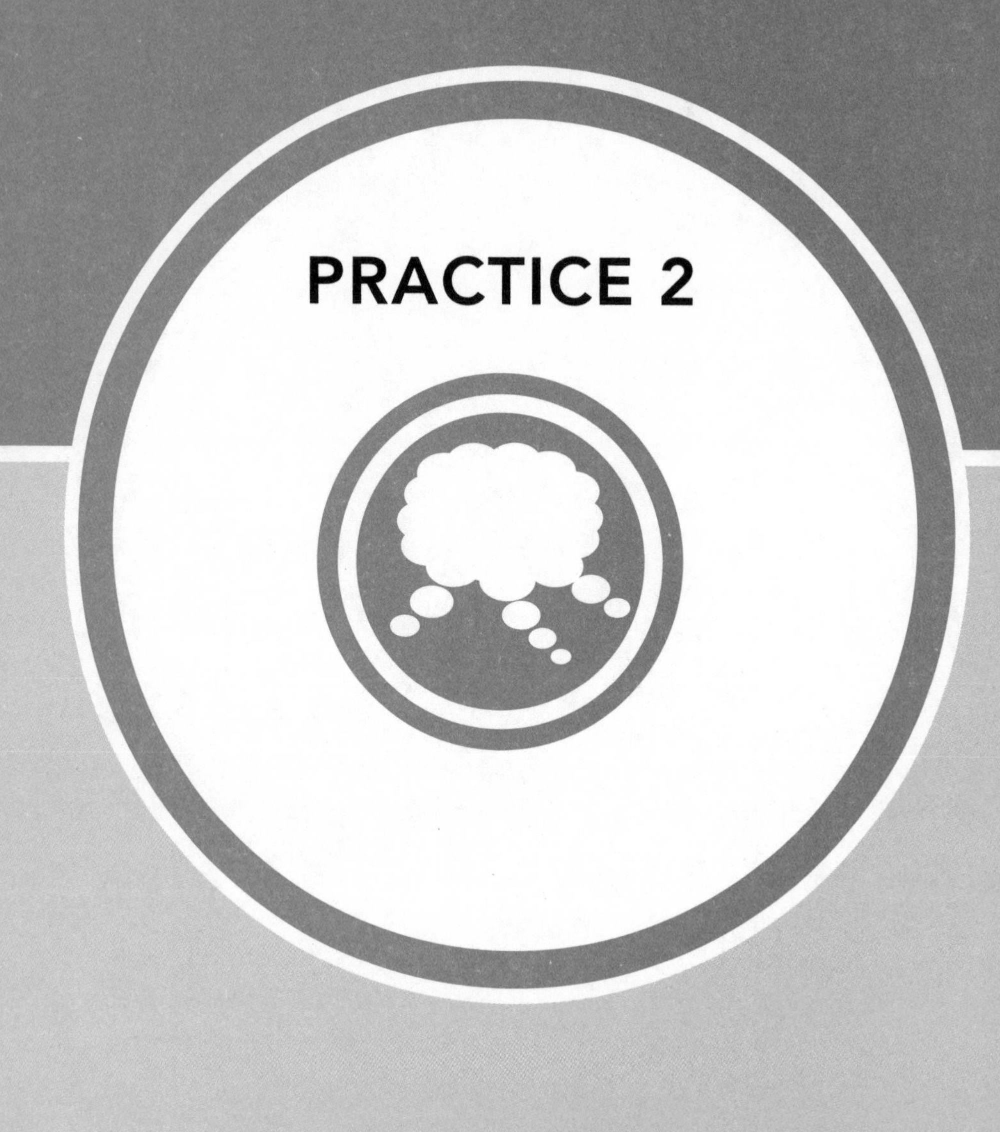

Inspire a Shared Vision

The future holds little certainty. There are no guarantees or easy paths to any destinations, and circumstances can change in a moment. Pioneering leaders rely upon an internal compass and a dream.

Leaders look forward to the future. They hold in their minds visions and ideas of what can be. They have a sense of what is uniquely possible if everyone works together for a common purpose. Leaders are positive about the future, and they passionately believe that people can make a difference.

But visions seen only by the leaders are insufficient to generating organized movement. They must help others to see the exciting future possibilities. Leaders breathe life into visions. They communicate hopes and dreams so that others clearly understand and share them as their own. They show others how their values and interests will be served by the long-term vision of the future.

Leaders are expressive, and they attract followers with their energy, optimism, and hope. With strong appeals and quiet persuasion, they develop enthusiastic supporters.

In the next two chapters we will explore how leaders:

- **Envision the Future by imagining exciting and ennobling possibilities.**
- **Enlist Others by appealing to shared aspirations.**

4

Commitment #3: Envision the Future

In his junior year at a southeastern university, Josh Scholl had an idea for a new research-related project. He felt there were many students who were doing amazing things in their field of study but he'd only hear about them here and there from friends; there was no single source of information on what was being accomplished. He found himself thinking about how great it would be to have such a source.

As a biology major Josh recognized that it was common for the sciences to regularly publish research, but there wasn't an avenue for students to deliver their research studies to audiences outside the sciences. He was sure he wasn't the only person on campus who would find this idea compelling. He felt certain there was interest among students in many disciplines to share their research or ongoing study projects; there was just no easy way to do it.

Josh decided to start a new campuswide journal for undergraduate students doing various kinds of research projects. He approached some faculty in his department about his idea and got a less than enthusiastic reception. They were much more interested in developing research opportunities for students in their own departments than having students spend time publishing work whose quality was beyond their departmental control.

This lack of support didn't stifle Josh. He formed a club to attract fellow students to discuss the possibilities. While he had an image of what the publication could be, he recognized early on that he also needed to listen to the ideas of others. "I wanted to be sure we developed a clear vision," Josh said, "one that many could connect with."

> If we were going to be successful, students had to want to contribute to the publication. I knew that we couldn't develop this in just one meeting. It was going to take a number of conversations. We would be challenged by differing views, but if we spent the time figuring out where we wanted to go and got really clear about it, it would guide our work.

Josh knew there might be distractions along the way that could push the group in a number of competing directions and that there would likely be a lot of trial and error. He felt that if the group was clear on their vision and they shared similar values concerning the project, these distractions would be manageable. The group spent a good deal of time in their early meetings talking about what the journal would stand for and what its purpose would be. "Those early discussions really helped us get the journal off the ground," Josh told us.

> I had the original idea, but it wasn't going to be "my" journal; it would belong to the campus community. By getting everyone involved in determining what the journal would be, we all had a clear sense of where we were going and it helped us work together through that tricky start-up phase every big new project faces.

Josh's story illustrates how major initiatives—whether a single project, campuswide program, or student movement—begin with one person's imagination. It doesn't matter what you call it—vision, purpose, mission, legacy, dream, aspiration, calling, or personal agenda—the result is the same. If you are going to be an exemplary leader, you have to be able to imagine the future you want for yourself and others. When you do that and when you feel passionate about the difference you want to make, you are much more likely to take that first step forward. But if you don't care about the future, or don't even have a clue about your hopes, dreams, and aspirations, there is probably no chance that you will lead others anywhere beyond where they currently are. In fact, it's very likely you may not even see the opportunity to lead that's right in front of you.

Exemplary leaders are forward looking. They are able to envision the future, to gaze across the horizon and realize the greater opportunities to come. They imagine that extraordinary change is possible, and that the ordinary could be transformed into something extraordinary, something that benefits their group, team, organization, or larger community. Leaders are able to develop an ideal and unique image of the future for the common good.

But that image of the future is not just about the leader's vision. It's a shared vision. Everyone has dreams, aspirations, and a desire for tomorrow to be better than today. When visions are shared they attract more people, sustain higher levels of motivation, and withstand more challenges than those that are the leader's exclusive idea. You have to make sure that what you can see is also something that others can see, and vice versa.

The second of The Five Practices of Exemplary Leadership is Inspire a Shared Vision. To do that leaders make a commitment to Envision the Future for themselves and others by mastering these two essentials:

- Imagine the possibilities
- Find a common purpose

Leaders begin with the end in mind by imagining what might be possible. Finding a common purpose inspires people to want to make that vision a reality.

IMAGINE THE POSSIBILITIES

"The human being is the only animal that thinks about the future," writes Daniel Gilbert, professor of psychology at Harvard University (italics his). "The greatest achievement of the human brain is its ability to imagine objects and episodes that do not exist in the realm of the real, and it is this ability that allows us to think about the future."[1] Being "forward looking" is an essential characteristic that people look for in their leaders, and in our studies, this quality is selected by more than two out of every three respondents in terms of what they look for in someone they would willingly follow. People don't generally expect this characteristic from their peers and from the data it is this quality of focusing on the future that most differentiates people who are seen as leaders from those who are not.[2]

Leaders are dreamers. Leaders are idealists. Leaders are possibility thinkers. All exemplary organizations, big or small, begin with the belief that what's merely an idea today can one day be made real. It's this belief that keeps leaders and their constituents moving through the difficult times. Turning possibility thinking into an inspiring vision—and one that is shared—is another one of your challenges as a leader.

When we ask people to tell us where their visions come from, they often have great difficulty in describing the process. And when they do provide an answer, typically it's generally about a feeling, a sense, even a gut reaction, rather than the result of some particularly logical or rational thinking process. Clarifying your vision, like clarifying your values, is a process of self-exploration and self-creation. It's an intuitive, emotional process. There's often no logic to it.

When Kirstyn Cole reflected on her personal-best leadership experience from her college years she noted that "being a leader often means going out on a ledge; it means being scared sometimes. But you shouldn't be afraid to see things differently because sometimes your perspective is the one that is necessary and enables you to lead." It can seem difficult, as a leader, to know where you want to take others. You may have a tendency to want to wait for the "right answer" to appear. Yet the right answer, as Kirstyn points out, may well reside within you already. It requires trusting yourself and that gut feeling you have about an idea you can't seem to let go. You just feel strongly about something, and that sense, that intuition, has to be fully explored. Visions come from the heart. They are reflections of your fundamental beliefs and assumptions about human nature, technology, economics, science, politics, art, and ethics.

A vision of the future is much like a literary or musical theme. It's the main message that you want to convey, it's the frequently recurring melody that you want people to remember, and whenever it's repeated it reminds the audience of the entire work. Every leader needs a theme, something on which they can structure the rest of the performance. Recall that for Taylor Putz it was about underage drinking, for Bethany Fristad it was about helping underprivileged children, for Kenzie Crane it was enriching the experiences of women joining sororities, and for Josh Scholl it was publishing student research. They could literally see what they wanted to happen; they saw how something that didn't exist or wasn't happening now could be possible in the future. Think about:

- What idea, feeling, aspiration, or concern grabs hold of you and won't let you go?
- What's your primary message?
- What's your recurring theme?
- What thoughts do you have that get stronger and louder when you think about where you want your group to go?
- What do you most want people to see every time they think about the future?

For many leaders, the answers to such questions don't come easily—at first. Fortunately there are ways you can improve your capacity to imagine exciting possibilities and to discover the central theme for *your* life, and the lives of others. You get better at imaging the future when you intentionally and consciously reflect on where you want to take others. This requires you to *reflect* on your past, *attend to* the present, *imagine* the future, and *feel* your passion.

Reflect on Your Past

As contradictory as it might seem, in aiming for the future you need to look back into your past. Looking backward can actually enable you to see farther than if you only stare straight ahead. Understanding the past can help you identify themes, patterns, and beliefs that both underscore why you care about certain matters now and explain why making them better into the future is such a high priority.[3] Student groups tend to look at those who came before them to see how things are done. They tend to repeat things, finding that the steep learning curve of doing something themselves the first time is discouraging. But leaders don't settle for replicating what was done in the past. They look to the past to find a platform from which to spring, to learn a better way to do something, maybe a more efficient way or even a new way altogether.

Christian Gbwardo was a full-time university student in Ghana when he founded an organization to combat corruption in Africa by introducing a perspective of ethical leadership to young people. Christian's passion for this organization—they called it "The Leadership Lab"—was rooted in his reflections about how the corruption he saw around him had come to be. "As I thought about those who have come into power," he told us, "I realized that they know little else."

> They have only been exposed to corruption and greed and assume, therefore, that is what government is meant to be. My father showed my family that corruption serves few and denies many. I grew up understanding that we are here to help each other, not take from each other. I realized the

> only way to stop this trend was to expose young people to an alternative as they become young adults, the way I was. They need to see that there is another way.

Looking into your past can reveal much about the future. Studies have shown there is a phenomenon called "the Janus Effect" after the Roman god with two faces, one that looks backward and the other forward. Your ability to look both to your past and your future for guidance opens up lots more exciting possibilities than doing one or the other alone.[4]

None of this is to say that the past *is* the future. That would be like trying to drive using only the rearview mirror. When you look deeply into your entire life history, even as a young person, you understand things about yourself, and about your world, that you cannot fully comprehend by looking at the future as a blank slate. It's difficult, if not impossible, to imagine going to a place you've never experienced, either actually or vicariously. Taking a journey into your past before exploring your future makes the trip so much more meaningful.

Attend to the Present

To envision the future, you have to look around and notice what's going on. Right now as you listen to the members of your team, club, or group, what are the hot topics of conversation? What are they saying they need and want? What are they saying that gets in the way of their doing the very best they can? What are they saying should be changed? Is there anything that they have suddenly stopped talking about that seems puzzling? What does all this tell you about where things are going? What's it telling you about what lies just around the corner?

Christian looked around at the extracurricular programs that high school students were currently attending and explored how he might build The Leadership Lab to have some of the same appeal. He looked at college-age programs at his university and at such programs in the United States when he was doing a study abroad program. He looked at the purpose, offerings, and popularity of many programs, took the best of what he saw for Africa, and began to build his program.

To be able to envision the future, you have to realize what's already going on. You have to spot the trends and patterns, and appreciate both the whole and the parts. You have to be able to clearly see at the same time the immediate situation your group is in and the greater possibilities available to them.

Imagining the future is like assembling a jigsaw puzzle. You see the pieces, and one by one you begin to figure out how they fit together into a whole. Similarly, with your vision, you need to rummage through the bits and bytes of data that accumulate daily and notice how they fit together into a picture of what's ahead. Envisioning the future is not about gazing into a crystal ball; it's about paying attention to the little things that are going on all around you and being able to recognize patterns that point to the future.

Imagine the Future

Even as you stop, look, and listen to messages in the present, you also need to raise your head and look out toward the horizon. Being forward looking is not the same as meeting the deadline for your current project. Leaders have to imagine what the future will hold. They have to be on the lookout for emerging developments, changes inside and outside their groups, such as new technologies, trends on campus, national and world news. They have to anticipate what might be coming just over the hill and around the corner.

There is no hard-and-fast rule as to how far into the future a leader should look. In fact, in school settings, most student leaders might have a time frame of the current academic year, or perhaps as far out as graduation. Contrast this perspective with supervisors who typically need to see at least a few years ahead, whereas middle managers need to see five or more years into the future, and the most senior level executives will need a horizon that's ten-plus years, or even more, into the future. What's critical is being able to not lose sight of the bigger picture while working on whatever you are currently doing.

The Leadership Lab began with just Christian and his wife, working with a few high school students that they knew in the neighborhood. Today the Leadership Lab has a leadership team of experts in various supporting fields, bound together by a common dedication to fighting corruption at the highest levels, and offers programs for hundreds of high school and college students to help the future leaders of Ghana identify with a healthy, ethical way of leading Africa into the future.

The domain of leaders is the future; they are asking themselves "what's new?" and "what's next?" even while they may be hunkering down in the present. Like Christian and his colleagues, you need to make choices today that are consistent with where you want to be in the future and, indeed, choices that tee you up for it. Master chess players study what has happened in the past, and play the game in the present, but make moves designed to get their pieces, and their opponents' pieces, into certain places for a future victory. This is the kind of thinking characterized by great thinkers, players, and leaders.

Visions are future oriented and are made real over different spans of time. It may take six months to create a new member recruitment and orientation process. It may take a couple of years to build your new group into one of the more respected student organizations on campus, just as it may take a decade to build a company that is one of the best places to work. It may take a lifetime to make neighborhoods safe again for children to walk alone. It may take a century to restore a forest destroyed by a wildfire. It may take generations to set a people free. It's pursuing a worthwhile change that matters, not how long it will take to make the change.

As a student leader, you have the opportunity to develop a forward-looking ability now so that you are experienced with visioning as you move into the workplace. It can seem unimportant to think about the future when you consider the relatively brief amount of time you are in school leading others. Yet, we know that leaders must be forward thinking all the time, regardless of the circumstances in which they find themselves. Even if you are leading others in a particular situation or project that might last only a year, you can still imagine what you want the group to be or look like at the end of that period. It takes practice to develop the ability to envision the future and it's a skill you will apply throughout your life. Why not start now?

The leader's job is to keep people focused on the future so that they will be eager to meet the daily challenges, work through the inevitable conflicts, and persevere to the end, which is exactly what Christine Mielke told us. While she was an undergraduate student, Christine launched Temptalia, now one of the most popular beauty blogs on the web, with over one million unique visitors each month. She told us that one of the most important reasons to be future oriented is so that "by keeping the big picture in mind you can help the group when they hit an obstacle or get hung up on details. Nobody gets left out wondering if what they are working on is making any difference in where we are going."

Imagination, asserted Nobel Prize–winning physicist Albert Einstein, is more important than intelligence, and this is even truer for leaders dealing with rapidly changing times. Give greater weight to thinking about what you're going to do after the current problem, task, assignment, project, or program has been completed. "What's next?" should be a question you ask yourself frequently. As a student, you are living in a culture where the goals are often short term; "If I can just get through this paper, examination, or semester" is the common mindset. But, if you're not thinking about what's happening after the completion of your longest-term project, then you're thinking only as long-term as everyone else. In other words, you're redundant! The leader's job is to think about the next project, and the one after that, and the one after that. This mindset can be very easy for student leaders to ignore. Your time in school, which may seem to last forever, is really a very short part of your life. Important time, surely, but short in the context of a whole lifetime. It is imperative to create time and space to think about the next things in your life, whether for your immediate school experience or those yet to come in your life beyond school.

Great football coaches, for example, demonstrate this beautifully. They aren't thinking about the current play on the field—that's the execution left up to the players, and they'll either be successful or not. What the coach is thinking about is the play after that, considering all the possibilities before even knowing the outcome of what's currently being executed. Similarly, chess players, poker players, even pool players aren't simply thinking about their next move. They are considering possible permutations that could emerge as the game unfolds. The same is true in all sports and games, and it's what you should be doing—thinking about what you and your group will be undertaking after what you're currently working on has been completed. As a leader you need to be thinking a few "moves" ahead of your team and picturing the future possibilities.

Whether it's through reading about trends, talking with others outside of your campus about issues they face, listening to international news sources, reading a variety of blogs, or watching different types of TED talks, a significant part of your job is developing a deep understanding of where things are going. Those who willingly follow you expect it. You have to spend more of today thinking more about tomorrow if your future is going to be an improvement over the present. And throughout the process of reflecting upon your past, attending to the present and imagining the future, you also need to keep in touch with what moves you, what you care about, where your passion is.

Feel Your Passion

Passion goes hand in hand with attention. People don't see possibilities when they don't feel any passion. Envisioning the future requires you to stay in touch with your deepest feelings. It's all about something that you find so important that you're willing to put in the time, suffer the inevitable setbacks, and make the necessary sacrifices. Everyone has concerns, desires, questions, propositions, arguments, hopes, and dreams—core issues that can help them organize their aspirations and actions. And every individual has a few things that are much more important to them than other things. Whatever yours are, you need to be able to name them so that you can talk about them with others. You have to step back and ask yourself, "What is my burning passion? What gets me up in the morning? What's grabbed hold of me and won't let go?"

This idea is exactly the kind of thinking that you should use to determine what you want to get involved in. Rather than joining groups or seeking experiences because you think it "looks good on your résumé," you should be looking for pursuits related to what you are passionate about. Leaders want to do something significant, to accomplish something that no one else has yet achieved. What that something is—your sense of meaning and purpose—has to come from within. No one can impose a self-motivating vision on you. That's why, just as we said about values, you must first clarify your own vision of the future before you can expect to enlist others in a shared vision.

Researchers in human motivation have long talked about two kinds of motivation—extrinsic and intrinsic.[5] People do things either because of external controls—the possibility of a tangible reward if they succeed or punishment if they don't—or because of an internal desire. People do something because they feel forced, or because they want to. People do something to please others, or because it pleases them. It's no surprise that intrinsic motivators are more likely to produce extraordinary results. The research is very clear on this subject: external motivation is more likely to create conditions of compliance or defiance; self-motivation produces far superior results. There's even an added bonus. People who are self-motivated will keep working toward a result even if there's no reward.[6] You've probably seen examples of this in sports. Even when it's obvious a team will lose the game, team members continue to play their hearts out because they are motivated from within. People who are externally controlled are likely to stop trying once the rewards or punishments are removed. It's a case of "Stop the pay, and stop the play."[7]

Exemplary leaders have a passion for something other than their own fame and fortune. They care about making a difference. If you don't care deeply for and about something how can you expect others to feel any sense of conviction? How can you expect others to feel passion if you're not energized and excited? How can you expect others to suffer through the long hours, hard work, absences from home, and personal sacrifices if you're not similarly committed? When Christine Mielke was asked to describe how she started her online blog she replied:

> My career—if you can really call it that, I think I have way too much fun for it to be a career!—began as a hobby, so it was and still is a very organic process. I just started doing something that I loved and was interested in, and by staying dedicated to it and finding ways to make it better, it ended up being much more successful than I ever thought possible.

And if you ask her if she ever gets tired of blogging several times each day, she'll say, "Nope—I just remember why I blog and who I blog for—the readers—and that I never want to let them down!" Christine feels passionately that "every person deserves to feel beautiful and confident from the inside out and free to express themselves" and her passion not only energizes her but inspires others to share this same vision.

When you feel your passion, as Christine clearly does, you know you are on to something very important. Your enthusiasm and drive spread to others. Finding something you truly believe in is the key to articulating a vision in the first place. Once you're in touch with this inner feeling, you can look and think beyond the constraints of your current role and view the possibilities available in the future.

FIND A COMMON PURPOSE

All too often, leaders have come to assume that it is solely their responsibility to be the visionaries. After all, if focusing on the future sets leaders apart, it's understandable that leaders would get the feeling that it's their job to embark alone on a quest to discover the future of their organization.

This is *not* what groups expect. Yes, leaders are expected to be forward looking, but they aren't expected to impose their vision of the future on others. People don't really want to listen to just the *leader's* vision. They want to hear about how their *own* visions and aspirations will come true, how their own hopes and dreams will be fulfilled. They want to see themselves in the picture of the future that the leader is painting. The key task for leaders is inspiring a *shared* vision, not selling their own particular view of the world. What this requires is finding common ground among the people who have to implement the vision. People in the group want to feel part of the process.[8]

Jade Orth began learning about leadership back in middle school. She believes the lessons she learned then (about giving back) drive what is important to her today. Her earlier experiences helped her define a vision for an event she initiated with a small group of students on her college campus to give something back to their community: a Veterans Day ceremony to recognize local veterans. Jade had several family members who were veterans and she brought others along into realizing her vision first by sharing with the group why she felt so strongly that it was important to have such a ceremony. Nothing was being done in Jade's college town to honor the substantial number of veterans there who had sacrificed much and gotten very little in return in terms of recognition and appreciation. In talking with the people around campus that she thought could help make the Veterans Day observance a reality, Jade shared her vision of making the ceremony an annual event. A group of supporters formed around this kernel of an idea, and people started to share their thoughts about how to sustain the program. Some of the ideas didn't work out and some did, but the group kept talking through their visions. Jade knew that she couldn't just "tell" others what to do. Through this sharing and discussion process they worked to keep the focus on the things that would make the event special rather than being concerned about who was having their idea heard or selected.

What Jade found out is something every leader must understand: nobody really likes being told what to do or where to go, no matter how worthwhile it might be. People want to be a part of the vision development process. The vast majority of people are just like Jade's team members. They want to walk with their leaders. They want to dream with them, invent with them, and be involved in creating their own futures.

This means that you have to stop taking the view that visions come from the top down. Jade said, "It doesn't always have to be my idea, nor should it be. The more people we have sharing ideas, the better ideas we will get. We accepted that with five or seven heads in a group we are going to get differing or conflicting views, but we approached our conversations with a give and take attitude and that worked pretty well." You have to start engaging others in a conversation about the future instead of delivering a monologue. You can't mobilize people to willingly travel to places they don't want to go. No matter how grand the dream of an individual, if others don't see themselves in it, realizing their own hopes and desires, they won't follow willingly. You must show others how they, too, will be served by the long-term vision of the future, how their specific needs can be satisfied.

Jade was clear in her mind about what she hoped to accomplish, and she also was careful to make sure others either shared in her ideas or had their own thoughts incorporated into the vision for the ceremony. Jade told us that there were many people involved in launching the Veterans Day celebration, from fellow students to campus officials to local veterans. She said she knew that she had to trust others and their commitment to the cause. Rather than giving orders, Jade told us, "I regularly checked with the group to be sure we were all still on board with the project and staying true to what our vision was. If we weren't I knew that I had a responsibility to keep us focused on our vision. I recognized that each person brought something special to the group, and I wanted to trust in and respect their ideas of where we should be going. It was about the collaboration."

Listen Deeply to Others

By knowing the members of your team, group, or organization, by listening to them, and by taking their advice you are able to give a voice to their feelings. That's what Jade did. You're then able to stand before others and say with assurance, "Here's what I heard you say that you want for yourselves. Here's how your own needs and interests will be served by all of us believing in this common cause." In a sense, leaders hold up a mirror and reflect back to others what they say they want most.

One of the challenges Jade faced was being part of two structured groups at her college: she was enrolled in a leadership class and was a member of student government, both of which had a stake in the event. She was able to help both groups come together and collaborate by understanding how each saw its role in the program. She talked regularly with both groups about their commitment to the program and also about what they were comfortable with and interested in doing. "I wanted to make sure both groups felt as comfortable as possible and felt that they could play the role they wanted in creating the event," she said. "I did that by listening a lot to others."

You need to strengthen your ability to hear what is important to others. The outlines of any vision do not come from a crystal ball. They originate from conversations with members of your team or club. They come from interactions with other students in classes, at campus events, and over meals. They're heard in the hallways, in meetings, and on social media. When Alvin Chen was a resident assistant for the Center for Talented Youth of Johns Hopkins University, he learned that "listening is one of the best things any leader can do." In launching the program's first international summer academic camp in Nanjing, China, there were many things that needed to be done and most of them for the first time in this new venue. Alvin and his team were, in his words, "learning as we went." His takeaway lesson was an appreciation for how "every stakeholder has a voice, and you should never underestimate or undervalue their opinions."

The best leaders, as Alvin and Jade attest, are great listeners. They listen carefully to what other people have to say and how they feel. They have to ask good (and often tough) questions, be open to ideas other than their own, and even lose arguments in favor of the common good. Through intense listening leaders get a sense of what people want, what they value, and what they dream about. This sensitivity to others is no trivial skill. It is a truly precious human ability.

Make It a Cause for Commitment

When you listen deeply, you can find out what gives work its meaning to others. People stay loyal to an organization, research finds, because they like the people they work with and they experience the work they are doing as challenging, meaningful, and purposeful.[9] When you listen with sensitivity to the aspirations of others you discover that there are some common values that link everyone together.[10] People of all ages, it turns out, want:

- A chance to be tested, to make it on their own
- A chance to take part in a social experiment
- A chance to do something well
- A chance to do something good
- A chance to change the way things are

Aren't these the essence of what most leadership challenges are all about? Research in the workplace suggests that people have a deep desire to make a difference. People want to know that they have done something on this earth, that there's a purpose to their existence. Work has become a place where people pursue meaning and identity. The same holds for participating in campus organizations, teams, and clubs. The best leaders satisfy this human desire by communicating the significance of the group's work so that people understand their own important role in creating it. When leaders clearly communicate a shared vision of an organization, they enrich those who work on its behalf. They elevate the human spirit.

When Ella Tepper served as one of the Campus Governors at her university, the group was charged with developing a program that would inform students about what student government could offer them and how they could get involved. In the past, these events had mostly highlighted free food and giveaways. Ella was determined to make the experience more meaningful, she told us.

> I'm a student too, and I knew that when I attended events like this, I wanted something more. I wanted to leave with more knowledge and have takeaways that were really useful. I wanted to create a way for people to talk about student government, ask questions, and learn.

Ella started by talking to the chief of staff about her ideas and then quickly went to the larger staff with a goal to create a program where students would leave with a good understanding of what student government did for them. They quickly got focused on how the event could be transformed into a space for meaningful conversations about student government. This focus became the cause that the team was committed to and they generated many good ideas about giveaways that would last and discussions that would truly inform. Together they came up with the idea of a safari. Each student got a passport to different areas where representatives from the different parts of student government were stationed to answer questions. Once the students circled through all the tables they got a bag of school supplies. The team, as Ella explained, had come up with a way to spark significant conversations about the purpose of student government and provide participating students with useful and lasting souvenirs of the experience.

> There is no way I would have come up with all the great ideas they had; and their commitment to design something that gave the students opportunities to ask questions and have meaningful dialogue was amazing. They were all so committed to helping students see the value of the student government they were part of. I may have been the leader, but they were the ones that made the event successful.

People commit to causes, not to plans. How else do you explain why people volunteer to rebuild communities ravaged by a tsunami, ride a bike from San Francisco to Los Angeles to raise money to fight AIDS, or rescue people from the rubble of a collapsed building after a tornado? How else do you explain why people work 24/7 to create the next big thing when the probability of failure is very high? People are not committing to the plan in any of these cases. There may not even be a plan to commit to. They are committing to something much bigger, something much more compelling than goals and milestones on a piece of paper. That's not to say that plans aren't important to executing on great dreams. They absolutely are. It's just to say that the plan isn't the thing that people are committing to.

Look Forward in Times of Rapid Change

In this digital age when the world is changing at warp speed, people often ask, "How can I have a vision of what's going to happen over the next semester or year, when I don't even know what's going to happen next week?" We can look to the business world for inspiration here. Venture capitalist Geoff Yang has taken risks on many new technology companies that are expected to move at a rapid pace. What type of innovators is he willing to back? "Men and women with great vision," he says. "They are able to recognize patterns when others see chaos in the marketplace. That's how they spot unexploited niche opportunities. And they are passionate about their ideas, which are revolutionary ways to change the way people live their lives or the way businesses operate. When they come to me they have conviction."[11]

Look at it this way. Imagine you're driving along the Pacific Coast Highway heading south from San Francisco on a bright, sunny day. The hills are on your left; the ocean, on your right. On some curves, the cliffs plunge several hundred feet to the water. You can see for miles and miles. You're cruising along at the speed limit, tunes blaring, top down, wind in your hair, and not a care in the world. Suddenly, without warning, you come around a bend in the road and there's a blanket of fog as thick as you've ever seen. What do you do?

We've asked this question many, many times, and here are some of the things people tell us:

- I slow way down.
- I turn my lights on.
- I grip the steering wheel with both hands.
- I tense up.
- I sit up straight or lean forward.
- I turn the music off.

Then you go around the next curve in the road, the fog lifts, and it's clear again. What do you do? Relax, speed up, turn the lights off, put the music back on, and enjoy the scenery.

This analogy illustrates the importance of clarity of vision. Are you able to go faster when it's foggy or when it's clear? How fast can you drive in the fog without risking your own or other people's lives? How comfortable are you riding in a car with someone who drives fast in the fog? The answers are obvious, aren't they? You're better able to go fast when your vision is clear. You're better able to anticipate the curves and bumps in the road when you can see ahead. No doubt, there are times in your life when you find yourself, metaphorically speaking, driving in the fog. When this happens you get nervous and unsure of what's ahead. You slow down. But as you continue forward the way becomes clearer and eventually you're able to speed up again.

Simply put, to become a leader you must be able to envision the future. The speed of change doesn't alter this fundamental truth. People want to follow only those who can see beyond today's problems and visualize a brighter tomorrow.

TAKE ACTION: ENVISION THE FUTURE

The most important role of vision in student organizational life is to give focus to the energy of others. To enable everyone involved and concerned with an effort to see more clearly what's ahead of them you must have and convey an exciting, worthwhile, and meaningful vision of the future. The path to clarity of vision begins with reflecting on the past, moves to attending to the present, and then involves imagining the future. And the guardrails along this path are your passions—what it is that you care about most deeply.

Although you have to be clear about your own vision before you can expect others to follow, you need to keep in mind that you can't effectively and authentically lead others to places they personally don't want to go. If the vision is to be attractive to more than an insignificant few, it must appeal to all who have a stake in it. Only *shared* visions have the magnetic power to sustain commitment over time, to keep people connected to the group or the cause rather than walk out the door in large numbers. Listen to the voices of all those in your groups; listen for their hopes, dreams, and aspirations. And because a common vision spans over time and keeps everyone focused on the future, it has to be about more than a task or job. It has to be a cause, something meaningful, and something that makes a difference in people's lives. Whether you're leading a community project, a fraternity or sorority, a campuswide event, or a national student movement, a shared vision sets the agenda and gives direction and purpose to all those involved.

The first commitment of Inspiring a Shared Vision requires *envisioning the future by imagining exciting and ennobling possibilities*. Here are some things you can do:

- Ask yourself what it is you care about, what drives you, where your passions lie.
- Think about all the things you want to accomplish. Can you say why these are so important to you? How do they connect to your values?
- Try to change the thinking about what you and others are doing; move it from being just an assignment, project, or event to becoming a "calling."
- What past experiences might be clues for understanding key themes in your life and for knowing what you find worthwhile? Make a list for each set of clues and see how they might connect.
- Stay curious about what is going on around you—especially things that aren't working well.
- Be the one who asks "what's next?" about every project long before it is completed.
- List five ways you can think about and find out about the future. Practice them all.
- Make a commitment to listen to others about what is important to their future.
- Come up with ways you can involve others in creating what could be possible; don't make it a process where you give out the orders about what to do.
- Get people on the same page, the same path, about where you all are going.

NOTES

1. D. Gilbert, *Stumbling on Happiness* (New York: Knopf, 2006), 5–6.
2. For an in-depth discussion of what people look for in their leaders, see J. M. Kouzes and B. Z. Posner, *Credibility: How Leaders Gain It and Lose It. Why People Demand It*, 2nd ed. (San Francisco: Jossey-Bass, 2011). Also see J. M. Kouzes and B. Z. Posner, *The Leadership Challenge: How to Make Extraordinary Things Happen in Organizations*, 5th ed. (San Francisco: Jossey-Bass, 2012). What's also

true is that the importance placed on "forward-looking" increases both with years of work experience and level in the organization.

3. J. P. Schuster, *The Power of Your Past; The Art of Recalling, Recasting, and Reclaiming* (San Francisco: Berrett-Koehler, 2011).
4. O. A. El Sawy, "Temporal Perspective and Managerial Attention: A Study of Chief Executive Strategic Behavior," unpublished doctoral dissertation, Stanford University, 1983. Also see O. A. El Sawy, "Temporal Biases in Strategic Attention," research paper, Marshall School of Business, University of Southern California, November 1988. See also J. T. Seaman, Jr., and G. D. Smith, "Your Company's History as a Leadership Tool," *Harvard Business Review* (December 2012): 44–52. For an example of learning from the past see E. Florian, "The Best Advice I Ever Got," *Fortune* (February 6, 2012): 14.
5. See E. L. Deci with R. Flaste, *Why We Do What We Do: Understanding Self-Motivation* (New York: Penguin, 1995). For another excellent treatment of this subject, see K. W. Thomas, *Intrinsic Motivation at Work: Building Energy and Commitment* (San Francisco: Berrett-Koehler, 2000); and for an extensive academic treatment, see C. Sansone and J. M. Harackiewicz (eds.), *Intrinsic and Extrinsic Motivation: The Search for Optimal Motivation and Performance* (New York: Academic Press, 2000).
6. D. Pink, *Drive: The Surprising Truth About What Motivates Us* (New York: Penguin Group, 2009); and L. Freifeld, "Why Cash Doesn't Motivate," *Training* 48, no. 4 (July/August 2011): 17–22.
7. Deci with Flaste, *Why We Do What We Do*, 25.
8. J. M. Kouzes and B. Z. Posner, "To Lead, Create a Shared Vision," *Harvard Business Review* (January 2009).
9. B. L. Kaye and S. Jordon-Evans, *Love 'Em or Lose 'Em: Getting Good People to Stay*, 4th ed. (San Francisco: Berrett-Koehler, 2008).
10. This list was originally shared with us in a telephone interview with Dave Berlew, November 14, 1994, based upon his research. See D. E. Berlew, "Leadership and Organizational Excitement," *California Management Review* 17, no. 2 (1974): 21–30. Others have reported similar findings about what employees want most at work.
11. As quoted in L. Ioannou, "Make Your Company an Idea Factory," *Fortune* (June 12, 2000): F264N–F264R.

5

Commitment #4: Enlist Others

Fabrice Guerrier's life in Haiti has exposed him to both extreme poverty and the immense wealth of the human spirit. This rich perspective goes far in inspiring others to develop a sense of belonging to something special—in Fabrice's case, channeling student energy and brainpower to address some of the world's thorniest problems.

"The current system this world is operating under is not only broken but outdated," Fabrice told us.

> We don't fully comprehend the scope and nature of our problems because of our short-minded nature, our nature to gravitate towards ideas and perspectives that mirror our own biases. Yet, we have the capacity to open our minds and apply our learning. Simply put, the problems that continue to plague humanity remain unresolved because we as a global community are not working together and more importantly, we are not asking the right questions. I wanted to find a way to work together.

When he started his undergraduate studies at a large state university in the United States, Fabrice was intent on finding a way to tap into the talent, the "genius," he saw in all his fellow students to explore ways to address some of the social imbalances he observed in the world. His vision was to use the students' collective brainpower, leveraging the differences in their experience, intellect, and ideology, to explore potential public policy, activism, and diplomatic solutions and in the process to awaken the genius within them individually and collectively to create a new age.

To enable others to share in this vision, Fabrice created the LEEHG (Leadership, Economics, Environment, Human Rights, and Geopolitics) Institute for Foreign Policy, a nonprofit student-run think tank. He believed the creative ideas of a committed group of students could provide the instruments to help sculpt the future. "'Awakening the Genius Within' is our motto," he told us. "We are all geniuses in our own ways. No matter who you are or where you come from, your existence on this planet is meaningful. Each person is an important piece of the puzzle for discovering solutions to our day-to-day societal problems." Armed with this message Fabrice began to enlist his fellow students, encouraging them to come together to share their unique perspectives, to learn, and to generate ideas.

The LEEHG Institute for Foreign Policy serves as the topical lens to build the critical analytical thinking skills Fabrice believes are essential to the group's mission to better understand the world, access the genius within, and generate ideas for change. In inviting people to be part of a global community, Fabrice appeals to them to become one of a group of individual "LEEHGeniuses" committed to the betterment and advancement of the human race. As the organization has grown, topical conferences have spun off to address the issues the group finds most compelling. Fabrice believes these conferences come into being like volunteer seeds in a garden:

> If you can enlist people and make them feel they are part of a community where they learn together and develop their voice, they use it! Our discussions generate ideas that engage them, tap into their emotions and brainpower, and build energy around a given topic.

Once such event was the Inaugural LEEHG Crisis Discussion Forum. The intent of this Forum was to give students an experience that would strengthen their critical thinking skills and enable them to learn what they would experience in the real-world practice of diplomacy. Forum participants addressed two ongoing crises: The Syrian Civil War and the unrest in Colombia between the government and the Revolutionary Armed Forces of Colombia (FARC). They formed small groups at the start of the forum and were assigned a role or position of some player within one of the situations. For example, participants might be assigned the role of an individual from a particular region, for instance, someone who represents an agency that is addressing a particular problem such as illegal drug trafficking or child soldier practices. Or they might be assigned the role of someone in a governmental position responsible for a specific geographic region. In playing out their roles, they were asked to represent their interests and work to implement policies that might resolve the issues that had a direct impact on them while learning about how those policies might affect others. As they engaged in interactive discussion, dialogue, and debate around the two scenarios, the students were observed by a panel of professors who offered immediate feedback on how well they represented their role and how effective their arguments were.

Events like this gave students a chance to come together and learn in real time about the many dimensions of complex world issues. Fabrice says that when they appreciate the power of learning in this way, these students often begin to enlist others: "Once they have had a chance to be part of this kind of compelling discussion, their minds begin to open and their energy and enthusiasm build as they witness the impact and influence they can have together. They naturally want to expand that potential by enlisting others into the group think tank."

In the personal-best leadership cases we collected, people talked about the need to get everyone on board with a vision and to Enlist Others in a dream. Like Fabrice, they had to communicate and build support for their project, idea, or cause. These leaders knew that in order to get extraordinary things done everyone had to deeply believe in and commit to a common purpose.

Part of Enlisting Others is building common ground on which everyone can agree. But equally important is the emotion that leaders have for the vision. Our research shows that in addition to expecting leaders to be forward-looking, people want their leaders to be *inspiring*. People need a lot of energy and excitement to sustain commitment to a distant dream. Leaders are expected to be a major source of that energy. People aren't going to follow someone who's only mildly enthusiastic about something. Leaders have to be *wildly* enthusiastic for people to give it their all.

Whether you're trying to mobilize a crowd in the grandstand or one person you're sharing a class assignment with, to Enlist Others you must act on these two essentials:

- Appeal to common ideals
- Animate the vision

Enlisting Others is all about igniting passion for a purpose, providing the emotional drive required to face the predictable ups and downs and to see the hard work through to the end. To make extraordinary things happen in groups you have to go beyond reason; you have to engage the hearts along with the minds of people in your group. You start by understanding their desire for something meaningful and significant.

APPEAL TO COMMON IDEALS

In every personal-best case leaders talked about ideals. They expressed a desire to make dramatic changes whatever their environment. They reached for something big, something meaningful and significant, and something that had never been done before.

Visions are about ideals. They're about hopes, dreams, and aspirations. They're about the strong desire to achieve something great.

They're ambitious. They're expressions of optimism. Can you imagine a leader enlisting others in a cause by saying, "I'd like you to join me in doing the ordinary"? We doubt many would want to go along. Visions are what stretch people to imagine exciting possibilities for their cause, whether it's simply a new approach to an old event or a revolutionary social change such as LEEHG's focus on "creating a new age."

When you communicate your vision of the future to your group, you need to talk about how they're going to make a difference, how they're going to have a positive impact on people and events. You need to show them how their long-term desires can be realized by being part of a common vision. You need to speak to the higher meaning and purpose of the work. You need to describe a compelling image of what the future could be like when people join together in a common cause.

Connect to What's Meaningful to Others

While enlisting others in the LEEHG Institute for Foreign Policy, Fabrice shared examples of the imbalances that existed in the world, and asked if others felt as he did that things needed to change. As the organization grew he built on the issues that clearly resonated with the Institute's members, understanding the importance that each student feel a personal connection to the work at hand. Fabrice encourages students to bring to the discussion table particular issues that concern them. "We form groups of interest such as The Syrian Crisis, or Inequities in South Africa," he explained.

In discussions and role plays on these topics students are able to express their passions and hone their ability to influence. Observing these sessions also helps students to learn about these topics and develop an informed opinion. The more they know, the better the chances are that they can come up with a possible solution.

Exemplary leaders don't impose their visions of the future on people; they help them recognize the vision that is already within them. They awaken dreams, breathe life into them, and arouse the belief that people can achieve something important. When they communicate a shared vision, they bring this into the conversation. What truly pulls people forward, especially in difficult times, is the possibility that what they are doing can make a real difference. People want to know that what they do matters.

Leaders help others to see that what they are doing matters and that their work can be something great, something that lifts them all up. Leaders believe the work they're doing makes a difference in other people's lives; that it is work done for the greater good and that it helps make things better for others.

Take Pride in Being Unique

Exemplary leaders also communicate what makes their group, organization, club, team, or project stand out and rise above all others. Compelling visions differentiate and set "us" apart from "them," and they must do so in order to attract and retain group members. People often leave groups because they don't know, understand, or believe in the vision of the group. There's no advantage in being just like everybody else. When people understand how they're truly distinctive and how they stand out in the crowd they're a lot more eager to voluntarily sign up and invest their energies.

Leaders get people excited about signing on to a group's vision by making certain that everyone involved feels that what they do is unique and believes that they play a crucial role regardless of titles or specific task responsibilities. The homepage of the LEEHG blog declares that the organization is dedicated to thinking differently and relying on the unique brain power of its members, who are referred to as "LEEHGeniuses." The intent is to instill a distinctive sense that each individual member in the organization is special as well as the group as a whole.

Feeling special fosters a sense of pride. It boosts the self-respect and self-esteem of everyone associated with the group. When people are proud to be part of your group's effort and serve its purpose, and when they feel that what they are doing is meaningful, they become enthusiastic ambassadors to the outside world. When people are proud to "be part of the team," they are more loyal and more likely to recruit their friends to be part of it as well. When the campus and community are proud to have you as a member, they're going to do everything they can to make you feel welcome.

David Chan Tar Wei knows a lot about promoting individual and collective pride. His college decided to start a new system of "houses" intended to spark greater school spirit and add more diversity to school life. David worked with a committee tasked with exploring various ideas for setting the new house groups apart from one another and thereby fostering greater house unity and pride. "The houses originally did not have unique ways to represent themselves," he explained, "and we felt strongly that things like house shirts and house crests could be used and accepted as formal symbols of identification." David and his committee went on to incorporate house outfits, insignia, and other distinguishing devices into almost every school event, from Orientation to Teachers' Day, to "create the house vibrancy and culture that we sought."

David's experience shows how feeling unique also makes it possible for smaller groups to have their own visions and still serve a larger, collective vision. While every subgroup within a larger organization—be it a religious institution, school, or volunteer association—must be aligned with the overall vision, each can express its distinctive purpose within the larger whole. How your student club or team carries out its daily functions must fit in with the vision of the school, youth organization, or university. Every function and every small group can differentiate itself by finding its most distinctive qualities. Each can be proud of its own ideal image of its future as it works toward the common future of the larger organization.

Align Your Dream with the People's Dream

In learning how to appeal to people's ideals, move their souls, and uplift their spirits—and your own—the Internet is a great resource. What is it that gets people engaged? The Arab Spring revolution in Egypt was sparked by people voicing their passion about their country via tweets and Facebook posts. Another great example is a classic YouTube video of social researcher Brené Brown. Her TED talk on "The Power of Vulnerability" took off because of the deep connection people felt for her research findings that, as counterintuitive as it seems, vulnerability is the birthplace of joy, creativity, belonging, and love, the things we treasure most.[1] Look online to see what gets people excited. Obviously there is a mountain of funny pet videos and celebrity bloopers to wade through, but when you find a piece like Brené Brown's, can you identify what made it go viral? What did she say that appealed to so many? Find a speech, a song, or performance that draws you in and speaks to your heart and your core values. What is it that grabs you and won't let go?

There is no better place to look than to the late Reverend Dr. Martin Luther King Jr., whose "I Have a Dream" speech tops the list of the best American public addresses of the twentieth century. On the US national holiday marking his birthday, this speech is replayed and young and old alike are reminded of the power of a clear and uplifting vision of the future. If you have never listened closely to Dr. King's words, take a few moments to read or hear them.[2]

Imagine that you are there on that hot and humid day—August 28, 1963—when on the steps of the Lincoln Memorial in Washington, DC, before a throng of 250,000, Martin Luther King Jr. proclaimed his dream to the world. Imagine that you're listening to Dr. King as thousands around you clap and applaud and cry out. Now try to better understand why this speech is so powerful and how he is capable of moving so many people.

We've asked thousands of people over the years to listen to Dr. King's famous "I Have a Dream" speech and then tell us what they heard, how they felt, and why they thought this speech remains so moving even today.[3] Below are many of their observations.

- It appeals to common interests. Most anyone in the audience or those who heard this speech afterward could find something personal to which they could relate. He knew his audience.
- It talks about traditional values of family, religion, and patriotism.
- It is full of images and word pictures. You can visualize the examples.
- People could relate to the examples. They were familiar and credible.
- It was personal. It revealed something about the speaker.
- It included everybody: all ages, genders, multiple religions and geographies.
- It used a lot of repetition.
- It was positive and hopeful, although no promises were made that it would be easy.
- The focus shifted from "I" to "we."
- It was filled with genuine emotion and passion.

These are the qualities that are key to success in enlisting others. To get others excited about your dream, you need to speak about meaning and purpose. You have to *show them* how *their* dreams will be realized. You have to connect your message to their values, their aspirations, their experiences, and their own lives. You have to show them that it's not about you, but that it's about them and their needs and the communities to which they belong, whether that is a university campus, a fraternity, a team, or a community group. The ability to tap into people's passion is rooted in fundamental values, cultural traditions, personal conviction, and a capacity to use words to create positive images of the future. To enlist others, you need to bring the vision to life. You have to make the purpose real and alive so that others can see it, hear it, taste it, touch it, feel it. You have to make the connection between an inspiring vision of the future and the personal aspirations and passions of the people with whom you are working.

You have to describe a compelling image about how people's dreams can be realized by enlisting in a common cause.

Admittedly, you don't give TED talks and you are not a Martin Luther King. Well, neither is Sheri Lee. As the editor of her school's yearbook, she needed to get everyone on the same page, motivating them to work hard all year long, generally producing smaller pieces of the overall project that would disappear into the yearbook a few days after the work was completed. As you read what she told her peers on the yearbook staff, think about how these remarks employ many of the same techniques utilized by Brown and King:

> Yearbook is something that I enjoy because we are making something that will be treasured for the rest of our lives. We are in charge of preserving all the memories that occur during this school year and it is up to us to make sure that there is a yearbook to hand out at the end of the year. Just think, every time that you look at this year's yearbook, you can see that all your hard work paid off in the pages that you created. When you are older, you can look back at and be proud that you were responsible for creating something so unique.

ANIMATE THE VISION

Leaders have to engage others to join in a cause and to want to move decisively forward. Part of motivating others is appealing to their ideals. Another part is animating the vision, essentially breathing life into it. To enlist others you have to help them *see* and *feel* how they are aligned with the vision. You have to paint a compelling picture of the future, one that helps the group believe in it. That's the only way your group will find the inspiration that moves them to commit their individual energy to keep going forward.

"But I'm not good at giving powerful presentations," you say. "I can't possibly do what those motivational speakers do." Many people initially respond this way. Most people don't see themselves as personally uplifting, and certainly don't get much encouragement for behaving this way in most organizations. Despite the acknowledged importance of compelling visions, our research finds that many people are uncomfortable with the leadership practice of Inspire a Shared Vision. Their discomfort comes mostly from having to publicly express their emotions, something many have not been taught and are unaccustomed to doing. We're not suggesting that sharing your feelings is easy to do, but don't underestimate your capacity to communicate with passion and enthusiasm.

People's perception of themselves as uninspiring is in sharp contrast to their performance when they talk about their personal-best leadership experiences or when they talk about their ideal futures—or even when they talk about a vacation they just took or an exciting sports event they just won or witnessed. When relating hopes, dreams, and successes, people are almost always emotionally expressive. Expressiveness comes naturally when talking about deep desires for the something that could be better in the future than it is today.

Most people have attributed something mystical to the process of being inspirational. They seem to see it as something that other people possess, but certainly not them. This assumption inhibits people far more than any lack of natural talent for being inspirational. It's not necessary to be a charismatic person to Inspire a Shared Vision. It is necessary, however, *to believe*—and to develop the skills to communicate that belief—in order to bring the vision to life. If you're going to lead, you have to recognize that your enthusiasm and expressiveness are incredibly important in your efforts to generate commitment in others.

Use Symbolic Language

During their 2012 season the San Jose Earthquakes soccer team had a knack for being down and then coming back to score and winning their games in the last few moments. When one of their players,

Stephen Lenhart, was asked about this he said, "Goonies never say die"—a reference to a popular 1980s film. At the start of the playoffs that year the team gave their fans headbands with that motto imprinted on them, and they stuck with that sentiment even in the following season, which was much less successful.

Leaders use metaphors and analogies to communicate a shared identity and give life to visions. They give examples, tell stories, and relate anecdotes; they draw word pictures; and they offer quotations and recite slogans. In other words, leaders embrace the power of symbolic language to help the group picture the possibilities—to hear it, to sense it, to recognize it.

Think about just one type of symbolic language: metaphors. Metaphors are everywhere—there are art metaphors, game and sports metaphors, war metaphors, science fiction metaphors, machine metaphors, and religious or spiritual metaphors. They influence what we think, what we invent, what we eat and drink, how we think, for whom we vote, and what we buy. Metaphors capture the energy and emotion that individuals feel and allow you to tap into that quickly and often. Your ability to enlist others in a common vision of the future will be greatly enhanced by learning to use metaphors and other symbolic speech elements.

For example, you can influence people's behavior simply by giving the task or the team a name that evokes the kind of behavior it implies. Notice how fraternities or sororities use words like *brothers* and *sisters*, and not simply *members*, to evoke the notion of being part of closely connected, much like members of a family. If you want people to act like a community, use language that evokes a feeling of community—words like *fellowship, neighborhood*, and *citizens*, for example. If you want them to act like Spiderman, "sticking" with things and working for the good of all, use language that cues those images. Words like these show you why paying close attention to the language you choose and the language you use will serve you well as a leader.

Make Images of the Future

Visions are images in the mind. They become real as leaders express those images to others. Just as architects make drawings and engineers build models, leaders find ways of giving expression to collective hopes for the future.

When you think about how people speak about the future, it typically includes words like *foresight, focus, forecasts, future scenarios, points of view*, and *perspectives*. The thing that these words have in common is that they are visual references. The word *vision* itself has at its root the verb "to see." Statements of vision, then, should not be statements at all. They should be pictures—word pictures. They're not facts and figures; they're images and impressions. For a vision to be shared it needs to be *seen* in the mind's eye.

In our workshops and classes we often illustrate the power of images with this simple exercise. We ask people to shout out the first thing that comes to mind when they hear the words *Paris, France*. The replies that pop out—the Eiffel Tower, the Louvre, the Arc de Triomphe, the Seine, Notre Dame, good food, wine, romance—are all images of real places and real sensations. No one calls out the square kilometers, population, or gross domestic product of Paris. Why? Because most of what we recall about important places or events are those things associated with our senses—sights, sounds, tastes, smells, tactile sensations, and feelings.

So what does this mean for leaders? To enlist others and inspire a shared vision, you must be able to draw upon that very natural mental process of creating images. When you speak about the future, you need to create pictures with words so that others get a mental image of what things will be like when you are at the end of your journey. When talking about going places you've never been you have to be able to imagine what they'll look like. You have to picture the possibilities (those who are more auditory by nature talk about those possibilities as a "calling"). Making the possibilities come alive is exactly what

David Mullenburg did when he recruited all the members of his senior class to go on an overnight backpacking trip. When we asked how he got people to sign up, David replied, "I told stories of past camping trips I had been on, how great they were, and painted a picture of how much fun we would all have."

Getting people to see a common future does not require some special power. Every one possesses this ability. You do it every time you return from a vacation and share the photos with your friends. If you doubt your own ability, try this exercise. Sit down with a few close friends and tell them about one of your favorite vacations. Describe the people you saw and met, the sights and sounds of the places you went, the smells and tastes of the food you ate. Show them the photos or videos if you have them. Observe their reactions—and your own. What's that experience like? We've done this activity many times, and people always report feeling energized and passionate. Those hearing about a place for the first time usually say something like, "After listening to you, I'd like to go there someday myself." By the way, this is often the way that members of your campus crew team convince people to join up: "Imagine how great it will be to go to bed early and get up in the morning before everyone else does, before the sun even rises, get out on a lake, and start rowing with your friends. If you can see this as fun, exciting, and rewarding, then you're a perfect candidate for the crew team!" Or water polo, ice hockey, or lots of other special activities!

Practice Positive Communication

To foster team spirit, breed optimism, promote resilience, and renew faith and confidence, leaders learn to look on the bright side. They keep hope alive. They strengthen others' belief that life's struggles will produce something meaningful and positive.

Alyssa Giagliani ran track and cross-country on the varsity team in her freshman year and remembers talking with the freshman team at the end of their first season. They had won the freshman division title race, and Alyssa asked them what they saw in their future. They said they didn't think they had a future in running; winning the title had probably just been a fluke.

The freshmen then asked Alyssa the same question right back, and she told them, "I see a great potential: the potential to be the first women's team in the history of our school to make the championships and win league titles and a division title." These aspirations had never crossed the freshman team's minds, Alyssa told us. "I could see that the freshmen, my future teammates, were enlightened by this idea and that they were willing to put in the hard work in order to attain those lofty goals."

Fast-forward to the varsity team's senior year. Alyssa lies in a hospital bed after a life-threatening auto accident. Her teammates tell her they don't have the heart to finish the season without her. Alyssa is flabbergasted and tells her team in no uncertain terms what she thinks about their quitting. She says that if they finish the season she will walk with them to the starting line the day of the championship race. "This way of getting my point across made my teammates realize that I was passionate about the team finishing what we started," she told us. That team didn't quit, Alyssa joined her teammates at the starting line, and they went on to become the first women's cross-country team in the school's history to advance to the championship meet and to win a major title.

People look for leaders who demonstrate an enthusiastic, genuine belief in the capacity of others, leaders who strengthen people's will, and who help support the needs of the group as they take on difficult tasks. They are drawn to leaders like Alyssa who express optimism for the future. People want leaders who remain passionate despite obstacles and setbacks. They want leaders with a positive, confident, can-do approach. Naysayers only stop forward progress; they do not start it. Researchers working with neural networks have documented that when people feel rebuffed or left out, the brain activates a site for registering physical pain.[4] People actually remember negative comments far more often, in greater detail, and with more intensity, than they do encouraging words. When negative remarks become a preoccupation, a person's brain loses mental efficiency. This is all the more reason for leaders to be positive.

A positive approach to life broadens people's ideas about future possibilities and these exciting options build on each other. Researchers have found that being positive opens you—your mind and your heart—and makes you more receptive to ideas and hence more creative.[5] You see more options, and hence you become more innovative. And that's not all. People who enjoy more positivity are better able to cope with difficulties, and are more resilient during times of high stress.[6] That's a vital capacity when dealing with challenges that people face as leaders in these uncertain and challenging times.

Express Your Emotions

In explaining why particular leaders have a magnetic effect, people often describe them as charismatic. But *charisma* has become such an overused and misused term that it's almost useless as a descriptor of leaders. Being charismatic is not a magical quality. It is simply a description of how people behave.

Social scientists have found that people who are perceived to be charismatic are just more animated than others.[7] They smile more, speak faster, pronounce words more clearly, and move their heads and bodies more often. Charisma, then, can better be understood as energy and expressiveness. The old saying that "enthusiasm is infectious" is certainly true for leaders. When you let your emotions show, without necessarily doing anything more, you will be viewed as expressive—that is, charismatic!

Emotions make things memorable. If you want to generate excitement among the members of your group, you need to communicate your emotions, both verbally and nonverbally. Having your messages remembered requires paying attention to adding emotion to your words and your behavior. Researchers have shown that "emotionally significant events create stronger, longer-lasting memories."[8] No doubt you've experienced this yourself when something emotionally significant has happened to you—a serious trauma, such as an accident, or a big surprise, such as winning a contest. But the events don't have to be real to be memorable. They can simply be stories. For example, in one experiment researchers showed subjects in two groups a series of twelve slides. The slide presentation was accompanied by a story, one line for each slide. For one group in the study the narrative was quite boring, for the other the narrative was emotionally moving. They didn't know when they watched the slides that they would be tested, but two weeks later they returned and took a test of how well they remembered the details of each slide. The groups did not differ in their memory of the first few or last few slides, but their recollection of the slides in the middle was significantly different. People who had listened to the emotionally arousing narrative remembered details better than the group that listened to the boring or more neutral story. If you want people to remember your message then you have to tap into their emotions; you have to arouse their feelings about the cause to which you want them to commit.

You don't need a complete narrative and you don't need slides. Just the words themselves can be equally effective as demonstrated in another laboratory experiment, where researchers asked subjects to learn to associate pairs of words. Some of the words in the pairs were used because they elicited strong emotional responses. Two weeks later, people remembered the emotionally arousing words better than they remembered the less arousing ones.[9] Whether it's a story or a word, you're more likely to remember the key messages when they're attached to something that triggers an emotional response. The reasons for this have to do with human physiology. People are wired to pay more attention to what excites them or scares them. Warm or cold. Use either word to describe someone else and our perceptions of their personalities are entirely different! Keep this in mind the next time you deliver any kind of presentation. It's not just the content that will make it stick; it's also how well you tap into people's emotions. People have to *feel* something to change. Thinking something isn't nearly enough to get things moving. Your job is to enable them to feel moved to change, and expressing emotions helps to do that.

Showing people a concrete example is better than telling them about an abstract principle, but that still leaves them on the outside looking in. If you can get them to experience what you are trying to explain, they will understand in a deeper way. For example, if you want your group or club to start a regular event where they work with underprivileged kids, can you take them to an ongoing event so they can experience firsthand the joy it brings to the kids?

The dramatic increase in the use of electronic technology also has an impact on the way people deliver messages. From podcasts to webcasts, social networking to video sharing, more and more people are turning to their digital devices and social media for information and connection. Because people remember things that have strong emotional content, social media has the potential for engaging people more than do e-mails, memos, and PowerPoint presentations. Leadership is a performing art, and this has become even truer as new technologies hit the market. It's no longer enough to write a good script—you've also got to put on a good show. And you've got to make it a show that people will remember.

Speak Genuinely

None of these suggestions about being more expressive will be of any value if you don't believe in what you're saying. If the vision is someone else's, and you don't own it, it will be very difficult for you to enlist others in it. If you have trouble imagining yourself actually living the future described in the vision, you'll certainly be unable to convince others that they ought to enlist in making it a reality. If you're not excited about the possibilities, you can't expect others to be. *The prerequisite to enlisting others in a shared vision is genuineness.*

Bailey Hamm had been a member of her sorority for three years and each year had run for an officer position. The first two times she lost the election to older, more experienced sisters. In her third attempt, she won a position but through some quirk in the bylaws lost it in a revote.

Bailey told us she never felt discouraged by the election outcomes. She was committed to what her sorority stood for and determined to find a way to continue to make the chapter better for its members. What was most important to her was to serve the women in her chapter whether she had a position or title or not.

Bailey eventually became her sorority's vice president for public relations and aspired to enhance the image of her sorority both within and outside the chapter. By this time she was a senior chapter member and felt it was important to communicate to her younger sisters, through her work and her words, who she was and the sincerity of her desire to lead and serve.

She often shared her personal story with the younger sorority members and explained why she believed the chapter could do great things and become stronger. She talked about how she had not been elected to three positions of leadership, and admitted it hadn't been easy for her to keep running for office. Still, she said, the sorority had done much for her and had the potential to make a huge difference in their lives and in the lives of their future sisters. She explained how important she believed it was for everyone to find a way to contribute to the group. Her efforts to become an officer in the organization had been a pretty big challenge, she admitted, yet all along she was out front about her intention to be part of her sorority's future, whether she held a position or not.

By being genuine and speaking from the heart about her vision for the chapter, she told us, "I wanted to show the other women that the choices I made after my election experiences were going to be true to who I was and what I thought our chapter stood for." Bailey used her circumstances as an example, not to dwell on the negative, but to speak genuinely and positively in showing her sisters that they can make a difference even when things are difficult. They might not see results in the next day or the next week, Bailey told them, but success would eventually come. And Bailey found the answers for how to talk to people not affiliated with the sorority system through the stories and insights she shared with her sisters: "Painting a positive picture of who we are and what we could do set me up to speak to people outside the sorority with conviction about what we stood for and what we could accomplish, and it energized people."

There's no one more believable than a person like Bailey with a deep passion for something. There's no one more fun to be around than someone who is openly excited about the magic that can happen. There's no one more determined than someone who believes fervently in an ideal. People want leaders who are upbeat, optimistic, and positive about the future. It's really the only way you can get people to willingly follow you to someplace they have never been before.

TAKE ACTION: ENLIST OTHERS

Leaders appeal to common ideals. They connect others to what is most meaningful in the shared vision. They lift people to higher levels of motivation and morality, and continuously reinforce that they can make a difference in the world. Exemplary leaders speak to what is unique and distinctive about the groups, projects, or causes they lead, making others feel proud to be a part of something extraordinary. And the best leaders understand that it's not their individual view of the future that's important; it's the aspirations of each and every person that matter most.

To last over time, visions must be compelling and memorable. Leaders must breathe life into visions, animating them so that others can experience what it would be like to live and work hard in that ideal and unique future. They use a variety of modes of expression to make their abstract visions concrete. Through skillful use of metaphors, symbols, word pictures, positive language, and personal energy leaders generate enthusiasm and excitement for the common vision. But above all, leaders must be convinced of the value of the shared vision and share that genuine belief with others. They must believe in what they are saying. If you don't truly believe in what you are doing or in what you want the group to do, how can you ever expect anyone else to believe in the cause or task? Authenticity is the key because people will only follow willingly if they sense that the vision is genuine.

Here are some actions you can take in order to demonstrate the second commitment of Inspire a Shared Vision, Enlist Others:

- Talk to others in your group and find out about their hopes, dreams, and aspirations for the future. Look for patterns and themes in their responses. Determine what their dreams have in common and how they align with your vision for the group.
- Speak about what your group can do specifically to bring the shared aspirations to life. Show that you listen to what they say by bringing their thoughts and ideas into the vision for the group. How will you rephrase or connect the dreams of others to your group's vision?
- Come up with ways to make sure that people are clear about what makes the group unique and how proud they can be about being distinctive.
- Show others how their long-term interests are served by them enlisting in a common vision, even if there may be some short-term sacrifices. Why should they persevere? How will there be a healthy self-interest in achieving a common good?
- Share metaphors, symbols, examples, stories, pictures, and words that represent the image of what you all aspire to become.
- Be positive, upbeat, and energetic when talking about the future of your organization.
- Be expressive. Use gestures, vary your tone of voice, and speak with authority. All these help others to experience your conviction for what you envision. And, if you haven't already done so, take a public speaking course.
- Acknowledge the emotions of others and validate them as important. When doing this, ask yourself if you are focusing more on the positive, productive emotions, or spending too much time on emotions that discourage and make people lose heart for the journey?
- When you get up each day remind yourself of the positive vision that you hold and the difference you are making. It will help sustain your excitement for what you are doing.

NOTES

1. Brené Brown, "The Power of Vulnerability," December 2010, http://www.ted.com/talks/brene_brown_on_vulnerability.html
2. "'I Have a Dream' Leads Top 100 Speeches of the Century," press release from the University of Wisconsin, December 15, 1999. Available online at www.news.wisc.edu/releases/3504.htmlorathttp://www.americanrhetoric.com/top100speechesall.html. See also: S. E. Lucas, M. J. Medhurst, *Words of a Century: The Top 100 American Speeches, 1900–1999.* (New York: Oxford University Press, 2008). Other leaders often seen on international lists of great speakers from recent history are Winston Churchill, Charles de Gaulle, Mahatma Gandhi, Vaclav Havel, Robert Kennedy, Nelson Mandela, Jawaharlal Nehru, Barack Obama, Ronald Reagan, Eleanor Roosevelt, Gloria Steinem, Mother Teresa, Margaret Thatcher, and Lech Walesa.
3. The audio version of the "I Have a Dream" speech that we have found to be most instructive is the version running 6 minutes and 11 seconds that contains the most famous passages. It is in the collection of *Greatest Speeches of All Time, Vol. 1*. You can download it from Amazon.com: http://www.amazon.com/Greatest-Speeches-All-Time-Vol/dp/B001L0RONE/ref=sr_1_cc_3?ie=UTF8&qid=1301516046&sr=1-3-catcorr. A printed version of this portion of the speech is in C. S. King (ed.), *The Words of Martin Luther King, Jr.* (New York: Newmarket Press, 1983), 95–98. A video can be viewed on YouTube at http://www.youtube.com/watch?v=smEqnnklfYs
4. D. Goleman, *Social Intelligence: The New Science of Human Relationships* (New York: Bantam, 2006).
5. Barbara L. Fredrickson, *Positivity: Groundbreaking Research Reveals How to Embrace the Hidden Strengths of Positive Emotions, Overcome Negativity, and Thrive* (New York: Crown Publishers, 2009), 21.
6. Fredrickson, *Positivity*, 60–65.
7. See, for example, H. S. Friedman, L. M. Prince, R. E. Riggio, and M. R. DiMatteo, "Understanding and Assessing Nonverbal Expressiveness: The Affective Communication Test," *Journal of Personality and Social Psychology* 39, no. 2 (1980): 333–351; D. Goleman, R. Boyatzis, and A. McKee, *Primal Leadership: Realizing the Power of Emotional Intelligence* (Boston: Harvard Business School Press, 2002); J. Conger, *Winning 'Em Over: A New Model for*

Management in the Age of Persuasion (New York: Simon & Schuster, 1998); and M. Greer, "The Science of Savoir Faire," *APA Monitor* 36, no. 1 (2005): 28.

8. J. L. McGaugh, *Memory and Emotion* (New York: Columbia University Press, 2003), 90. Also see R. Maxwell and R. Dickman, *The Elements of Persuasion: Use Storytelling to Pitch Better Ideas, Sell Faster, & Win More Business* (New York: HarperCollins, 2007), especially pages 122–150 on "Sticky Stories: Memory, Emotions and Markets."
9. McGaugh, *Memory and Emotion*, 92.

PRACTICE 3

Challenge the Process

Challenge is the crucible for greatness. People do their best when there's the chance to change the way things are. Maintaining the status quo breeds mediocrity. Leaders seek and accept challenging opportunities to test their abilities. They move others to exceed their self-perceived limits. They seize initiative and make something meaningful happen. Leaders treat every assignment as an adventure.

Most innovations do not originate from leaders—they come from the people closest to the work. They also come from *outsight*, meaning that exemplary leaders look for good ideas everywhere. They listen, take advice, and learn.

Progress is not made in giant leaps. It's made incrementally. Exemplary leaders move forward in small steps with little victories. They turn adversity into advantage and setbacks into successes. They persevere with grit and determination

Leaders venture out. They test and they take risks with bold ideas. And because risk taking involves mistakes and failure, leaders accept and grow from the inevitable disappointments. They treat these as learning opportunities.

In the next two chapters, we will see how leaders:

- **Search for Opportunities by seizing the initiative and by looking outward for innovative ways to improve.**
- **Experiment and Take Risks by constantly generating small wins and learning from experience.**

6

Commitment #5: Search for Opportunities

Logan Hall, an agricultural education major at his university, had been a member of a five-county 4-H Council in high school. 4-H is one of the largest youth development organizations in the United States with more than six million high school aged members. The organization focuses on personal development through learning by doing. Logan told us that 4-H is an opportunity for youth to learn life skills that they will be able to apply in all their future endeavors.

In his senior year Logan ran for the 4-H State Council in Pennsylvania, was elected, and became part of that leadership group. The State Council's role was to advance the purpose and vision of 4-H and to promote it throughout 67 counties in Pennsylvania. In addition they provided various research-based leadership training programs and curricula to local councils and their officers. That year, Logan's state leadership group influenced more than 110,000 other students with their events and training at 4-H clubs in his state.

The challenges and logistics involved in identifying and meeting the needs of other students from all across the state were not small. Logan and his team were concerned about how they could possibly meet the needs of all of these students, leaders, and chapters. "We realized we needed help and we had to find it ourselves," Logan told us. "So, we decided to look outside our state. We contacted the 4-H State Council in Tennessee and looked at what they had been doing to better serve their local and county councils. We asked them a lot of questions to learn what they did in their 4-H clubs."

To make the most of the opportunity to learn from the Tennessee group, Logan had to let go of the way his own council had been doing things, and he also had to let go of the way he wanted things to be done. "I still had my vision," he said, "but now I was realizing that we had a great group of resources available to the group. We needed to figure out how we could take that vision and reach a large mass of people. The vision shifted and we stepped into new territory with tons of opportunity." What Logan developed with his team by searching for a new perspective was not just new ideas, but a long-lasting network of supporters that they could continue to call on and collaborate with. This network was an added bonus to looking outside their group to find new and better ways to do things.

Challenge opens the doors to making extraordinary things happen. Leaders like Logan understand that you don't get anyplace different if you just keep doing the same things over and over again. Getting out of routines and ruts requires treating every project, assignment, or job as an adventure. This involves lifting your head up and looking all around, and being willing to invest your time and energy in finding out about other possibilities.

Sometimes challenges find leaders and sometimes leaders find challenges; most often, it's a little of each. What Logan did is what all exemplary leaders do. They look outwards, beyond the easy answer or the established pattern. They convince others to take seriously the challenges and opportunities that lie ahead of them in the future. They serve as a catalyst for change, challenging the way things have been done and convincing others that new practices need to be incorporated to achieve greater levels of success. This involves a lot more than simply complaining about the way things are, and it's not about pushing back for the sake of pushing back or for the sake of being controversial. It is about proactively looking for options that might lead to a better way of doing things.

The personal-best leadership cases are all about changing the way things have always been done and improving them, about doing things that have never been done before, and about going to places that you or your group haven't yet discovered or figured out. The work of leaders is about change. And we don't mean you need to seek change just for the sake of changing things. We mean changing the way things are being done today in order to achieve results beyond expectations—and that can't be done by good intentions alone. All change requires that leaders actively seek ways to make things better, to grow, innovate, and improve. Exemplary leaders make the commitment to Search for Opportunities to make extraordinary things happen. They make sure they engage in these two essentials:

- **Seize the initiative**
- **Exercise outsight**

Sometimes leaders have to shake things up. Other times they just have to harness the uncertainty that surrounds them. Either way, leaders make things happen. And to make new things happen they rely on outsight to actively seek innovative ideas from beyond the boundaries of familiar experience.

SEIZE THE INITIATIVE

When students recall their personal-best leadership experiences they always think about some kind of challenge. Why? The reason is that challenges are where greatness can take hold and grow. When things are stable and secure, people are not severely tested. They may perform well, do well in school, and even achieve some recognition. But certainty and routine breed complacency and generate average performance. Certainty and routine really are all about being average. In contrast, hardships have a way of making people come face-to-face with who they really are and what they're capable of becoming.

Also significant about the emphasis on change in these leadership stories is that we don't ask people to tell us about *change;* we ask them to tell us about their personal-best leadership experiences. They can discuss any leadership experience they choose—past or present; unofficial or official; in any functional area; in any school, community, sport, religious, or volunteer organization. But they choose to talk about times of change, underscoring the fact that leadership demands changing the same old business-as-usual environment.

The study of leadership is the study of guiding others through adversity, uncertainty, hardship, disruption, transformation, transition, recovery, new beginnings, and other significant challenges. It's the study of people who triumph against overwhelming odds, who take initiative when there is apathy, who confront the established organization with opportunity, who mobilize people and groups in the face of strong resistance. It's also the study of how people actively seek to change the status quo and inspire others to new possibilities. Leadership, challenge, and seizing the initiative are all linked.

Make Something Happen

Alec Loeb joined his fraternity as a freshman. His goal from the start was to hold a leadership position at some point in his fraternity tenure, and he started on that path by accepting the position of Philanthropy Chair. "I was raised in a family where giving back to the community was a way of life," Alec told us, "so I was well suited to the position. When I took the position I knew there was a retiring chair who could help me find my way. But then, he got an unexpected opportunity to take a semester abroad, and we never got a chance to go over anything. I was really left to figure it all out myself."

There were several events that had been traditions with the fraternity that Alec knew he would be expected to continue. The first up was an annual Oyster Roast. Alec found out that in previous years the most they had raised from this event was $2,000. He found himself thinking, "I know we can do better than that."

> I started to talk to the brothers about what makes students come to an event like this and asked about how they got the word out. The answers were pretty vague and definitely not adventurous, with suggestions like "We put flyers up . . . word of mouth . . . we get our girlfriends to spread the word." I decided to try something new. Why not see if some of the local bars would be willing to sell tickets for us, or at the very least donate food? What if we could get a few of the past brothers or even famous university alumni to donate to the cause? You never know until you ask, right?

These ideas worked out, and as a result the Oyster Roast made $5,600 for charity, almost triple what it had made the year before. This experience taught Alec an important lesson: "If you can think of ways to improve the process you should take it."

If you are going to lead others, you have to stop simply going through the motions when it comes to the job, project, or assignment you've been asked to do. It's a lesson all leaders need to learn. Even if you're on the right track, you're likely to get run over if you just sit there. To do your best as a leader you have to seize the initiative to change the way things are.

Some standard practices, policies, and procedures serve an important role in how things get done in an organization; others may simply be "this is the way it's always been done" and need to be challenged. In Alec's example, there was an expectation set by the title he had been elected to: "Philanthropy Chair." Certain events had been done every year and were expected to continue, but the bottom line was that it wasn't the particular event that mattered; the point was to raise as much money as possible for good causes. Keeping that goal in mind allowed Alec to try something new. That the previous chair was unavailable to him actually worked in his favor, he said, freeing his thinking and empowering him to try new approaches.

> There was nobody watching over my shoulder saying, "I did it this way, why are you changing it?" There was just an expectation to plan an event and it was up to me to make it happen. Once I started thinking about how it could be done and talking to people about those ideas, I got excited about the possibilities and tried some new things.

New jobs and new assignments are ideal opportunities for asking probing questions and challenging the way things are done. They are the times when you're expected to ask, "Why do we do this, and why do we do that?" But don't just do it when you're new to the job or assignment. Make asking those questions a routine part of your leadership. Treat today as if it were your first day. Ask yourself, "If I were just starting this responsibility, what makes sense about how things are done and what might I do differently?" Ask questions if you don't understand why things are done the way they are so that you can determine whether an old routine should stay in place or should be done differently. Then take action. This is how you'll continuously uncover needed improvements.

And don't stop at what you can find on your own. Ask those around you about what gets in the group's way of achieving its best. Promise to look into what they say and get back to them; then kick the possibilities around some more with them. Keep looking for things that don't seem right or simply could be better. Ask questions, and then ask some more.

Leaders are restless. They don't like the status quo. They want to make something happen. They want to change the "same old, same old" environment. Research shows that students who rate high on proactivity are not only considered by their peers to be better leaders, but they are more engaged in extracurricular and civic activities targeted toward bringing about positive change. Proactivity consistently produces better results than reactivity or inactivity.[1] Everyone performs better when they take charge of change rather than allowing it to buffet them about.

Leaders look outside their defined circle of responsibility and see opportunities where others don't. This occurs when you undertake an action that produces a result when it wasn't necessarily your job to take that action. It takes place when you don't wait for permission or instructions before jumping in. You make something happen when you notice what isn't working, create a solution for the problem, gain buy-in from others, and implement the desired outcome.

As Alec's experience shows, you need to give everyone on your team the chance to search for better ways of doing things and give them the chance to step forward and take initiative. The data show that students are significantly more engaged in the organizations when they report that their leader "challenges people to try out new and innovative ways to do their work."

Encourage Initiative in Others

Change requires leadership, and every person in the group, not just the leader, can come up with creative ideas and suggest improvements in a team's processes.

Before Kelly Estes went to work for the Santa Clara County Human Relations Commission, she was a summer intern at a law firm. Kelly told us that on the first day she and the other interns took part in an orientation and were trained in the work they were to do. Many of the interns were disappointed with the type of work they were assigned: mostly performing data input and simple office tasks.

Kelly knew she was in for an intriguing summer when on that first day she heard nothing but reactions like "This sucks!" or "This is going to be one long summer" and "We should all just quit now and go on vacation." In addition, Kelly saw a real lack of interest and motivation in some of the full-time employees. It seemed everyone was looking for ways to do as little as possible and people were spending time doing whatever they wanted.

Kelly was determined to remove herself from all the naysayers and try to figure out how she could work in a more professional environment. "I had seen more professionalism at day-care centers," Kelly told us. "Right away, I decided that I didn't want to make a waste of my summer and, that even in the worst situations, there was always an opportunity to shine."

This was a turning point for Kelly to challenge the process and to consider how she might influence others at the firm. Kelly took the initiative and started walking around the office, introducing herself to anyone she could. She went the extra mile to meet the staff throughout the firm. Kelly started her assignment correlating data for various attorneys and secretaries and would ask questions when something didn't seem right. Others began to notice her initiative and were happy to have someone on board who would try to resolve issues rather than ignore them, leaving them to turn into bigger problems.

After a few weeks, the other interns saw that Kelly had developed very positive relationships with many in the firm and started asking her what she had been doing. She explained that she asked questions and offered ideas on what they could do in their departments. While she admitted that her direct boss wasn't too excited about her taking the initiative to dive more deeply into the firm's business, Kelly said she wouldn't let that stop her determination to do a good job. Besides, others in the firm were very appreciative of her efforts. She told us that other interns soon began following suit and the partners began noticing how much more efficiently work was completed and that the "status quo" was now different in some of the departments. The other interns who followed Kelly's lead began enjoying their work and ended up having a great summer experience. They were not only influenced themselves by Kelly's initiative and her drive to try a different approach, but as a group they wound up having a positive influence on the work style within a number of departments.

Leaders like Kelly take the initiative themselves and in doing so encourage initiative in others. They want people to speak up, to offer suggestions for improvement, and to be straightforward with their perspective and feedback. Yet when it comes to situations that involve high uncertainty, high risk, and high challenge, many people feel reluctant to act, afraid they might make matters worse. They get scared. There are a number of ways you can create conditions so that others will be ready and willing to make things happen in both good times and bad.

First, promote a "can-do" attitude by providing opportunities for people to slowly and steadily gain skills. Helping someone learn or simply talking things through in your time together is crucial to building people's ability and confidence so they feel ready to do something about the situations they face. It's tempting to say, "I don't have time to show someone how to do this! It's easier if I just do it myself," or even "If I want it done right, I'll do it myself," but this short-term thinking will cause problems down the road. The best leaders know that taking the time to help someone learn can strengthen the group in the long term. People can't be effective when they haven't been given the tools they need to perform, whether that's knowledge or a skill.

Another form of preparation is mental simulation.[2] Playing a scenario through in your mind until you can picture it frame by frame is a great way to encourage and support the efforts of others. Asking people to imagine how things will be done before they need to be done helps them feel confident that they can act when the time comes. It's much the same as practicing fire drills, except you run them in your head.

In addition, find ways for people to stretch themselves. Give people a chance to learn and grow, but take it one step at a time, at a level where they feel they can succeed. Give people too much too soon and they will fail, and if they fail too often, they'll quit trying. Increase people's challenges slowly but steadily, and as people get better and build their self-confidence, they will continue moving the bar upward in terms of their skills, abilities, and confidence. Leaders encourage initiative by providing visibility and access to role models, especially when the role model is a peer who is successful at meeting the new challenges. Seeing someone like you succeed in doing something new and different is an effective way to encourage others to do it, too, as long as you put it in a light that is positive and encouraging, rather than demeaning. Comparing people can shut down an initiative in a minute and once it shuts down, it's very difficult to restart.

Challenge with Purpose

Leaders don't challenge for challenge's sake. They don't try to change things just for the sake of change. Leaders who simply criticize new thoughts and ideas, or point out problems with what others have to contribute without offering any kind of alternate options, are not leading by Challenging the Process. They are simply complaining. Leaders challenge, often with great passion, because they want people to live life *on* purpose and *with* purpose. What gets people through the hard times, the scary times—the times when they don't think they can even get up in the morning or take another step—is a sense of meaning and purpose. The motivation to deal with the challenges and uncertainties of life and work comes from the inside, and not from something that others hold out in front of you as some kind of reward. Leaders raise challenges to resolve and improve the situation, not simply complain.

The evidence from our research, and from studies by many others, is that if people are going to do their best, they must be internally motivated.[3] Their tasks or projects must be engaging and meaningful. When it comes to excellence, it's definitely not "What gets rewarded gets done," it's "What *is* rewarding gets done." Think about your own level of engagement when you're doing an assignment that is rewarding rather than doing an assignment just for the grade. Why do people push their own limits to get extraordinary things done? And for that matter, why do people do so many things for nothing? Why do they volunteer to collect toys and clothing, raise money for worthy causes, or help children in need? Why do some risk their lives to save others or defend liberty? Extrinsic rewards certainly can't explain these actions. Leaders understand they must find what motivates people internally; they must tap into their hearts and minds.

Arlene Blum knows firsthand the importance of challenging with purpose. Arlene earned a doctorate in biophysical chemistry and has intertwined her career as a scientist with a life of climbing mountains. She's had more than three hundred successful ascents. Her most significant challenge—and the one for which she is best known—was not the highest mountain she's ever climbed. It was the challenge of leading the first all-woman team up Annapurna I, the tenth-highest mountain in the world.

"The question everyone asks mountain climbers is 'Why?'" Arlene explains, "and when they learn about the lengthy and difficult preparation involved, they ask it even more insistently."

> For us, the answer was much more than "because it is there." We all had experienced the exhilaration, the joy, and the warm camaraderie of the heights, and now we were on our way to an ultimate objective for a climber—the world's tenth-highest peak. But as women, we faced a challenge even greater than the mountain. We had to believe in ourselves enough to make the attempt in spite of social convention and two hundred years of climbing history in which women were usually relegated to the sidelines.[4]

In talking about what separates those who make a successful ascent from those who don't, Arlene says, "The real dividing line is passion. As long as you believe what you're doing is meaningful, you can cut through fear and exhaustion and take the next step."[5] This applies to all leaders. It's not about the climb; it's about the meaning it fulfills.

EXERCISE OUTSIGHT

Leaders understand that new ideas are available from many sources. The ability to stay open to new ideas and to stay curious about what is possible demands that you look for answers beyond what you already know. Insight is important, and people rely on it to guide their thinking. But your insight is limited by your attitude. If you think you have all the answers, would you look for new ones? By contrast, if you think you have some ideas that are good yet still ask for more input from other people, places, and sources, you will be more open and receptive to what *could be*. That process of looking outside yourself—and outside your familiar world—for inspiration is what we call exercising "outsight," the capacity to perceive external things.

Logan Hall's personal-best leadership experience recounted at the beginning of this chapter clearly demonstrates one of the ways leaders commonly use outsight to search for opportunities to grow, innovate, and improve. Logan knew that his 4-H Pennsylvania State Council needed help, but instead of jumping right in and possibly reinventing the wheel, Logan and his team looked around to see how other councils had addressed similar issues. In their case, they reviewed the curriculum and leadership lessons a fellow council in Tennessee had created, identified speakers they had used, and explored what might be adapted to work for them in Pennsylvania. "The Tennessee students," Logan explained, "put it all on the table for us. We found ways to use many of their ideas and in the process we began to understand their vision, how it connected to ours, and how we could collaborate. All we had to do was ask them."

According to our research, when students indicate that their leader "searches outside the formal boundaries of his/her organization for innovative ways to improve what we do," as Logan and his fellow 4-H leaders did, those students are significantly more excited and proud about their organization than students who view their leaders as constrained by current and past decisions.

Look Outside Your Experience

Studies into how the brain processes information suggest that in order to see things differently and creatively, you have to bombard your brain with things it has never encountered. This kind of novelty is vital because the brain, evolved for efficiency, routinely takes perceptual shortcuts to save energy. Perceiving information in the usual way doesn't require much energy, so you have to force yourself to break free of preexisting views to get your brain to recategorize information. Moving beyond habitual thinking patterns is the starting point to imagining truly new ideas.[6]

The human mind is surprisingly good at supporting its ways of viewing the world. It is also adept at rationalizing away evidence that disproves those views. One way to adjust this limiting lens is by expanding your hands-on experiences. Consider what one North American specialty retailer did in seeking to reinvent its store format while improving the experience of its customers:

> To jump-start creativity in its people, the company sent out several groups of three to four employees to experience retail concepts very different from its own. Some went to Sephora, a beauty product retailer that features more than 200 brands and a sales model that encourages associates to offer honest

> product advice, without a particular allegiance to any of them. Others went to the Blues Jean Bar, an intimate boutique retailer that aspires to turn the impersonal experience of digging through piles of jeans into a cozy occasion reminiscent of a night at a neighborhood pub. Still others visited a gourmet chocolate shop. . . By visiting the other retailers and seeing firsthand how they operated, the retailer's employees were able to relax their strongly held views about their own company's operations. This transformation, in turn, led them to identify new retail concepts they hadn't thought of before, including organizing a key product by color (instead of by manufacturer) and changing the design of stores to center the shopping experience around advice from expert stylists.[7]

The process of moving outside your usual thinking patterns doesn't have to be as elaborate as this retailer's, and it can take place right where you are today, on campus or off. Leaders find ways to look outside the particular program, department, or chapter they are in to find out, and even experience, what other groups like theirs are doing. Alec Loeb did this when his Philanthropy Chair predecessor left campus before Alec could get the details of his approach to the traditional Oyster Roast. Instead of scrambling to recreate an event exactly as it had been done before, Alec relied on a what-if attitude: what if we try something different?

There's also an example of looking outside one's own experience in Kelly Estes's story. She had no experience in legal matters, and in fact her summer internship was her first exposure to the practice of law. She could have just done her assigned work, but she felt that there was more she could do that would help her develop as a person and a leader—not to mention acquiring more skills. By venturing outside her appointed duties and exploring other departments within the firm, Kelly essentially did, internally, the same thing that you saw with the employees who sought firsthand experience with the retailing approaches at Sephora, the Blue Jean Bar, and the gourmet chocolate shop. By lifting her eyes up and looking around her larger surroundings, she found opportunities to make a real difference in the firm's work. By the way, Kelly's boss, who initially hadn't approved of her going outside her routine responsibilities, called her the "best intern ever" at the end of the summer; by the next summer, Kelly had job offers from several departments within the firm.

Leaders like Alec and Kelly understand that innovation requires more listening and greater communications than routine work does. Successful innovations take hard work, constant communication, and the willingness to say "What if?" You have to establish relationships, network, be connected, and be willing to look outside the ordinary no matter where you are. To change any routine environment you find yourself in requires staying in touch with the world around you. As the saying goes, if you want a different result, you have to try doing something different.

Look Out for Good Ideas

On a visit to Northern California, we stumbled across some extremely important advice for leaders. Exploring the Mendocino coast we picked up a pamphlet describing a particular stretch of shoreline. Printed boldly across the top of the first page was this warning: "Never turn your back on the ocean." And what's the reason you shouldn't turn your back on the ocean to look inland to catch a view of the town? Because a rogue wave may come along when your back is turned and sweep you out to sea, as many unsuspecting tourists can attest. This warning holds lifesaving advice for travelers and for leaders alike. When you take your eyes off the external realities, turning inward to admire the colorful scenery in your own group, team, or organization, you may be swept away by the swirling currents of change.

New ideas often come from insight, the ability to see into the nature of things. Outsight is an even more important source, and when you master this ability you become aware and knowledgeable about what goes on around you. With the benefits of outsight you have a much better chance of seeing opportunities for change and new ways of doing things. So, put yourself into new situations. Confront existing theories and models. Have a curious attitude toward others' opinions and insights. These are methods that will keep your eyes and ears open to new ideas. Remain receptive and expose yourself to broader views. Be willing to hear, consider, and accept ideas from sources outside your group or immediate circle of friends or classmates. If you never turn your back on what is happening outside the boundaries of your group or organization you will not be caught by surprise when the waves of change roll in.

Treat Every Experience as an Adventure

Leaders personally seize the initiative, encourage others to do the same, and actively look everywhere for great ideas. But that doesn't mean you have to wait to be the president of the club or the captain of the team to make things better or change the environment. When we asked people to tell us who initiated the projects that they selected as their personal bests, we assumed that the majority of people would name themselves. Surprisingly, that's not what we found. Someone else initiated more than half the cases. If leaders seize the initiative, then how can we call people leaders when they're assigned the jobs and tasks they undertake? Doesn't this contradict all that we've said about how leaders behave? No, it does not.

The fact that over half the personal-best cases were not self-initiated should be a relief to anyone who thought they had to start all the change themselves, and it should be encouragement to everyone in the group to appreciate that responsibility for new ideas and improvement is *everyone's business*. If the only times people reported doing their best were when they got to choose the projects themselves or when they were the elected head of the group, the majority of leadership opportunities would evaporate—as would most social and organizational changes. The reality is that much of what people do is assigned; few get to start everything from scratch. That's just a fact of being part of a group or organization.

People who become leaders don't always seek the challenges they face. Challenges also seek leaders. Stuff happens on campus, on teams, in communities, and in people's lives. It's not so important whether you find the challenges or they find you. What's important are the choices you make as you address those challenges. What's important is the purpose you find for challenging the way things are. So, the question is: When opportunity knocks, are you prepared to answer the door? Just as important, are you ready to open the door, go outside, and look for an opportunity?

Be an adventurer, an explorer. Treat every day as if it were your first day "on the job." Approach every new assignment as an opportunity to start over. Concentrate on ways to constantly improve your whole group. Identify projects that you've always wanted to undertake but never have. Ask your team members to do the same. Do you know everyone in your group? Come up with a way to get to know them all. Where on campus have you not been? Make a plan to check out those places. Go sit in on a class in a discipline other than yours. Visit a student group like yours on another campus.

Also look for organizations on campus that support the spirit of adventure. On the campus of The University of North Carolina, for example, the Campus Y houses The CUBE, a hub for social innovation. The CUBE is an experiential learning lab where aspiring social entrepreneurs can test ideas, take risks, experience accountability, and incorporate feedback into their social enterprise. It is a community that includes undergraduate and graduate students, faculty, staff, and alumni across many disciplines, a place where people who share the same passion can meet and learn from each other. The CUBE is the place on campus where outsight comes naturally because it brings together people who can look outside the boundaries of their organizations and work to see what others are doing, Conversations there take on the spirit of adventure, giving people a chance to see possibilities that they might never have envisioned on their own.

You don't have to have the support of an organization like The CUBE to pick up on what's going on around you and come up with ways of challenging the status quo. Take it from Kyle Harvey, who worked one summer in an internship at a high-end reseller of printers. One of his responsibilities was working in the warehouse, helping with managing the company's inventory.

Historically the company had simply counted the products in stock and logged them in a book. However, there were always hundreds of parts left over or unaccounted for because they had been mislabeled or stocked in an unorganized manner. Kyle began to think about where he had learned other ways to organize bits of merchandise and equipment. He wondered if there might not be something he had learned in school and from his other work experiences that would help to make his employer's inventory process more efficient and more accurate.

By thinking about how he would approach designing the inventory system from scratch, Kyle came up with the idea of cataloguing the parts by both their part number and the product that they would eventually go into. It took a month for Kyle and his five coworkers to set up the system and reorganize the warehouse. Once installed, the brand-new system gave the technicians quicker access to needed parts, and it helped management keep tighter tabs on the company's property. Had Kyle not treated his internship as an opening to apply his experience with other systems to the inventory-management problem, the company would have stayed stuck in the same old way of doing things and Kyle would have missed an important opportunity to develop his leadership skill of Challenging the Process.

Leaders like Kyle are always on the lookout for opportunities to use new ideas, wherever they are. If you're serious about trying new approaches and helping others to be adventurous, make finding new ideas a personal priority. Encourage others to open their eyes and ears to the world outside the boundaries they know. Collect suggestions from everyone you can, in your organizations or outside them. Use social media to draw ideas from an even wider field.

Encourage your group to spend some time in meetings thinking about new ways you might be able to do some part of a project or some task or event your group does on a regular basis. If you put on annual events or activities, suspend looking at the notebooks and files from past years and treat an event as if it were the very first time you've ever planned it. If you know groups at other schools or organizations that do similar events, call them to talk about how they do things. Look at other groups on your campus that have a reputation for doing things really well or that seem very organized and efficient. Meet with their leaders to get ideas on how they do things. Find out if they have had challenges or faced difficult situations similar to yours. Search around the Internet for videos or stories and "how-tos" on things similar to what you are addressing in your group. Sometimes new ideas spring from things you come across by accident and aren't even related to what you're working on. Keep your eyes and ears open, no matter where you are. You can never tell where or when you'll come across the next great idea.

TAKE ACTION: SEARCH FOR OPPORTUNITIES

Leaders who are dedicated to making extraordinary things happen are open to receiving ideas from anyone and anywhere. They are skilled at using their outsight to constantly survey the landscape in search of new ideas. And because they are proactive they don't just ride the waves of change, they make the waves that others ride.

You don't have to change history, but you do have to avoid the attitude that "we've always done it this way." You need to be proactive, constantly inviting and creating new initiatives. Leaders, by definition, are out in front of change, not behind it trying to catch up. Innovation and leadership are nearly synonymous. This means that your focus needs to be less on the routine and daily actions of your group and much more on the untested and untried. And when searching for opportunities to grow and improve, the most innovative ideas are most often not your own. They're elsewhere, and the best leaders look all around them for the unexpected places, and people, in which great new ideas are hiding. Exemplary leadership requires outsight, not just insight. That's where the future is.

Whether you are trying a new approach or taking on a project that's never been done before, change is an adventure. It tests your will and your skill. It's tough, but it's also stimulating. The challenge of change introduces you to yourself. To get the best from yourself and others, you must understand what gives meaning and purpose to your work.

Here are some suggestions further exploring the first commitment of Challenge the Process, *searching for opportunities by seizing the initiative and looking outward for innovative ways to improve.*

- Always ask: "What's new? What's next? What's better?"
- Make it a daily exercise to ask yourself each morning, "How can I do better or differently what I did yesterday or plan to do today?" If there is something you're not happy with, try a different approach.
- Be restless. Don't let routines become your main focus or your way of acting with your group.

(*Continued*)

- Put yourself in new situations. Take on a new project at least every few months if not more often.
- What is one thing that has been bugging you the most about your group; can you focus on something to change within that area?
- Go on the Internet each day and search for something related to what you do. Visit sites that are totally unrelated to what you are involved in now and see how this might spark your imagination.
- Design tasks and projects so that they are meaningful. Be sure to tap into the purpose the project serves and not just the fact that it's new and different.
- Get firsthand experiences outside your comfort zone and skill set. Find something off the beaten path that you think you can learn from and apply it to your goals, your major, and the groups you lead.
- Make idea gathering part of your daily, weekly, and monthly schedule.
- Talk with people outside your group; get others around you to do the same. Then bring back what all of you learned, share it, and talk about how you can apply these lessons to your assignments and projects.
- Try this task: Assign each one of your group members to find two or three ways another organization is doing something well that your group isn't. What can you learn from their experiences to your own situations and challenges?

NOTES

1. T. S. Bateman and J. M. Crant, "The Proactive Component of Organizational Behavior: Measures and Correlates," *Journal of Organizational Behavior* 14 (1993): 103–118; T. S. Bateman and J. M. Crant, "Proactive Behavior: Meaning, Impact, Recommendations," *Business Horizons* 42, no. 3 (May-June 1999):

63–70; and J. M. Crant, "Proactive Behavior in Organizations," *Journal of Management* 26, no. 3 (2000): 435–463. See also, for example: J. M. Crant, "The Proactive Personality Scale and Objective Job Performance Among Real Estate Agents," *Journal of Applied Psychology* 80, no. 4 (August 1995): 532–537; J. A. Thompson, "Proactive Personality and Job Performance: A Social Capital Perspective," *Journal of Applied Psychology* 90, no. 5 (2005), 1011–1017; S. E. Seibert and M. L. Braimer, "What Do Proactive People Do? A Longitudinal Model Linking Proactive Personality and Career Success," *Personnel Psychology* 54 (2001): 845–875; D. Goetsch, *Effective Leadership: Ten Steps for Technical Professions* (Englewood Cliffs, NJ: Prentice-Hall, 2004); and D. J. Brown, R. T. Cober, K. Kane, P. E. Levy, and J. Shalhoop, "Proactive Personality and the Successful Job Search: A Field Investigation of College Graduates," *Journal of Applied Psychology* 91, no. 3 (2006), 717–726.

2. For detailed information on mental simulation, see G. Klein, *Sources of Power: How People Make Decisions* (Cambridge, MA: MIT Press, 1999), 45–77; see also G. Klein, *The Power of Intuition: How to Use Your Gut Feelings to Make Better Decisions at Work* (New York: Currency, 2004).
3. See E. L. Deci with R. Flaste, *Why We Do What We Do: Understanding Self-Motivation* (New York: Penguin, 1995). See also D. Pink (2011), *Drive: The Surprising Truth About What Motivates You* (New York: Riverhead Press) and K. W. Thomas, *Intrinsic Motivation at Work: What Really Drives Employee Engagement* (San Francisco: Berrett-Koehler, 2009).
4. A. Blum, *Annapurna: A Woman's Place*, Twentieth Anniversary Edition (San Francisco: Sierra Club Books, 1998), 3. See also A. Blum, *Breaking Trail: A Climbing Life* (New York: Scribner, 2005).
5. P. LaBarre, "How to Make It to the Top," *Fast Company* (September 1998): 72.
6. G. Berns, *Iconoclast: A Neuroscientist Reveals How to Think Differently* (Cambridge, MA: Harvard Business School Press, 2008).
7. M. M. Capozzi, R. Dye, and A. Howe, "Sparking Creativity in Teams: An Executive's Guide," *McKinsey Quarterly* (April 2011).

7

Commitment #6: Experiment and Take Risks

Heather McDougall is the executive director of the student exchange program Leadership exCHANGE and associate dean of their Global Leadership Program (GLP) that has taught and trained over a thousand students from more than eighty countries.

"We are experiencing amazing success, but believe me, it's been a long road," Heather told us.

> It all started when I went to the Czech Republic as a graduate student. The experience was life changing for me. I realized how much we had to learn from other cultures and how that knowledge could inform how we learn to grow and develop as leaders. It seemed such a missed opportunity to learn about leadership on campus and not incorporate the learning I got when I was taken to a different environment and given the opportunity to work with people.

Heather decided to design a program that would do just that, and she created a curriculum, activities, and everything else that was needed. She took it to the university where she had received her undergraduate degree and offered it to them. The response was lukewarm, with a half-hearted promise: "We'll get back to you." Heather went back to her graduate studies and waited. When a couple of months had passed, she called the university and got the same response. Months more and still no response, and by then it was too late to get students engaged for the summer. Heather then decided to take her program to the Travel Abroad group at the university where she was doing her graduate work and she met with the same resistance. Later that year, while doing a summer internship with the YWCA, she offered the program to them, but the response was once again, "Well, we'll see."

"I was so frustrated at this point," Heather told us, "that my roommate at the time suggested I stop going through existing entities to find a home for the program and simply do it myself. My response was immediate and clear: 'No way. I can't do that!' But my roommate was so positive and knew the steps needed and helped me get set up."

When Heather thought her program was good to go, she started spreading the word via the Internet, connecting with any college or university she thought might be interested. By then she was living full time in Prague and getting online required hopping from Internet café to Internet café. "It was slow and tedious work," she said. "After several months I only had five people signed up and I thought it might fail again."

Heather had gotten married in the midst of all this and her husband was still back in the States. When she called him one night feeling especially discouraged, he encouraged her to hang in there and also said he'd support whatever she chose to do. "Maybe it was the notion of quitting after all the years of work," Heather said, "but something clicked and I said to myself, 'You're feeling sorry for yourself and you need to get over it and figure out another way to make this work!' I had experimented with a lot of different approaches and I knew I was getting closer to a success."

Heather decided that if she could get just eight people to participate she could run a pilot. She ended up with seven students from the United States and one from Finland. Having the Finnish student in the group was a risk because the program had been designed for US students, but it also ended up being a gift pointing the way to internationalizing the student body for the next session. Heather created a revised curriculum based on what they all learned from the pilot and kept growing and developing the program from there. If something worked well, she kept it; if it didn't, she changed it, growing the program with each iteration.

Today each Global Leadership Program typically includes students from at least ten, and sometimes up to twenty, countries.[1] "By living and learning alongside young people from around the world," Heather says,

> . . . students have the unique opportunity to gain firsthand knowledge not only of the country where they are studying but a wide range of cultures. In this environment, they discover the true meaning of global citizenship. I am so proud of this program and what it has become. I had no idea how hard it was going to be to get off the ground, but I knew I believed in it and the impact it could have. I simply hit a point where I knew I would never give up and just found a way to move past each roadblock and I am mighty glad I did.

To achieve the extraordinary, you have to be willing, just like Heather, to do things that have never been done before. Every single personal best we have heard and read speaks to the need to take risks with bold ideas. Nothing new and nothing great is achieved by doing things the way you've always done them. You have to test unproven strategies. You have to break out of the norms that box you in. You have to do the things you think you cannot. You have to venture beyond the limitations you normally place on yourself. Making extraordinary things happen in organizations demands a willingness to experiment and take risks.

Leaders have to take this one step further. Not only do they have to be willing to test bold ideas and take calculated risks, they also have to get others to join them on these adventures in uncertainty. It's one thing to set off alone into the unknown, it's entirely another to get others to follow you. The difference between an exemplary leader and an individual risk taker is that leaders are able to create the conditions where people *want to* join with them in the struggle.

Leaders make risk safe, as contradictory as that might sound. They create a climate where calculated risk taking is encouraged, where people feel supported in trying new things in pursuit of a common goal. They make experiments learning opportunities. They place little bets, not all-in wagers where they can lose everything in one move. They're bold, but not foolish. More often than not, they see change as starting small, using pilot or test projects, as Heather did, and gaining momentum. The vision may be grand and distant, but the way to get there is by putting one foot in front of the other. These small, visible steps are more likely to win early victories and they certainly gain early supporters. Of course, when you experiment, not everything works out as intended. There are mistakes and false starts. They are part of the process of innovation. What's critical, therefore, is that leaders promote learning from these experiences.

Exemplary leaders make the commitment to Experiment and Take Risks. They know that it's essential to:

- **Generate small wins**
- **Learn from experience**

These essentials can help leaders transform challenge into an exploration, uncertainty into a sense of adventure, fear into resolve, and risk into reward. They are the keys to making progress that becomes unstoppable.

GENERATE SMALL WINS

Amanda Itliong is currently director of the Center for Student Leadership, Ethics, and Public Service at North Carolina State

University, and the personal-best leadership experience she told us about was when she became vice president of her undergraduate chapter of the National Society of Collegiate Scholars. She described this organization as "one of those honor societies that doesn't do much except induct students with a certain GPA, collect dues from them, and then induct more people the next year." She and her fellow officers quickly realized that the organization had a lot of money from all those years of dues collected that hadn't been spent on anything.

"We looked to the mission of our organization for ideas about what we could do with the money," she told us. The group had been founded on the concept of supporting academic and service excellence, and so they started to brainstorm ways that they might be able to fulfill that aspiration. They decided that the arts was an area where their school didn't offer many opportunities for students to showcase their work and found that funding for community arts in their city was scarce. They came up with a plan to hold a student-created fashion and arts showcase called "Diversion" to benefit a nonprofit that taught the arts and entrepreneurship to low-income kids in the area. "Even though we were really excited about the plan," Amanda told us, "we knew it was going to be difficult to get other people on board and involved in the process because our group didn't usually do anything and all of a sudden we were planning a huge event."

Planning a large arts event was a big risk for the group because it would require a lot of approvals, support, and volunteers from their school and the community at large. So they broke the task down into lots of little pieces.

First, they started a forum for people to learn about the general idea for the event and to contribute their personal perspectives on the project. They literally drew a detailed picture of the way they envisioned the auditorium during "Diversion" and described all of the possibilities of what would be there and what it could look like. They then started working with people all over campus to find out how to connect to the interests and values of other groups and individuals that they would need for support. Little by little, they got people to say "yes," again and again. As Amanda told us:

> The Art Department quickly got on board because we included in our idea a small gallery that was open before the show and during intermission and also gave them space to advertise their academic programs to students. The multicultural groups were excited to showcase their music and dance talents while helping a local good cause at the same time. With the input and brainstorms from so many people we were able to create a really amazing vision.

From those early small wins, Amanda said, "We went on to host a sold-out event that was fun for everyone! The arts became very visible through the event and a local charity received significant funding. Since we had used the organization's saved funds for all production costs, every cent we raised through ticket sales went to the nonprofit."

Leaders face situations similar to Amanda's all the time. How do you achieve something no one has ever done before? How do you get something new started? How do you turn around a losing team? Or address the campus safety problem? How do you work to solve even larger problems such as child trafficking, or global climate change? These are such daunting challenges that you can get stuck even before you get started. Framing the challenge as something too big can actually have the effect of dampening motivation.

Break It Down

So how do you do it? How do you get people to want to move in a new direction, break old mindsets, or change existing behavior patterns in order to tackle big problems and attempt extraordinary performance? You take it step by step, one bit at a time. Just as Amanda and her colleagues did in turning "Diversions" from concept to reality, you make progress incrementally. You break the long journey down into milestones. You start doing little things that create a sense of forward momentum. You move people forward step-by-step through the generation of "small wins."

A small win has been defined as "a concrete, complete, implemented outcome of moderate importance."[2] Small wins form the basis for a consistent pattern of winning that attracts people who want to be part of a successful group. Although planting one tree won't stop global warming, planting one million trees can make a difference, and it's that first tree that gets things started. Small wins identify the place to begin. For Heather and the Global Leadership Program, the small win was the very first group involving only eight students. The success of that trip, the stories collected and shared, helped recruiting for future groups. The success in one country was also the impetus for programs in other countries. Small wins can make a project seem doable even with limited time and budget. They minimize the cost of trying and reduce the risks of failing. What's exciting about this process is that once a small win has been accomplished, natural forces are set in motion that favors progress over setbacks.

Leaders have grand visions about the future, and they get there one step at a time, building momentum as well as the strength and the resolve to continue forward along the journey. Small wins play an important role in Challenging the Process because they produce the kind of visible results that attract people to be connected to a successful group or team. We see this demonstrated when a sports team begins to win games after a losing streak. When the team starts to succeed, people jump on the bandwagon. Small wins build people's confidence and reinforce their natural desire to feel successful. Because additional energy, and even resources, may gravitate to winners, they position you well to strive for a slightly larger win next time. A series of small wins therefore provides a foundation of stable building blocks.

Each win preserves gains and makes it harder to return to preexisting conditions.

Small wins produce results because they actively make people feel like winners and make it easier for others to want to go along with their ideas and requests. If people can see that you are asking them to do something that they're quite capable of doing, they feel some assurance that they can be successful at the task. If people aren't overwhelmed by a task, their energy goes into getting the job done, instead of wondering, "How will we ever solve that problem?"

Small wins produce results because they build personal and group commitment to a course of action. By identifying little ways that people can succeed, you make people want to be involved and stay involved because they see that what they are doing is making a difference. Small wins build confidence and create a positive environment, which go a long way to combat apathy or group turnover. They give people great reasons to stick around and keep working.

Leaders know they have to break down big problems into small, doable actions. They also know that they have to try a lot of little things when initiating something new before they get it right. Not every new approach works, and the best way to ensure success is to experiment with a lot of ideas, not just one or two big ones. Successful leaders help others to see how breaking the journey into measurable milestones can move them forward. Anyone who has ever played a team sport understands this. No game is won without ups and downs, and no game is won without preparation. Each practice, each play that's rehearsed, is a step toward the larger success. Sometimes you have the advantage, sometimes you don't, but if you learn from your experience, you strengthen the odds of an eventual victory.

"Big things are done by doing lots of small things," as we heard over and over in the personal-best cases we collected. When you break a big project down into pieces you're also creating the possibility to make progress by experimenting with lots of little things. Whatever you call your experiments—a practice, dry run, trial mode, demo, rehearsal, pilot project, test drive—all are methods about trying lots of little things in the service of something much bigger. These are the tactics that continually generate lots of possibilities for small wins.

Build Psychological Hardiness

Before you can take that first step toward your goal, however, you have to take a step forward in your attitude. For example, Heather McDougall told us that she lost her momentum several times in starting the Global Leadership Program, becoming frustrated and ready to give up. Her initial battle was with herself. She told us how she had to stop feeling sorry for herself and realize that she had the capacity to search a little harder, to give it one more day to see if she could find the students she needed to make the program work. She was determined to follow through on all her hard work and not give up. She took charge and began doing things that would lead, gradually, to the program she had dreamed of many years before.

The same is true for Amanda Itliong and other leaders in the personal-best stories we collected. The tenacious quality these leaders display is what social psychologists refer to as *psychological hardiness;* it's about the persistence and resilience that move them forward against the tide. The circumstances weren't always as long and drawn out as Heather's experience with the Global Leadership Program, but the conditions people faced during their personal-best leadership experiences were filled with their own significant uncertainties and stressors. Although 95 percent of the cases were described as exciting, about 20 percent of leaders also called the experiences frustrating, and approximately 15 percent said that their experiences aroused fear or anxiety. The very first thing Heather said in relaying her story was, "My success came after years of setbacks and tears, but out of it came a great experience." Heather faced multiple setbacks in getting started toward her dream of creating a global leadership exchange program. When she was feeling as though the whole idea was just too much for her, she didn't quit. She simply changed her focus to what she could do: a very small pilot class. Once that class happened things began to change. Remember how Heather related how discouraged she was at one time? She said, "I was so tired of it all and thought, I just can't do it anymore." But that didn't last too long. She found a way to keep on going.

> I thought, OK, if you stopped feeling sorry for yourself what could you do? I was in a small college that often had tiny classes and I knew I could run a pilot with just a very few students, so I decided to do that. We ended up with just eight students, but it worked and it was a great experience for them. After that, we simply asked, what next? How can we make this better? We had the momentum and the confidence that we could define and take that next step.

Even though the overwhelming emotions associated with personal-best cases are positive, we can't overlook the fact that they were also filled with tension. But instead of being debilitated by the stress of a difficult experience, exemplary leaders said they were challenged and energized by it. The ability to grow and thrive under stressful, risk-abundant situations is highly dependent on how you view change.

Amanda Rossi told us about one of her fellow swim instructors, Bryan, who was in charge of a junior lifeguard program. The program was held at a local pool center for fifty to sixty children. Every year the program became more and more successful, which eventually led to a long waiting list of up to thirty children trying to get in. The pool supervisors felt that there was no way to expand the program due to the limited amount of space in the pools, and the amount of money it would cost to add another lifeguard as an instructor. Bryan hated seeing the kids turned away and had an idea on how to increase the enrollment for the program. He thought they could get more people into the program by splitting the children into two separate groups, with one having swim practice in the morning while the other group was doing exercises poolside. The two groups would meet up for lunch, and then switch. This arrangement meant that the program could potentially add about ten more children to each group. By adding more children, they could increase their profit and make their clients happy.

Excited about the possibility of getting more kids into the program, Bryan immediately proposed his idea to his supervisor who listened but quickly dismissed it saying there was no way it could be done that summer. Bryan felt the idea was sacked because it came from "a young kid," but instead of getting discouraged and worrying about the supervisor's reaction to his idea, he decided to work on a way to convince his supervisor of the major benefits of increasing the enrollment for the program.

Because the supervisor had said they couldn't pursue the idea for the upcoming summer, Bryan knew that he had a year to change her mind. His first task was to research the information about the costs included in running the junior lifeguard program, and the costs of adding another instructor. Bryan took it upon himself to learn about the program's financial structure and to research ways to make his idea become a reality. He chose not to view his supervisor's rejection as the end to his vision; instead he was motivated by the challenge of convincing her that the program could be expanded.

After researching all the current expenses, Bryan calculated the costs of adding another instructor and about twenty more children to the program. Bryan also calculated the increased revenue that would accompany the increase in enrollment. After collecting all the necessary information, he approached his supervisor again. He illustrated that the increased revenue from expanding the program far outweighed the added costs, and that the program could indeed expand profitably. Once again, the supervisor didn't take his idea seriously, and once again Bryan didn't stress out; he met the challenge with increased enthusiasm, seeing it as an opportunity to learn even more about what he needed to do to convince the supervisor. He decided to engage the rest of the lifeguards in the discussion. He asked each instructor what they felt about the idea, getting their input and support so that when he spoke to the supervisor again, there would be a unified voice of the very people who would be dealing with the increased workload. It took almost a full year, but eventually Bryan's idea was embraced and the program was successfully expanded.

People like Bryan, who experience a high degree of stress and yet are able to cope with it in a positive manner, have a distinctive attitude toward stress: they are psychologically hardy.[3] Researchers over the last forty years have discovered that people who exhibit this attitude are much more likely to withstand serious challenges and bounce back from failure than those low in hardiness.[4] And the good news is that hardiness doesn't have anything to do with age—and it is an attitude that people can learn and that leaders can support.

Your view of events contributes to your ability to cope with change and stress. Psychological hardiness comes from how you think and act in terms of *commitment, control*, and *challenge*. Think back to what Heather, Amanda, and Bryan did when facing their challenges. To turn adversity into advantage first you need to *commit* yourself to what's happening. You have to become involved, engaged, and curious. As we saw in Bryan's story, you have to act; you can't sit back and wait for something to happen. When you commit you'll find the people and the situations much more meaningful and worthwhile to you. You also have to take *control* of your own life, which is what Heather eventually decided to do. You need to make an effort to influence what is going on. Though all your attempts may not be successful, you can't sink into powerlessness or passivity. Finally, if you are going to be psychologically hardy you need to view *challenge* as an opportunity to learn from both negative and positive experiences. You can't play it safe, which was the realization that Amanda came to. Always choosing the easy path or avoiding uncertainty is not only unrealistic, it also can be paralyzing. Personal improvement and fulfillment comes through the continual process of getting engaged in the uncertainties of life. With a hardy attitude, you can transform stressful times into positive opportunities for growth and renewal. What's more, you can help your team feel the same way.

LEARN FROM EXPERIENCE

Whenever you're challenging the status quo, whenever you're tackling demanding problems, whenever you're making meaningful changes, whenever you're confronting adversity, you will sometimes fail. Despite how much you see challenge as an opportunity, despite how focused you can be, despite how driven you are to succeed, there will be setbacks.

People never get it right the first time—not in sports, not in games, not in school. Yes, it's something that leaders are told that they must do, but it's neither realistic nor useful advice. Sure, everyone wants and perhaps expects you to get it right *every time*, but not when you're trying to do things you have never done before. When you engage in something new and different you make a lot of mistakes. Everyone does.

Over and over again, people in our studies tell us how important mistakes and failure have been to their success. Without mistakes they'd be unable to know what they can and cannot do (at least at this moment). Without those experiences, people said, they would have been unable to achieve their aspirations. It may seem ironic, but many share the thought that the overall quality of work improves when people have a chance to fail. Studies on innovation make the point: "Success does not breed success. It breeds failure. It is failure which breeds success."[5]

James E. West, research professor at Johns Hopkins University, has secured nearly fifty domestic and more than two hundred foreign patents. Yet, in spite of all his successes he says, "I think I've had more failures than successes, but I don't see the failures as mistakes because I always learned something from those experiences. I see them as having not achieved the initial goal, nothing more than that."[6] Or consider how professional basketball hall of famer Michael Jordan explains his success. "I've missed more than 9000 shots in my career. I've lost almost 300 games. Twenty-six times, I've been trusted to take the game winning shot and missed. I'VE FAILED over and over again in my life. And that is why I SUCCEED."

To be sure, failure can be costly. For the individual who leads a failed project, it can mean a poor grade that reflects badly in class. For someone leading a campus event, it can mean being overlooked the next time or perhaps being assigned a different, less desirable role within the organization. For athletes, it can mean a loss for the team. Regardless of the situation, there is no significant success without the possibility of failure.

Failure is never the objective of any endeavor. The objective is to succeed, and success always requires some amount of learning. And learning always involves mistakes, errors, miscalculations, and the like along the way. Learning happens when people can openly talk about what went wrong as well as what went right. Leaders don't look for someone to blame when the inevitable mistakes are made in the name of innovation. They ask, "What can be learned from the experience?"

Be an Active Learner

Insight Dubai is an interactive conference that brings together sixty young women from around the world and pairs them up with Dubai Women's College students for five days of sharing, learning, and growing together. Participants develop global awareness, intercultural understanding, and leadership skills through working together in small groups. Marie Jones was one of ten representatives to the conference from the United States. The experience was so profound that Marie applied to return the following year as a facilitator, and was chosen.

Marie's assignment was to lead a group of sixteen women, eight from Dubai and eight from other countries. Marie knew from her own experience that even though she would be leading the group's work together, she would not be standing in front of them lecturing. Marie understood that she needed to get all sixteen participants in her group talking, sharing, and eventually shaping the experience themselves if it was going to be meaningful for each of them. "We all learned so much from each other when I was a participant because we were all actively engaged in the conversations we had," she told us. "I was determined to build that same kind of experience as the facilitator, and the key was active listening and active learning."

Active listening started with Marie herself. She said it was important for her to be fully present with the women so that she could understand their perspective and experience. "Knowing these women helped me put them into groups that would be effective—for example, mixing up the backgrounds and putting the more reserved in the group with women who were very inclusive," she told us. "I knew it would take some time to get to know them so I kept an open door policy which led to many late night talks, but it was worth it." Marie also knew that each woman brought a unique perspective to the conference based on her personality, background, and life experiences. As the group's leader Marie was committed to bringing those perspectives into the room so the women could all learn from each other. The key to this, she believed, was to have them actively engaged, drawing on what they knew from their experiences and what they were learning at the conference. Marie put her participants into small groups, each group working on an issue or topic they needed to carefully think through. For example, one group had a deep discussion on the moral code and religious law of Islam and what the implications would be on businesswomen in the Middle East in the next ten years. No matter what issue the small groups were considering, each had to come up with a list of concerns and recommendations on how they might be addressed. Marie told us that she "challenged them all to make sure each voice in their group was heard, and to come together as one voice in the end." She also asked the small groups to take time at the end of each session to reflect on what they had learned and how they had learned. "The feedback I got was very similar to my own experience as a participant in Insight Dubai. Being fully engaged in your learning helps you understand how you learn. That is so valuable."

Learning is the master skill. Our research has found a strong correlation between engagement in learning and leadership effectiveness.[7] And other scholars have reported that the single best predictor of success in future roles is learning "agility."[8] When you fully engage in learning—when you throw yourself completely into experimenting, reflecting, reading, or getting advice or coaching—you are going to experience the satisfaction of improvement and the taste of success.

More is more when it comes to learning. It's clear that exemplary leaders approach each new and unfamiliar experience with a willingness to learn, an appreciation of the importance of learning, and the recognition that learning necessarily involves making some mistakes. In Marie's work as an Insight Dubai facilitator, she needed to stay fully present to catch the topics that emerged and open them to debate without letting a particular topic or person dominate. "Sometimes it worked," she said, "and other times, I recognized it wasn't the best choice and I'd need to shut it down and move on. I like to think I got better as we went along." In Bryan's case, he had to learn about the costs of running the junior lifeguard program and figure out how much they could charge for it. He had to learn what would be involved in expanding the program and determine the additional resources required.

Building your capacity to be an active learner begins with developing a *growth mindset.* The foundational belief of this mindset is that people can learn through their efforts. In contrast, those with a *fixed mindset* believe that people's basic qualities are immutable, carved in stone.[9] Individuals with a growth mindset, for example, believe people can learn to be better leaders. Those with the fixed mindsets think leaders are born, and that no amount of training is going to make you any better than you naturally are.

In study after study, researchers have found that when working on simulated business problems, those individuals with fixed mindsets gave up more quickly and performed more poorly than those with growth mindsets.[10] The same is true for students, athletes on the playing field, teachers in the classroom, and partners in relationships.[11] Mindsets, not skill sets, make the critical difference in taking on challenging situations.

In order to develop your own growth mindset, and to nourish it in others, you need to embrace the challenges you face. That's where the learning is. When you encounter setbacks—and they will be inevitable—you have to persist. Recognize that it's because of your effort and persistence, and that of others, that mastery is achieved. It's neither raw talent nor good fortune that leads to becoming the best; it's hard work that gets you there, bolstered by psychological hardiness. Ask for feedback about how you're doing. Learn from the constructive criticism you get from others. And view the success of others around you as inspiration and not as a threat. When you believe that you can continuously learn, you will.

Create an Environment for Learning

Promoting learning and nurturing a growth mindset requires that you create a climate of inquiry and openness, of patience and encouragement. Studies of top performers strongly suggest that people have to have a supportive environment in order to become the best they can be. Researchers have found, in fact, that when there are high-quality relationships in a group—relationships characterized by positive regard for others and a sense of mutuality and trust—people engage in more of the behaviors that lead to learning and hence growth.[12]

A good area to explore, then, is what you can do as a leader to create a supportive environment. Think about how you can support learning by offering people encouraging words when they try something new, by providing understanding and patience when they fall short of targets, and by giving helpful suggestions as they try to learn from their experience and bounce back from mistakes. This idea isn't limited to just a working environment; it's true for any kind of setting where people seek to achieve something exciting together.

Marie Jones recognized that to maximize their learning it was essential for all members of her Insight Dubai group to both contribute and be heard. To create an environment that supported those goals she worked with the team to establish a set of guidelines they could all agree to. During the process, if someone began to dominate the conversation or cut someone off, or if people were not contributing, these guidelines became the touchstone for the group, allowing them to self-correct and move back to the learning environment they were committed to. Marie also used the design of the group process to support the kind of learning environment they wanted. "I knew I didn't want to be doing all the talking in the front of the room," Marie told us, "so when we had new topics to discuss, the sub-groups each had a specific part to explore and then share their understanding with the whole group. That way we all learned together from each other."

Creating a climate for learning doesn't come instantly, and sometimes, it requires a conscious change in your leadership behaviors. Leaders with high expectations demand a lot from themselves and from others. High expectations can motivate people to stretch themselves and promote learning and greater self-development. Leaders with high expectations can also become overly demanding and downright bossy. They can exhibit impatience, frustration, and anger, causing people to become defensive, less open, and less willing to take risks. For younger leaders, if not dealt with appropriately, these demanding behaviors can transform into leaders taking over, doing more things themselves, or trying to do it all—none of which leads to extraordinary achievements.

People generally know that they don't always get it right the first time they try something and appreciate that learning new things can be a bit scary. They don't want to embarrass themselves or look stupid in front of their peers. To create a climate for learning you have to make it safe for others to try, to fail, and to learn from their experiences. Make it a habit to ask, "What can we learn?" as often as you can from each project experience, and build upon people's experiences so that mistakes are not repeated but are learned from.

The truth is that failures and disappointments cannot be completely avoided. It's how you handle them when they arise that will ultimately determine your eventual effectiveness and success. You have to be honest with yourself and with others. You have to own up to your mistakes and reflect on your experiences so that you gain the learning necessary to be better the next time around. It's true for you, and also true for your constituents.

Strengthen Resilience

It takes determination and strength to deal with the adversities of life and leadership. You can't let the setbacks get you down or the roadblocks get in your way. You can't become overly discouraged when things don't go according to plan. You can't give up when the resistance builds or people criticize your ideas. Neither can you let yourself get distracted by other tempting new projects that divert your attention. You can't lose focus or move on too quickly. You have to stick with it. You must never give up. Heather's and Bryan's successes would never have happened if they had allowed the frustration they were feeling to shut them down. In both of their situations, the lack of follow-through from others actually spurred on what needed to happen: to build the teams needed to make their programs come about.

The ability to recover quickly from setbacks and continue to pursue a vision of the future is often referred to as resilience. Others have called it "grit." Grit is defined as "perseverance and passion for long-term goals," and it "entails working strenuously toward challenges, maintaining effort and interest over years despite failure, adversity, and plateaus in progress."[13] Showing grit involves setting goals, being obsessed with an idea or project, maintaining focus, sticking with things that take a long time to complete, overcoming setbacks, and the like. Empirical studies, whether with students, cadets in the military, working professionals, artists, teachers, and others, document convincingly that people with the most grit are the ones most likely to achieve positive outcomes. The more grit you demonstrate, the better you do.

The good news is that these qualities of resilience and grit can be developed and strengthened, much like growth mindsets. People with resilience bounce back and those with grit simply don't give up. These folks interpret setbacks as temporary, local, and changeable.[14] Essentially, people who are resilient, even in times of great stress and adversity, remain committed to moving forward by believing that what has happened isn't going to be permanent and that they can do something about the outcome the next time around. As every basketball player knows, 100 percent of the shots not taken don't go in. So you better keep shooting if you want to make a basket.

You can do a number of things to strengthen resilience for yourself, as well as others. For example, when a failure or setback occurs, don't blame yourself or the people around you working on the project. Instead look for the circumstances that contributed to the failure and convey a belief that this particular situation is likely to be temporary, not permanent. Emphasize that the failure or setback means a problem only in this one instance and not in every case. When success occurs you should attribute success to the individuals in the group. Hold and express the belief that many more victories are out there and be optimistic that good fortune will come eventually and be with your team for a long time. Resilience is further strengthened when you assign people tasks that are challenging but within their skill level, and when you encourage them to see change as full of possibilities.[15]

The personal-best examples involved change and stressful events in the leaders' lives, but they had passion and they persevered. They didn't give up despite the failures and setbacks. Even in the toughest of times people can experience meaningfulness and accomplishment. They can overcome great odds. They can make progress. They can change the way things are. It's your responsibility as a leader to create the conditions and environment for them to experience these feelings as members of your group.

TAKE ACTION: EXPERIMENT AND TAKE RISKS

Change is the work of leaders. It's what they do. You may have been asked in your school, organization, or community to run an event or head up a project. Students too often take the view of "Just get it done!" But *leaders* want more. They are always looking for ways to get it done *better*—continuously improving, growing, and innovating. They know that the way things are done today won't get people to the better tomorrow they envision. So, they experiment. They tinker. They shake things up. They ask, "What can we change that might make things better?"

Change can overwhelm, frighten, and immobilize some people. Exemplary leaders, however, view change as a challenge that can be successfully overcome. They believe, and get others to believe, that every individual can influence outcomes and control their own lives. They make sure that the meaning and purpose of change is clearly understood, and they create a strong sense of commitment to the mission.

To get things moving in the right direction, you need to break the tasks down into small wins, setting short-term goals or milestones. Take it one step at a time. A little-things approach gets people started, gets them moving, makes progress imaginable, builds commitment, and creates momentum.

Whenever you try new things, big or small, stuff happens. Mistakes are made, and failures occur. No one ever gets it right the first time—and maybe not the second or third time either. That's why exemplary leaders create an environment that encourages learning. People have to know that when they experiment and take risks they won't be punished for failure. Instead it'll be treated as a learning experience. The truth is that the best leaders are the best learners. You need a growth mindset, believing that everyone can improve when they put in the effort to learn. You also need to create a learning climate—one in which everyone is encouraged to share successes and failures, and views continuous improvement as a routine way of doing things. This entails building psychological hardiness, persisting despite the odds. You have to have grit. Exemplary leaders make it a practice to create a climate in which others feel strong and proficient, capable of flourishing even under the most adverse circumstances.

The second commitment of Challenge the Process requires leaders to *experiment and take risks by constantly generating small wins and learning from experience*. Here are some things you can do:

- Figure out how you can keep people focused on what they can control in their lives and in the tasks or work you all do together. Ask yourself what's holding you and your group back. What obstacles are you putting in your own way? What can you control and what have you decided you can't do anything about?
- Help people find work and tasks that are meaningful for them and will show how their contributions make a difference. What are some of the "little things" in a project that people can do, succeed at, and see the difference it makes in the bigger picture?
- Emphasize how personal fulfillment results from constantly challenging yourself to improve. What do you feel when you see improvement in yourself? How can you use that emotion to motivate yourself?
- Break big projects down into achievable steps. Remind people of the progress they are making every day and how any setbacks are only temporary.
- Continuously experiment with new ideas. Test them out in a way that will build confidence in the group, and mark learning.
- What do you think about failure? Do you try to avoid it? Can you think back to times when you did fail and learned something valuable from it? How can this understanding help you deal better with failure now and in the future?
- Whenever mistakes are made always ask, "What can we learn from this experience?"
- Discuss and reflect on successes and failures, recording the lessons learned and making sure that everyone is aware of them.
- At the end of each day, see if you can find just one thing (big or small) that you learned. Keep a record of these and look at the list each month to see how you're changing and growing.
- Repeat frequently this mantra: Never give up.

NOTES

1. For more information on Heather's program, see http://www.globalleaders.info
2. Weick, K. E., "Small Wins: Redefining the Scale of Social Problems." *American Psychologist* 39, no. 1 (1984): 43. Karl attributes the concept of small wins to author Tom Peters who wrote about it in his doctoral dissertation at Stanford University. For a related treatment of this topic, see P. Sims, *Little Bets: How Breakthrough Ideas Emerge from Small Discoveries* (New York: Free Press, 2011), 141–152.
3. The research on psychological hardiness has looked at groups as diverse as corporate managers, entrepreneurs, students, nurses, lawyers, and combat soldiers. For a history of the research see S. R. Salvatore, "The Story of Hardiness: Twenty Years of Theorizing, Research, and Practice," *Consulting Psychology Journal: Practices and* Research 54, no. 3 (2002): 175–185. Also see: S. R. Maddi and S. C. Kobasa, *The Hardy Executive: Health Under Stress* (Chicago: Dorsey Press, 1984); S. R. Maddi and D. M. Khoshaba, "Hardiness and Mental Health," *Journal of Personality Assessment* 67 (1994): 265–274; and S. R. Maddi and D. M. Khoshaba, *Resilience at Work: How to Succeed No Matter What Life Throws at You* (New York: AMACOM, 2005).
4. See R. A. Bruce and R. F. Sinclair, "Exploring the Psychological Hardiness of Entrepreneurs," *Frontiers of Entrepreneurship Research* 29, no. 6: 5; P. T. Bartone, R. R. Roland, J. J. Picano, and T. J. Williams, "Psychological Hardiness Predicts Success in US Army Special Forces Candidates," *International Journal of Selection and Assessment* 16, no. 1 (2008): 78–81; and P. T. Bartone, "Resilience Under Military Operational Stress: Can Leaders Influence Hardiness," *Military Psychology* 18 (2006): S141–S148.
5. M. Maidique, "Why Products Succeed and Why Products Fail," presentation to the Executive Seminar in Corporate Excellence, Santa Clara University, May 29, 1985; see also M. Maidique and B. J. Zinger, "The New Product Learning Cycle," *Research Policy* 14 (1985): 299–313; G. A. Moore, *Crossing the Chasm: Marketing and Selling High-Tech Products to Mainstream Customers* (New York: HarperBusiness, 1999); and C. M. Christensen, S. D. Anthony, and E. A Roth, *Seeing What's Next: Using the Theories of Innovation to Predict Industry Change* (Boston: Harvard Business School Press, 2004). See also J. McGregor, "How Failure Breeds Success," *Business Week*, July 10, 2006: 42–50. McGregor writes, "The best companies embrace their mistakes and learn from them."
6. T. L. O'Brien, "Are U.S. Innovators Losing Their Competitive Edge?" *New York Times*, November 13, 2005: 3.

7. L. M. Brown and B. Z. Posner, "Exploring the Relationship Between Learning and Leadership," *Leadership & Organization Development Journal* (May 2001): 274–280. Also see, J. M. Kouzes and B. Z. Posner, *The Truth About Leadership: The No-Fads, Heart-of-the-Matter Facts You Need to Know* (San Francisco: Jossey-Bass, 2010), 119–135.
8. Learning agility has been defined as "the ability to reflect on experience and then engage in new behaviors based on those reflections." Robert W. Eichinger, Michael M. Lombardo, and Dave Ulrich. *100 Things You Need to Know: Best Practices for Managers & HR* (Minneapolis, MN: Lominger, 2004), 492.
9. C. S. Dweck, *Mindset: The New Psychology of Success* (New York: Random House, 2006), 6–7.
10. J. Barash, M. Capozzi, and L. Mendonca, "How Companies Approach Innovation: A McKinsey Global Survey," *The McKinsey Quarterly* (October 2007). Available from https://www.mckinseyquarterly.com/How_companies_approach_innovation_A_McKinsey_Global_Survey_2009
11. A. Bandura and R. E. Wood, "Effects of Perceived Controllability and Performance Standards on Self-Regulation of Complex Decision Making," *Journal of Personality and Social Psychology* 56 (1989): 805–814. Also, see C. Dweck, *Mindset*, for a discussion of numerous research studies in these and other domains.
12. Abraham Carmeli, Daphna Brueller, and Jane E. Dutton, "Learning Behaviours in the Workplace: The Role of High-Quality Interpersonal Relationships and Psychological Safety," *Systems Research and Behavioral Science Systems Research* 26 (2009): 81–98.
13. A. L. Duckworth, C. Peterson, M. D. Matthews, and D. R. Kelly, "Personality Processes and Individual Differences" in *Journal of Personality and Social Psychology* 92, no. 6 (2007): 1087–1088.
14. M.E.P. Seligman, "Building Resilience" in *Harvard Business Review* (April 2011): 101–106. For a more complete treatment of this subject see M.E.P. Seligman, *Flourish: A Visionary New Understanding of Happiness and Well-being* (New York: Free Press, 2011).
15. It may be difficult to overcome a habitual pattern of avoidance, but it is possible to learn to cope assertively with stressful events through counseling and educational programs. For example, see Maddi and Kobasa, *The Hardy Executive*; D. M. Khoshaba and S. R. Maddi, "Early Experiences in Hardiness Development," *Consulting Psychology Journal* 51 (1999): 106–116; S. R. Maddi, S. Kahn, and

K. L. Maddi, "The Effectiveness of Hardiness Training," *Consulting Psychology Journal* 50 (1998): 78–86; Maddi and Khoshaba, *Resilience at Work;* K. Reivish and A. Shatte, *The Resilience Factor: 7 Keys to Finding Your Inner Strength and Overcoming Life's Hurdles* (New York: Broadway Books, 2003); and J. D. Margolis and P. G. Stoltz, "How to Bounce Back from Adversity," *Harvard Business Review* 88, no. 1, (January-February, 2010); 86–92.

PRACTICE 4

Enable Others to Act

Leaders know that they can't do it alone. It takes partners to make extraordinary things happen in organizations.

Leaders invest in creating trustworthy relationships. They build spirited and cohesive teams, teams that feel like family. They actively involve others in planning and give them discretion to make their own decisions. Leaders make others feel like owners, not hired hands.

Leaders develop collaborative goals and cooperative relationships within the group. They are considerate of the needs and interests of others. They know that these relationships are the keys that unlock support. They bring people together, creating an atmosphere where people understand that they have a shared fate and should treat others as they would like to be treated. They make sure that everyone wins.

Mutual respect is what sustains extraordinary group efforts. Leaders nurture self-esteem in others. They make others feel strong, capable, and confident to take initiative and responsibility. They build the skills and abilities of their constituents to deliver on commitments. They create a climate where people feel in control of their own lives.

In the next two chapters, we will explore how leaders:

- **Foster Collaboration by building trust and facilitating relationships.**
- **Strengthen Others by increasing self-determination and developing competence.**

8

Commitment #7: Foster Collaboration

Saima Saddiqi was in the first class of a brand-new college of medicine. It was a small class of only sixty-four, and she quickly learned that she shared with many classmates a deep commitment to learning, to excellence in medicine, and to serving the community. From the many opportunities to help shape a college culture that aligned with those shared values, one of her first efforts was to work to streamline the process of starting student organizations. Saima found others who shared the idea that student organizations could extend their opportunities for learning, and they focused on making the process for starting a new organization clear and simple. They reviewed the existing protocols, redlined as much as they possibly could, and made the process quicker and more manageable. Eighteen dynamic organizations were soon created that today thrive and support each other. "What we all learned in this process," Saima told us, "is that together we can define what the college culture is. *We* define it—not the faculty, not the deans, but we the students."

Through these student organizations, Saima and her classmates were able to expand their medical education curriculum. They started by cataloging the things they wanted to know about that might not be available through the normal academic channels of such a small college.

Then they worked together with the new student organizations to make relevant learning experiences available. One example: the college had not been able to have a pediatric neonatologist on its faculty, but the students found one to come speak regularly to the Pediatrics Club.

The faculty had at first been unprepared for the energy, enthusiasm, and commitment the students shared for the programs they had put together. It wasn't long, however, before faculty encouraged and supported their efforts, deepening the emerging culture of innovative student-powered learning. Today, they are very open to the students' ideas and let them run with new projects; they trust the students to come up with novel and effective ways to enrich their medical school education through student-developed programs.

When you create a climate of trust as Saima and her team did among the student organizations and with the faculty, you create an environment that allows people to freely contribute and innovate. You nurture open exchanges of ideas and truthful discussions of issues. You motivate people to go beyond compliance and inspire them to reach for the best in themselves. And you nurture the belief that people can rely on you to do what's in everyone's best interests. An example of how all this came to life at her school, Saima told us, was their Community Health Fair.

To honor their commitment to community service, Saima and her classmates had decided to hold a Health Fair to serve the uninsured or underinsured members of their community, some of whom were illegal aliens. No surprise, but the big stumbling block was legal liability. Saima and her team knew that this obstacle could only be met by working with the faculty and coordinating effectively with the local Department of Health.

"The faculty had faith in our abilities to pull something like this off," Saima told us, because of the good relationships built when the students were setting up the first student-sponsored educational programs. "They were incredibly supportive in helping us find a way to make the insurance issue work." Of course, considering the size of the undertaking, it would also take more than just a handful of medical students to make the Health Fair a success, and they would have to get lots of people to feel excited to be part of the project. One of the ways she encouraged classmates to feel confident about joining the project was to "constantly remind them about our commitment to serve and our ability to 'make things happen.'" Eventually, more than a third of the student body volunteered to help out in one way or another. "There was no doubt in my mind that the students who got involved were committed to this," Saima said. "The students who stood up and voiced their enthusiasm for helping with the Health Fair wanted to be seen as students at a college that doesn't see itself as elite but as part of community and willing to do the right thing."

The passion was there, but the Health Fair still needed the support of the local health department. The Health Fair team needed to forge a relationship with the department that would be "productive and mutually beneficial," one that would be open to serving their community in a special way. With the commitment of so many students in evidence, Saima and the project team sat down with health department officials at their office. "We discussed the tremendous need we all saw and quickly knew we were on the same page. We talked about how by working collaboratively we could make this happen," she said.

In the end, the Health Fair was a success, a clear reason being that so many players were fully committed to working together to meet the challenge. Without the faculty helping to navigate the legal waters, the health department getting ready to receive a whole new set of clients, and the students volunteering their time and medical skills, the Health Fair simply would not have happened. The project team needed all those people to make it work and as its leader Saima needed to help everyone feel connected and part of something important and meaningful.

Saima's experience is a good illustration of something that all exemplary leaders know: Leadership is not a solo pursuit. It's a team effort.

When talking about personal bests, and when talking about leaders they admire, people speak passionately about teamwork and cooperation as the interpersonal route to success, especially when conditions are extremely challenging and urgent. Leaders of all ages, from all economic sectors, and from around the globe, continue to tell us, "You can't do it alone."

Exemplary leaders understand that to create a climate where people work together effectively, they need to do several things. They must determine what people will need to do their work. They must also make sure the team is clear on their purpose, and last but not least, they must make sure the team is built around mutual respect. Leaders make trust and teamwork a priority.

Exemplary leaders make the commitment to Foster Collaboration by engaging in these essentials:

- Create a climate of trust
- Facilitate relationships

Collaboration has always been a key element for success in any extraordinary endeavor. Leaders, no matter what age, must find a way to invite and encourage collaboration and teamwork. They must be trustworthy themselves, and build relationships with others and between people that are based on mutual trust and respect.

CREATE A CLIMATE OF TRUST

Think about the leaders who engage you. Chances are it's because, as Saima did, they make you feel part of something important and that the hard work you contribute will help everyone connect to the cause, project, or team. They have a "WE not I" philosophy.

However, "we" can't happen without trust. It's the central issue in human relationships. Without trust you cannot lead. Without trust you can't get people to believe in you or in each other. Without trust you cannot get extraordinary things done. Individuals who are unable to trust others fail to become leaders, precisely because they can't bear to be dependent on the words and works of others. Either they end up doing all the work themselves, or they become overly controlling. Their obvious lack of trust in others results in others' lack of trust in them. To build and sustain social connections you have to be able to trust others and others have to trust you.

When you create a climate of trust, you create an environment that allows people to freely contribute and innovate. You nurture an open exchange of ideas and a truthful discussion of issues. You motivate people to go beyond compliance and inspire them to reach for the best in themselves. And you nurture the belief that people can rely on you to do what's in everyone's best interests. To get these kinds of results you have to ante up first in the game of trust. You have to listen and learn from others, and you have to share information and resources with others. Trust comes first, and following comes second.

Be the First to Trust

Building trust is a process that begins when someone (either you or the other party) is willing to risk being the first to open up, being the first to show vulnerability, and being the first to let go of control—and then reciprocating these actions. Generally it is leaders who go first. If you want the high levels of performance that come with trust and collaboration, you will have to demonstrate your trust in others before asking them to trust you. But the payoff is huge, no matter what your organization or where you are located. Consider what these students from around the world told us it meant to them to know that their leader trusted them:

- "I am a hard worker as a rule of thumb but Alex's trust in me made me work even harder, because I did not want to disappoint him." (Canada)

- "Since Bob put his trust in me, I made sure that I would not fail." (Hong Kong)
- "His telling me that he trusted my judgment made me more than double my efforts to make sure that I didn't let him down and truly earned his respect." (South Africa)
- "This trust gave me more confidence in myself, which encouraged me to do even better and gave me a sense of power." (China)
- "I was excited to work with him because I felt that he trusted my abilities. Not only did I feel compelled to reciprocate Wilson's trust but I also felt empowered to explore new avenues." (Germany)
- "Knowing that she trusted me to handle this situation on my own gave me the confidence that I could be successful even though I had never done something like this before." (Australia)
- "When she told me that she trusted me to do the right thing; well, that's exactly what I was going to make sure happened." (United States)
- "I felt empowered and trusted at the same time. It made me want to work harder in order to show that I deserved this trust." (Chile)

Going first is a scary proposition, even if you realize that you can't be successful all on your own. When these leaders demonstrated that they trusted their fellow students, they were taking a chance. They were betting that their confidence wouldn't be betrayed, and that the information, resources, and power that they shared would not be taken advantage of. In letting go, delegating responsibility and leadership to others, you're taking the risk that others can be relied on to do what's right, and to care about the outcomes as much as you do. It's intriguing that considerable self-confidence is one of the prerequisites for being able to trust others.

When Jordan Goff started working with a class group in one of his business courses he quickly had to develop the confidence that he could trust others. As many students know from their own experiences, working on class projects as a group can be stressful, frustrating, disorganized, and challenging because of the various levels of commitment of the people in the group. Jordan knew that he couldn't do the project all alone and that he needed others to complete the task successfully, but he was concerned that other members of the group wouldn't live up to his expectations.

Eventually Jordan was overwhelmed by the work and decided to take a chance on his classmate Stanley by asking him to take over an important piece of the project. Stanley did not disappoint, turning in great quality work ahead of schedule. That's when it dawned on Jordan that he needed to give up power and create an atmosphere where others can feel a sense of their own power within the group to get things done. When Jordan began to trust others with carrying out important details of the project, taking into account their individual skills, abilities, needs, and interests, their trust in him grew. By going first, by showing that he trusted Stanley to succeed, Jordan demonstrated to his classmates that he was confident that they could learn from and support one another and instilled confidence and competence within every member of the project team.

Trust is the central issue in human relationships within and outside organizations, and it is essential for getting things done. Student leaders who do not trust others end up doing all the work themselves, or they supervise the work so closely that they become control freaks. Both are a recipe for burnout, and they undermine the confidence of others on the team, dampening their motivation. But as the experiences of so many students from around the world have shown, trust is contagious. When you trust others, they are much more likely to trust you. They are much more likely to work as hard as they can to make certain that they live up to the trust that they have been shown. But should you choose not to trust, understand that distrust is equally contagious. If you exhibit distrust, others will respond accordingly and hesitate to place their trust in you or in their colleagues. It's up to you to set the example.

Self-disclosure is one way to demonstrate trust. Letting others know what you stand for, what you value, what you want, what you hope for, and what you're willing (and not willing) to do discloses information about yourself. You can't be certain that other people will appreciate your openness, agree with your dreams, or interpret your words and actions in the way you intend. But once you take the risk of being open, others are more likely to take a similar risk and be willing to work toward mutual understanding.

Trust can be built in many ways, but in the end, trust can't be forced. If someone is bent on misunderstanding you and refuses to perceive you as either well intentioned or competent, there may be little you can do to change that perception. You have to remember that placing trust in others is the safer bet with most people most of the time. Trust begets trust. It's a reciprocal process. When you are first to trust, others are more likely to trust you.

Show Concern for Others

Ike Opara was a sophomore on his college soccer team when he was heavily pursued to enter the Major League Soccer draft at the end of the year as a projected top-three pick. While Ike acknowledged that it was a terrific honor, he just didn't feel quite right about it. He had been part of his university's team that had taken the national championship the year before and if he entered the draft he would be leaving when they were all deeply connected and thriving as a team. They had a good opportunity to win another national title and Ike felt as though his departure might jeopardize the team's chances of achieving that goal. "I wanted to help us win again if we could," he told us. "These were my best friends, I counted on them and they counted on me."

When Ike talked with his teammates and his coach, everyone was very supportive of whichever decision he might make. "That's the thing about a team," he said, "we're all connected." He also knew he was taking a risk financially and professionally by not going pro after his sophomore year. Uncontrollable factors, like a serious injury, could hinder his development or even end his career prematurely. After taking all these factors into account, Ike chose to embark on his professional journey one year later. "I'm grateful it all worked out," he said. "I got to spend another year as part of great team with great people, many of whom I still consider good friends, and I got a year further in my academics."[1]

The concern you show for others is one of the clearest and most unambiguous signals of your trust. When others know you will put their interests ahead of your own, they won't hesitate to trust you.[2] But that doesn't happen automatically. It's something people have to see in your actions. Ike's decision to stay in school and play on the soccer team for another year was a crystal-clear demonstration of his values, how he could be trusted, and how he had placed his own trust in his teammates. He listened to others, paid attention to their ideas and concerns, and was open to their influence. When you show your openness to the ideas of other people and your interest in their concerns, your constituents will be more open to *yours*.

The simple act of listening to what other people have to say and appreciating their unique points of view demonstrates your respect for them and their ideas. Being sensitive to what others are going through creates a bond between people that makes it easier to accept another's guidance and advice. These actions build mutual empathy and understanding, which in turn increase trust. Leaders demonstrate how powerful listening and empathy can be in building trust. You need to see the world through others' eyes, and make sure that you consider alternative viewpoints. Those who follow you have to feel they can talk freely with you about their difficulties. They have to believe that you'll be caring and constructive in your responses so that they'll be open to sharing their ideas, their frustrations, and their dreams with you. They won't do that if they don't feel that you know them.

Share Knowledge and Information

To willingly follow your lead, people have to believe that you know what you're talking about and that you know what you're doing. One way you can demonstrate this is by sharing what you know and encouraging others to do the same. Leaders who play this role of knowledge builder set the example for how team members should behave toward each other. As a result, team members trust in each other and in the leader increases, along with their performance.[3]

That's exactly what happened with Gregory Smith's university debate team. The team had grown so fast that it didn't have enough coaches to help all the students prepare and compete. Gregory and another senior on the team stepped in to assist by sharing lessons from their more extensive debate experience and by coaching the younger competitors. "I led practice every Thursday night, working with anyone who wanted to improve their performance," Gregory told us. He also began teaching an undergraduate-level public speaking class.

Gregory saw the teaching and coaching he was doing not just as a one-way transfer of his knowledge and skills to the debate team but as a matter of "building communication bridges" within the team. He told us that:

> One of the greatest needs I filled on my team was being a sounding board for teammates—whether critiquing an event, or just listening and encouraging teammates with their problems, because even non-speech difficulties can distract them from their best performance or infect the team when ignored.

Gregory also pointed out that "I was certainly not alone in seeing and acting on this need on my team." Others began to follow his lead, and people started to open up with one another and share information and insights about what they were learning from their practice and tournament experiences. All this, combined with the team's already high motivation and "willingness to work together," Gregory told us, "catapulted us from being a mediocre debate team into being one of the best in the country."

Leaders like Gregory know that trust among team members goes up when knowledge and information is shared, and the fact that performance increases as a result underscores how important it is for leaders to stay focused on the needs of their team. If you show a willingness to trust others with information they will be more inclined to overcome any doubts they might have about sharing information in return. But if you withhold information—or if you're overly concerned about protecting your turf and keeping things to yourself—you can quickly lose their trust. Trust, once lost, is very difficult to regain.

FACILITATE RELATIONSHIPS

"You can't do it alone" is the leader's mantra. Indeed, you really can't be much of a leader if no one wants to follow in the same direction with you. What defines leaders, quite simply, is that they have followers. And what makes people willing to follow is, paradoxically, that leaders turn their followers into leaders. Leaders have the best interests of others in their hearts, and trusting in any other person, including a leader, is evidence of a caring relationship. Leadership is a relationship that needs to be nurtured and treasured. When leaders can get the people on their team, in their class, or in their community to trust one another, the strength of these relationships facilitates the ability of everyone to work together for the collective good. When this is the case, asking for help and sharing information come naturally, and setting a common goal becomes almost intuitive.

Kerrin McCarthey was a college sophomore when she got involved in a peer advisory board for a program dedicated to mentoring younger students on her campus. As a member of the board, she was responsible for helping to guide the program and the other mentors who worked with a small group of students throughout the year. The previous boards' practice had been to have all of the students attend a retreat to kick off the program and then meet with their mentors on a regular basis to talk about all sorts of things related to the college experience and how to be more successful. Kerrin immediately saw that one of the program's difficulties was that students really didn't seem as excited and involved a few months into it as they had been right after the retreat. She felt this had a great deal to do with the fact that solid relationships were not developed, either among the mentors or with the students they served. There also was a general lack of trust in the mentoring process and even in the value and worthiness of the program itself.

Kerrin talked with her fellow board members to get their perceptions, and then she started consulting the mentors. "It was very awkward at first to talk with others and get them to open up about what they were feeling and thinking," she told us. "I realized that maybe we hadn't developed much trust yet so that everyone could feel comfortable sharing their thoughts." In her conversations with the board members and the mentors, Kerrin communicated first that she "felt honored to have their trust" and that she would do whatever it took to help them believe in her and in the program. She shared some of her personal experiences, both from times when she was being mentored and when she served as a mentor, thinking that this would help others feel more relaxed in sharing what was on their minds. She believed that if they thought she wasn't trying to judge or criticize then they might open up and talk about what was on their minds. She asked sincere questions about their experience, what they thought the program needed, and how the mentors could better help and work with their mentees. They also talked about what might be keeping other students from getting more involved.

The result of all of Kerrin's probing seemed to come down to the core issue that no one had taken the time to develop genuine relationships with one another. After all the sense of camaraderie from the kick-off retreat wore off, the students didn't care about much else because they didn't see their mentors really caring. Kerrin continued seeking out stories and ideas of what would help the mentors and students get what they wanted from the program and began to get everyone more personally involved in ongoing regular gatherings. As a result, the mentors grew much more committed to the program because they really wanted to be a part of it and make a difference rather than just going through the motions. Seeing the mentors' newfound dedication, the students grew more enthusiastic and started finding more value from the mentoring experience. Soon they became advocates for the program, encouraging their friends and other students to participate.

Leaders like Kerrin understand that relationships are necessary in order to get people to collaborate, relying and depending on each other. People have to know that they need each other to be successful. The best leaders create an environment where people know they can count on each other. They encourage people to talk about the goals they have and the roles each person can take in achieving those goals, and they create projects or tasks where people work together, not in isolation. All of these practices played a big part in the turnaround of Kerrin's mentoring program.

Develop Cooperative Goals and Roles

In the previous chapter, we told you a little about Insight Dubai. This annual conference brings together sixty young women from around the world and pairs them with sixty students from the Dubai Women's College for five days of lectures, workshops, and discussion on global topics. The overarching goal of the conference is for these young women to share and learn and grow together by getting to know each other and the cultures they represent.

This goal is clearly stated at the beginning of the conference, when the students are reminded that the conference is focused on inclusion and therefore they should make it a priority to spend time with students from different backgrounds. Rana Korayem, the lead facilitator for the 2013 conference, explained:

> I said in the opening session that Insight Dubai was a journey with a final destination of greater understanding, deeper knowledge, and lasting friendships. Everything we do throughout these five days is focused on that. I described my first conference experience, when I arrived to see so many women with different attire, different languages, yet all coming together to share as women. That is the goal of Insight Dubai, that is the gift of Insight Dubai.

Throughout the conference participants work together in small groups to develop their global awareness, intercultural understanding, and leadership skills. They spend time getting to know each other and determining the best ways to share their knowledge and perspectives while collaborating on developing proposed solutions to substantial global issues.

For a group of people to have a positive experience together at events such as Insight Dubai, or in sports or campus clubs, classroom assignments, community service projects, and the like, they must have shared goals that provide a specific reason for working together. The most basic ingredient in every collective achievement is a common goal. Common purpose binds people into cooperative efforts. It creates a sense of interdependence, a condition in which everyone knows that they cannot succeed unless everyone else succeeds, or at least that they can't succeed unless they coordinate their efforts. If there's not a sense that "we're all in this together"—that the success of one depends on the success of the other—then it's virtually impossible to create the conditions for positive teamwork. If you want individuals or groups to work cooperatively you have to give them a good reason to do so, and that good reason is generally expressed as a goal that can only be accomplished by working together.

Keeping individuals focused on a common goal promotes a stronger sense of teamwork than emphasizing individual objectives. For cooperation to succeed, you must also design roles so that every person's contributions matter for the outcome. You have to get everyone to clearly understand that unless they each contribute whatever they can, the project or team fails to be as successful as it could be. It's like putting together a jigsaw puzzle. Each person has a piece, and if even one piece is missing the puzzle is impossible to complete.

What's more, fostering collaborative goals and roles means making sure that there aren't any in-groups or out-groups, any "us versus them," or competition for attention among members. People have to identify with the group they are part of in order to work together. Schools create identity with mascots, uniform colors, unique gestures, and songs. Fraternities and sororities do it with Greek letters, handshakes, special symbols, ceremonies, and rituals. Project teams do it with special names for product versions, insider jokes, badges, and the like. Make sure that everyone feels that they are part of one team. It multiplies the strength of their feeling that it's "all for one, and one for all."

Support Standards of Reciprocity

In any effective long-term relationship, there must be a sense of reciprocity. If one partner always gives and the other always takes, the one who gives will feel taken advantage of and the one who takes will feel superior. In such an atmosphere, cooperation is virtually impossible. University of Michigan political scientist Robert Axelrod demonstrated the power of reciprocity in the well-known study of the "Prisoner's Dilemma."[4] The dilemma is this: two parties (individuals or groups) are confronted with a series of situations in which they must decide whether or not to cooperate. They don't know in advance what the other party will do. There are two basic strategies—cooperate or compete—and four possible outcomes based on the choices players make: win-lose, lose-win, lose-lose, and win-win.

The maximum *individual* payoff comes when the first player selects an uncooperative strategy and the second player chooses to cooperate in good faith. In this "I win but you lose" approach, one party gains at the other's expense. If both parties choose not to cooperate and attempt to maximize individual payoffs, then both lose. If both parties choose to cooperate, both win, though the individual payoff for a cooperative move is less than for a competitive one (in the short run).

Scientists from around the world submitted their strategies for winning in a computer simulation of this test of win-win versus win-lose strategies. "Amazingly enough," says Axelrod, "the winner was the simplest of all strategies submitted: cooperate on the first move and then do whatever the other player did on the previous move. This strategy succeeded by eliciting cooperation from others, not by defeating them."[5] Simply put, people who reciprocate are more likely to be successful than those who try to maximize individual advantage. Cooperation wins over selfishness in the long run.

The dilemmas that can be successfully solved by this strategy are not restricted to theoretical research. Similar predicaments happen every day: Should I try to maximize my own personal gain? What price might I pay for this action? Should I give up a little for the sake of others? Will others take advantage of me if I'm cooperative? Shouldn't I be competitive—try to be the best, because that's how you get ahead? Reciprocity turns out to be the most successful approach for such daily decisions, because it shows both a willingness to be cooperative and an unwillingness to be taken advantage of. As a long-term strategy, reciprocity minimizes the risk of escalation: if people know that you'll respond in kind, why would they start trouble? And if people know that you'll reciprocate, they know that the best way to deal with you is to cooperate and become recipients of your cooperation.

It's less stressful to work with others when you understand how they will behave in response. When you treat others as you'd like for them to treat you, it's likely they'll repay you over and over again. Once you help others to succeed, acknowledge their accomplishments, and help them shine, they'll never forget it.

Structure Projects to Promote Joint Effort

Leaders structure projects and assignments in a way that supports and facilitates relationships by promoting joint effort. People are more likely to cooperate if the payoffs for working *together* are greater than for independent work. Certainly each individual within the group has a distinct role, but on great teams everyone knows that if they only do their individual parts well they are unlikely to achieve the group's goal. After all, if you could do it alone, why would you need a team? Soccer isn't a one-on-eleven sport; hockey isn't one-on-six; baseball isn't one-on-nine; basketball isn't one-on-five. They require team effort—as do all organizational achievements.

Cooperative behavior requires individuals to understand that by working together they will be able to accomplish something that no one can accomplish on their own. When Kjerstin Lewis made the commitment to lead a fundraiser and event for her church's youth mission trip, realizing that she wasn't going to have the backing and support of the new youth director, she quickly appreciated the importance of collaboration and cooperative effort.

> I knew I couldn't do it by myself. I knew I was going to have to take some risks. I was going to have to "put myself out

> there," and recognize that this event wasn't about me. If we were going to get anything done, we were going to all have to do it together. We didn't have a lot of time to pull this off so we had to work together as one group and that required us to believe in each other.

Kjerstin knew things wouldn't always go as planned, but if the group communicated and shared and stayed true to the goals, the little glitches could be overcome because they were committed to working together as a connected group of individuals, not just as individuals in a group. Leaders help people to realize that by working together they can complete the project faster than by thinking about any short-term (or individual) victories resulting from doing their own thing, or complaining, blaming, or competing with others for scarce resources.

Support Face-to-Face Interactions

Group goals, identity, reciprocity, and promoting joint efforts are all important for collaboration to occur, but positive face-to-face interactions and sincere, high-quality interpersonal communications are also vital. People function more easily as a team when they can have some amount of face time with each other. This is true not only locally, but also in globally distributed relationships. Getting to know others firsthand is vital to cultivating trust and collaboration. It's the leader's responsibility to provide frequent and lasting opportunities for team members to connect between disciplines, across groups, and among peers.

Technology and social media can certainly enhance communications. Virtual connections are no doubt a great part of your life. And no organization could function if people always had to be in the same room together to exchange information, make decisions, or resolve disputes. Still, a text message, online post, or video-conference doesn't get you the same results as an intimate in-person conversation.

To foster collaboration among team members when you connect virtually, you need to communicate clearly and sincerely; keeping in mind that you have to initially build trust with others. For example, rather than texting the person across the hall, talk with her face-to-face first and continue that quality communication, if you have to, online. And be sure to work as hard as you can to get the members of your group together in front of each other as often as possible. Firsthand experience with another human being is simply a more reliable way of creating identification, increasing adaptability, and reducing misunderstandings than virtual connections.[6]

There obviously are limits to virtual trust. Virtual trust, like virtual reality, is one step removed from the real thing. Human beings are social animals; it's in our nature to want to interact.[7] If you mainly know the members of your group virtually, you probably don't know them well enough to trust them with really important things. You will have to reconcile the benefits of virtual meeting time with the knowledge that building trust depends on getting to know one another deeply.

Another benefit of frequent face-to-face interactions is the way they promote continuity of relationships in the group. In other words, knowing that you'll have to deal again with someone in person tomorrow, next week, or in another class next semester ensures that you won't easily forget about how you've treated them, and how they've treated you. This makes the consequences of today's actions on tomorrow's contacts that much more pronounced. In addition, frequent interactions between people promote positive feelings about one another. Begin with the assumption that in the future you'll be interacting with these people again in some way and that these relationships will be important to your mutual success. By making this assumption, everyone will be more motivated to make sure that things work out well in the short run.

TAKE ACTION: FOSTER COLLABORATION

"You can't do it alone" is the mantra of exemplary leaders—and for good reason. You simply can't make extraordinary things happen by yourself. Collaboration is the key skill that enables classrooms, clubs, teams, and communities to function effectively. Collaboration is sustained when you create a climate of trust and facilitate effective long-term relationships within your group. You have to promote a sense of mutual dependence—feeling part of a group in which everyone knows they need the others to be successful. Without that sense of "we're all in this together" it's virtually impossible to keep effective teamwork going.

Trust is the lifeblood of collaborative teamwork. To create and sustain the conditions for long-lasting connections, you have to be able to trust others, they have to trust you, and they have to trust each other. Without trust you cannot lead; you cannot get great things accomplished. Share information and knowledge freely with people in your group, show that you understand their needs and interests, be open and receptive to their ideas, make use of their abilities and expertise, and—most of all—demonstrate you trust them before you ask them to trust you.

The challenge of facilitating relationships is making sure everyone recognizes how much they need each other to excel—how interdependent they really are. Cooperative goals and roles contribute to a sense of collective purpose, and the best incentive for people to work to achieve shared goals is the knowledge that you and others will do the same. Help begets help just as trust begets trust. Structure projects to reward joint efforts. Get people interacting and encourage communication through face-to-face interactions as often as possible to reinforce the durability of relationships.

Exemplary leaders Foster Collaboration *by building trust and facilitating relationships*. Here are ways you can live out this commitment:

- Tell people in your group, "I trust you." Saying it matters, and, obviously, you'd better mean it, and, most important, demonstrate it by your actions.
- Extend trust to others first, even if they haven't already shown it to you. Share information about yourself—your hopes, your strengths, your fears, your mistakes—the things that make you who you are.
- Ask others for help and assistance when needed.
- Spend time getting to know those in your group and find out what makes them tick. What can you do today to build a closer relationship with one person in your group?
- Show concern for the problems, plans, and dreams others have. Ask them what bugs them, what they aspire to, and where they see themselves five years down the road.
- Listen, listen, and listen some more.
- Share with others what you know, answer their questions, connect them to resources they need, and introduce them to others who might be helpful.
- Clearly, and frequently, communicate the common goal that you are all striving to achieve, the shared values that are important, and the larger purpose of which everyone is a part.
- Do someone a favor, as if you were paying it forward. If they do one for you, say thank you. Then reciprocate.
- Structure projects and assignments so that there is a common goal that requires people to cooperate and help each other out. Decide how you will make visible the fact that people are interdependent with one another for success.
- Find ways to get people into meaningful conversations where they can get to know each other. If one approach doesn't work, try something else.

NOTES

1. Ike Opara was a member of Wake Forest's 2007 NCAA College Cup Championship team. They lost in the semifinals the following year. Ike was named ACC Defensive Player of the year in 2008 and 2009. He was drafted in the first round (third overall) of the 2010 MLS SuperDraft by the San Jose Earthquakes and traded to Sporting Kansas City from San Jose in 2012.
2. See, for example, P. S. Shockley-Zalabak, S. Morreale, and M. Hackman, *Building the High-Trust Organization: Strategies for Supporting Five Key Dimensions of Trust* (San Francisco: Jossey-Bass, 2010).
3. P. Lee, N. Gillespie, L. Mann, and A. Wearing, "Leadership and Trust: Their Effect on Knowledge Sharing and Team Performance," *Management Learning* 41, no. 4 (2010); 473–491.
4. R. Axelrod, *The Evolution of Cooperation: Revised Edition* (New York: Basic Books, 2006). See also W. Poundstone, *Prisoner's Dilemma: John Von Neumann, Game Theory, and the Puzzle of the Bomb* (New York: Anchor, 1993). These findings were replicated in an extensive probability analysis, which used high-powered computing to run hundreds of "games" and found that cooperativeness, rather than selfishness, won in the end. For more information, see: C. Adami and A. Hintze, "Evolutionary Instability of Zero-Determinant Strategies Demonstrates That Winning Is Not Everything," *Nature Communications* 4, no. 2193 (2013). Available online at http://dx.doi.org/ 10.1038/ncomms3193.
5. Axelrod, *The Evolution of Cooperation*, 20, 190.
6. M. Mortesen and T. Beyene, "Firsthand Experience and The Subsequent Role of Reflected Knowledge in Cultivating Trust in Global Collaboration," MIT Sloan School Working Paper 4735–09, April 29, 2009. Available online at http://ssrn.com/abstract=1395732. See also: D. Cohen and L. Prusak, *In Good Company: How Social Capital Makes Organizations Work* (Boston: Harvard Business School Press, 2001), 20.
7. D. Brooks, *The Social Animal: Hidden Sources of Love, Character, and Achievement.* (New York: Random House, 2011).

9

Commitment #8: Strengthen Others

Francis Appeadu-Mensah attended the African Leadership Academy in South Africa, a two-year academic program that prepares Africa's young men and women to be future leaders and make a difference in their communities. Students are nominated to attend from countries throughout Africa, and Francis was deeply honored by the opportunity to represent Ghana and develop himself as a leader. "I saw it as a chance to find out all I could about myself," he said "and bring that wisdom back to my family and community."

When we asked Francis about a personal-best leadership experience during his time at the Academy, he told us about being appointed the director of the Drama Club. He modestly shared that he thought he had been appointed only because he had attended all the meetings the previous year, but he also told us that he was committed to leading the club because he saw its potential to help students find new avenues for personal expression. "I knew there was a great deal of interest and untapped talent in the student community," he explained. "I believed that success for the club depended on getting those people involved so they could explore and eventually share those talents with everyone."

The crucial first step, Francis quickly realized, was getting people to make the commitment to show up and participate. He appealed to the club members with that message, telling them that showing up mattered more than anything else. It was up to each of them individually, but if they attended club meetings they would learn from being engaged in the club's activities and have fun too. To support that promise, he created several committees: writing, directing, acting, poetry. Rather than assign students to committees, Francis invited them to participate in any committee they wished in order to help them discover their passions and their strengths. Francis told them, "This is a place where you can explore and decide where your talent lies. The only requirement is showing up to share that talent."

Francis promoted the vision of the Drama Club as a place where new talent is discovered and every voice is heard. But, to be heard, he explained to its members, they had to first show up. Then he would make it a point of involving every person in a way that helped him or her grow. "We needed each other," he said.

> We were in this together and we needed to help each other and help the club to grow. If someone had only acted in plays before but had a desire to direct one, I encouraged them to come to the meetings and they would have a chance to do that. It was amazing to see the talent that emerged.

When people were new to the club, or simply not sure what part of the club they wanted to explore, Francis would pull them aside after rehearsals and ask, "What did you think?" or "What would you do if you were directing this scene?" or "How would you have delivered this speech if you were the actor?" Francis recognized that people need new opportunities to grow and learn and he was committed to offering those. His questions sent the message that people's opinions mattered and built their confidence to express themselves. Over time, the club became stronger as members began to take on new roles and get involved in multiple aspects of theater production. "At the end of my term we were selected as 'Best Club' on the campus," Francis told us. "We all got to go out to a restaurant together and celebrate each and every member. I think that celebration helped inspire the next Club Director, who built on our 'show up, learn together, and share your talent' philosophy."

Exemplary leaders like Francis make a commitment to Strengthen Others. They enable people to take ownership of and responsibility for their success by enhancing their competence and their confidence in their abilities, by listening to their ideas and acting upon them, by involving them in important decisions, and by acknowledging and giving credit for their contributions. You want people to take initiative and be self-directed. In Francis's experience, by creating various committees with an open invitation to explore any facet of a dramatic production, he encouraged his colleagues to explore and try new things, learning new skills, and strengthening their overall capability and confidence.

Creating a climate in which people are fully engaged and feel in control of their own lives is at the heart of Strengthening Others. Exemplary leaders build an environment that both develops people's abilities to perform a task and develops their self-confidence in completing it. In a climate of competence and confidence, people don't hesitate to hold themselves personally accountable for results, and they feel profound ownership for their achievements.

To Strengthen Others exemplary leaders engage in two essentials. They:

- Enhance self-determination
- Develop competence and confidence

When you engage in these two essentials, you can significantly increase people's belief in their own ability to make a difference. You move from being *in control* to *giving over control* to others, becoming their coach. You help others learn new skills and develop existing talents, and you provide the institutional supports required for ongoing growth and change. In the final analysis, you are turning your constituents into leaders.

ENHANCE SELF-DETERMINATION

Long before *empowerment* became a popular word, exemplary leaders understood how important it was that others felt strong, capable, and useful. People who feel weak, incompetent, and insignificant consistently underperform and are typically quite unhappy.

People who are not confident about their ability to influence tend to hang onto whatever pieces of power they have. To get a better sense of how it feels to be powerless as well as powerful, we've asked thousands of people over the past thirty years to tell us about their own experiences of being in these situations. Think of actions or situations that have made you feel powerless, weak, or insignificant, like a pawn in someone else's game. Are they similar to what others have reported as shown in Actions and Conditions That Students Say Make Them Feel *Powerless?*

Actions and Conditions That Students Say Make Them Feel *Powerless*

- No one was interested in, listened to, or paid attention to my opinion.
- People ignored me or wouldn't answer my questions.
- People attacked me personally while I was making a presentation.
- The leader argued with me in front of my peers—even called me names.

(*Continued*)

- My decisions were not supported by others, even though they said they would back me up.
- Someone else took credit for my work.
- Things I needed to know were withheld and I wasn't part of the conversation on things that mattered to what I was doing.
- No one seemed to care very much whether I succeeded or failed.
- Others in the group didn't feel that I could handle the work and made me feel insignificant.
- I was pushed to do things the leader wasn't willing to do him- or herself.
- I was given responsibility but no authority to actually make decisions or hold others accountable.
- The tasks assigned to me were trivial and relatively unimportant in the scheme of things.
- People made negative remarks about my performance.
- Our leader played favorites, and I wasn't one of them!

Now think about what it was like at times when you felt powerful—strong, effective, valuable, like the creator of your own experience. Is what you remember similar to what others experienced, as recalled in Actions and Conditions That Students Say Make Them Feel *Powerful*?

Actions and Conditions That Students Say Make Them Feel *Powerful*

- Information was shared with me.
- I was asked to take on an important project even though I had never done this before.
- I was able to make choices and use my own judgment to make decisions.

- My coach and mentor told me that I had great potential and that she believed in me.
- People asked for my opinion and listened to what I had to say; in fact, my ideas often carried the day.
- The leader had my back, and supported the decisions that I made.
- I was given responsibility for handling a difficult situation.
- I was visible because the leader let everyone know in the organization that I was the one who had both the knowledge and authority to make the project successful.
- The organization helped me learn how to do my job more effectively.
- Others expressed positive sentiments that I was capable of doing a great job.
- I was appreciated for my accomplishments, especially from people that I respected.
- Our leader made time to let me know how I was doing and where I could be improving.
- I was given the chance to learn new skills and the opportunities to apply them.

People everywhere share a fundamental need: to be in control of their own life. When you feel controlled by others, when you believe that you lack support or resources, you show little commitment to give it your all. Even though you may go along with things you still realize how much more you could contribute, if you wanted to.

Consider what people report when we ask them to think about either the worst or the best leader they have ever worked for and the percentage of their talents that each leader utilized.

We've asked this question to a wide variety of people: undergraduate students, US Coast Guard commanders, senior human resources executives, graduate students in higher education administration, marketing executives with a global cosmetics firm, palliative medicine physicians, and community organizers. The responses from each group have not varied all that much. Generally what we've found is that when we ask people to think about their worst leaders and to indicate the percentage of their talents used, we get a range of responses from 2 to 40 percent, with an average of about 31 percent. In other words, our research shows that people report that in their experience, their worst leaders tapped less than a third of their available energy and talents.

This percentage is in sharp contrast to what people report when they think about their best leader. The best leaders bring out on average 95 percent of people's talent, and the *bottom* of the range was the *top* of the range for the worst leaders. In fact, many people say that these leaders got more than 100 percent of their talents! We know that it's mathematically impossible to get more than 100 percent of one's talents, yet people shake their heads and say, "No, they really did get me to do more than I thought I was capable of doing or that it was possible to do." By the way, these findings are relatively equivalent when we ask high school students to answer the same question, but this time in relation to their best teachers (rather than leaders).

There's clearly a difference between how we behave around our best and our worst leaders. As illustrated in Figure 9.1, the best leaders get more than three times the amount of talent, energy, commitment, and motivation from people compared to their counterparts at the other end of the spectrum.

The most effective leaders exemplify the actions that make people feel powerful.[1] They increase the level of self-determination that makes people, both figuratively and literally, powerful.[2] Self-determination can be enhanced in a number of ways, based on three core principles that ensure that people are able to decide for themselves: choice, latitude, and personal accountability.

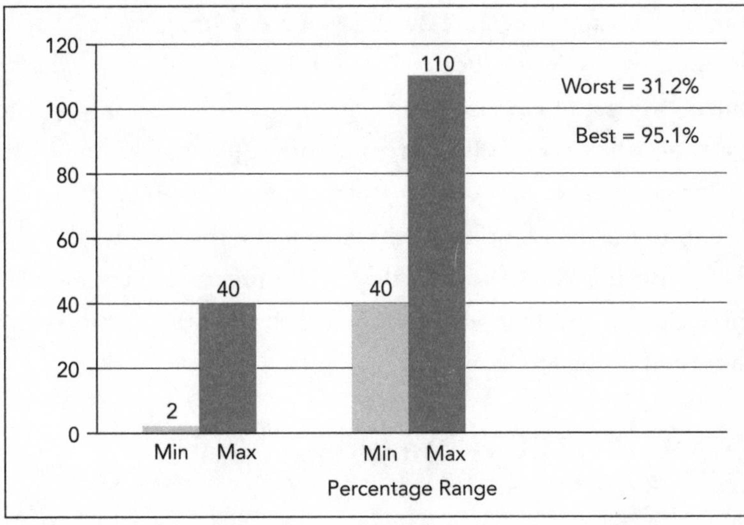

Figure 9.1: The Best Leaders Bring Out Two to Three Times the Talents in Others Compared to the Worst Leaders

Provide Choices

Exemplary leaders set standards and hold everyone accountable for shared values and visions, yet they also give people the opportunity to make choices about how they will get the job done.

You want people to take initiative and be self-directed. Francis organized the African Leadership Academy's Drama Club so that students could think about the available opportunities, explore and try several of them out, and make their own choices about where their talents and interests might best be deployed. He didn't assign people to committees, based upon his own intuition or simply where "warm bodies" were needed, but left spaces open for people to choose for themselves. That way, nobody got slotted into a role or position, but could explore their options.

Leaders want people to think for themselves and take action rather than continually asking someone else, "What should I do?"

This ability cannot be developed if you are telling people what to do and how to do it. They really can't learn to act independently unless they get to exercise some degree of choice. The only way to create an efficient and effective group of people who can meet the challenges that are part of trying new things is by giving them the chance to use their best judgment in applying their knowledge and skills. This implies, of course, that you've prepared them to make these choices and that you've grounded them with the values and the vision of the group.

Structure Work to Offer Latitude

Every year the students in a leadership development program at a large eastern university participate in the annual homecoming week festivities. One of the major events of the week is the homecoming parade, for which groups across campus build floats on large flatbed semi-trucks based on the theme for the year. Designing and building their parade float has always been a group effort for the leadership program students, but the process was not always well planned out and their floats didn't measure up to what the other student groups put in the parade.

The year Dan Samuels was a new float committee cochair he and his committee members recalled how challenging it had been building the floats in previous years. At the beginning of previous float projects, conversations typically progressed from talking about what had been created in prior years to tossing around new ideas with great enthusiasm. It was common to start with a high level of energy, Dan said, then the momentum would quickly wane as confusion set in around who would play what role, who would oversee the work, how the subcommittees would get more students involved, how much time would be required, and on and on. Dan was determined to prevent that from happening, and set out to make the group's float for that year—and the process of creating it—the best one yet. "I'd been involved in the homecoming float project a couple of times," he told us, "and people getting confused and losing interest didn't seem logical to me because as construction on the float progresses it gets to be even more exciting and fun." When Dan began talking to students who had started strong in years past and then dropped off, he learned that they just didn't feel like they were contributing in a significant way, that there were plenty of others who could do what they had been assigned to do. "That made me realize," he said, "that I needed to help people feel like their unique contribution was valued and that we were counting on each and every one of them."

As in the past, the float committee spent a lot of time brainstorming designs and choosing one that they thought best fit that year's homecoming theme. Dan decided that the traditional process needed something else to draw students in. So he asked some members of the committee to build a model of the float they envisioned. They could then use the model to encourage students to sign up for specific parts of the float project rather than having people show up night after night and just jump in sawing, hammering, and painting as they had done in years past.

Once the students had signed up for the portion of the float they wanted to work on, Dan led a smaller group to create a list of the specific tasks that needed to be done. The students could then pick from the list the work they wanted to do, factoring in the time they realistically had to contribute and what they thought they'd be good at doing. This strategy made a huge difference in how everyone engaged in the project. With everyone having a choice about what they would do and being asked to be honest about the time they had to contribute, Dan and his committee were able to spread the work out more efficiently and avoid the chaos and disengagement that had characterized their float building in the past. "There was no way people could fade away because they had signed up for the job they wanted and had committed to it," Dan explained. "Students signing up for the float also really liked the fact that they weren't assigned something, but had a chance to provide input on what they wanted to do."

By providing them latitude on the roles they would play, Dan was able to influence the attitude students brought to the project. As a result most kept their commitment. Plus, by giving people the opportunity to sign up for as much or as little as they realistically could do, their commitment was stronger. The float committee had far fewer no-shows than in any previous year. People weren't overcommitted and they knew what they were doing, so nobody bailed. There was much less frustration and much more efficiency and organization in the planning and construction process. "Everyone seemed to simply enjoy their work much more," Dan told us. "The enthusiasm kept on going and the whole process was fun."

Having latitude in how they do their work strengthens people. Each person grows when they are allowed to try new things and make decisions that affect how they do their work without having to check with someone else.[3] Effective leaders are not control freaks. Nor are they rigidly glued to a standard set of rules, procedures, or schedules. You need to give people a great deal of freedom and choice in deciding how to do their work. The payoff will be significant. Data from the Student Leadership Practices Inventory shows that the more that people agree that this is what their leaders are doing, they are significantly more engaged in their organizations, feeling more productive and appreciated.

Foster Accountability

It turns out that when people take personal responsibility and are held accountable for their actions others are much more interested in working with them and are more motivated to cooperate. Individual accountability is important in every collaborative effort. Everyone has to do their part for a group to function effectively.

Mykell Bates had played soccer from the age of fourteen and was chosen captain of the US Under-17 national team when he was just fifteen years old. When he went on to college his soccer playing continued and in his sophomore year Mykell was chosen captain of his school's men's soccer team. Being captain of a college team meant many more organizational duties than Mykell was used to, off the field as well as leading the team on the field. "At first I tried to do it all," Mykell told us, "but then it occurred to me, we depend on each other on the field, so shouldn't I depend on them off the field too?"

Mykell began to reach out to the players to be accountable for some of the communication duties on the team. "We all play an important part in our success on the field," he explained, "so all I was asking for was that same level of accountability and connection to the team off the field. When I'd ask a player 'Hey, can you text the guys about the team meeting tonight?' they always stepped up." Slowly Mykell began passing on responsibilities to more members of the team. Ultimately, it became clear that spreading out some of the tasks allowed for a much more efficient way of doing things, and helped all those who contributed feel accountable for the successful operation of the team.

What Mykell was doing with his team is what leaders do to foster accountability: they consciously create an environment where team members count on one another to get done what needs to get done. This doesn't mean they are autocratic or controlling. His teammate Brandon Zimmerman told us, "Mykell was not directive in handing out tasks; he would simply ask for your help and you would want to help him. He trusted that I could do the job that needed to be done and I didn't want to break that trust. It was mutual respect, for each other and for the good of the team."

Leaders like Mykell know that the more freedom of choice people have, the more personal responsibility they must accept. There's also a bonus: the more people believe that everyone else is taking responsibility for their parts of the project—and have the ability to do it—the more trusting and the more cooperative they're going to be. It's also true that people will be more confident in doing their part on a project when they believe others will do theirs.

Some students believe that teams and other cooperative experiences minimize individual accountability. They argue that if their classmates are encouraged to work collectively, somehow they'll take less responsibility for their own actions than if they are encouraged to compete or to do things on their own. Think about a group project for a class. If there are a lot people in the group, do you think that people are less likely to worry about what happens if they don't do their part? It's true that some people become lazy or distracted when working in groups, blowing things off while others do their jobs for them. But this doesn't last for long, because people quickly get tired of carrying the extra load. Either the slacker steps up to the responsibility, or the team wants that person out—provided the team has shared goals and shared accountability.[4]

Individual accountability strengthens any group assignment. People are more likely to be personally accountable when they believe in the task they are being asked to do. Here are a few suggestions on how you can foster individual accountability in group projects.

Remember to provide as many of the necessary resources as possible for people to perform autonomously. There's no worse feeling than to have lots of responsibility for doing something but nothing to do it with. People want to feel their efforts contribute in a meaningful way to the success of the whole.

Ideas for Fostering Individual Accountability

- Make certain that everyone in your group, no matter the task, has someone they are serving (that is, feel responsible to).
- Find ways to ensure that everyone is part of the decision-making process.
- Keep people posted and up to date on what is going on.
- Remove or reduce unnecessary decision-making steps.
- Eliminate as many rules as possible.
- Decrease the amount of routine work.
- Ask group members to do things that are not part of their regular routine.
- Support others when they make choices and decisions on their own.
- Encourage creative solutions to problems.
- Define roles more broadly—as projects, not tasks.
- Provide greater freedom of access to information.

COACH FOR COMPETENCE AND CONFIDENCE

Choice, latitude, and accountability inspire people's sense of power and control over their lives. But as necessary as enhancing self-determination is, it's not enough. Without the knowledge, skills, information, and resources to do a job well, and without feeling competent to do the job, people feel overwhelmed and discouraged. And even if they have the resources, there may be times when people don't have the confidence that they know how to use them or are even allowed to use them; they may fear that they won't be backed up if their use of resources doesn't produce the necessary results.

What Mykell Bates did, when he asked his soccer teammates to step up and take over some of the operational tasks for the soccer team, had another benefit beyond fostering accountability. By spreading responsibilities among the group, each teammate could specialize and perfect one thing rather than having one person to take it all on. Mykell learned that giving others responsibilities enhances their skills and self-confidence. Teammate Brandon Zimmerman shared another takeaway from his experience with Mykell: "I have a job building sheds and Mykell's leadership showed me that one thing I can do starting next week at work is pass on some of the building responsibilities to others. I have always liked doing everything myself, but I am sure the guys I am working with can do just as well as I can, if not better in some cases. I can coach them through it, and that will build their capabilities and confidence, eventually making us a stronger work team."

It's no secret that sharing power the way Mykell did results in higher performance for the group as a whole. Developing competence and building confidence for all members of the group is essential. To make extraordinary things happen you must invest in strengthening the capacity and the resolve of every single person in your group.

Think about a time when the challenge you faced was greater than the skills that you had. How did you feel when the challenge was high but your skill was low? If you're like most people, you felt anxious, nervous, scared, and the like. Now think of a time when your level of skill was greater than the level of challenge in the job. How did you feel? Bored and apathetic are the most common responses. Do you do your best work when you're anxious or bored? Of course not. You do it when the challenge you face is just slightly greater than your current level of skill. That's when you feel stretched but not stressed out. What's true for you is just as true for the other people you work with.

Exemplary leaders strive to create the conditions that make it possible for others to perform effortlessly and expertly despite the difficulty of the experience. That means you need to continuously assess the capacity of individuals and the group to meet the challenges they face. That requires attention to the skill power and the willpower of each person you lead.

Share Information

People may be reluctant to be accountable, in part because they aren't sure about how to do certain things, or because they are simply afraid to make mistakes. Developing the competence and confidence of each member in a group is a virtuous cycle making everyone involved feel more qualified, more capable, more effective, and like leaders in their own right. This is your job as a leader. And that was the job that Christina Belge took on when she was placed on her university's Energy Task Force, along with faculty and staff across the campus.

The year before Christina joined the task force, there had been an initiative led by the Student Alliance for a Green Earth (SAGE) to institute a "Green Fee," but it had not been enacted because the university president felt there was insufficient evidence of overall student support. Christina's task force came up with numerous green projects, policy plans, and publicity efforts to make the school more environmentally friendly. "This was a fantastic effort," Christina said, "but I knew it would go nowhere if there was no funding. I had to take action." She wrote a resolution for a $10 "Green Fee" designed to fund various projects and promotional efforts to boost environmental awareness and responsibility on campus. She presented the "Green Fee" resolution to the school's student senate, with a well-defined outline of how the $200,000 would be spent.

The senate was hesitant, feeling the previous student body survey needed to be redone to provide evidence of support. So Christina and SAGE, along with other supportive students across campus, reached out again to educate the student body about this fee. They were competing at the time with a proposal from athletics to raise the athletic fee and appeared to be outnumbered and outspent every step of the way. "But we didn't stop," Christina told us. "We had a lot of good information on something we believed the student body really cared about and we believed that if we could share it with the students we'd have a fair shot." Their knowledge sharing paid off big time. Armed with facts and figures about the impact of the projects the Green Fee would fund, students overwhelmingly supported it, with 75 percent of them eventually approving the fee increase.

Christina's experience tells us that sharing information with others is a crucial task for leaders who want to make extraordinary things happen. Plus, sharing information consistently shows up in our research as one of the leadership actions that makes people feel powerful; not sharing information was frequently cited as making people feel powerless. Making people smarter is the job of every leader. If the people in your group aren't growing and learning from the projects and activities they are involved in, they're likely to leave and find better opportunities.

Organize Work to Build Competence and Ownership

A leader's job is to enrich the responsibilities of the group members so that they experience variety in their task assignments and opportunities to make meaningful decisions about how things get done. You need to make sure that everyone feels well represented on the committees, teams, and problem-solving groups dealing with the important matters in your organization. Involve them in programs, meetings, and decisions that have a direct impact on what they are being asked to do.

Dan Samuels learned this lesson from his experience in building his group's homecoming float. Traditionally, the job assignments had been organized by broad task: construction, painting, decorating, and so forth. Students would sign up for one general type of task and that was it. Dan's approach was to divide the float project work into subparts; the committee used the float model they had built to have students match themselves to the tasks associated with separate parts of the model. This approach created many different opportunities for students to paint, for example, or to decorate, or to do construction. And they could sign up for multiple tasks, so if they had painted in the past, they might choose to do that again, but if they also wanted to try something new and learn a new skill or work with someone else, they could sign up to do something different on another part of the model. "In the past people were encouraged to sign up for something they felt they knew how to do, or had done before, like painting," Dan explained. "The result was that often people just got sick of painting, they felt pigeonholed." He thought, why not let people try a new skill? If they are good at painting they could do that, but maybe they want to learn how to do some of the construction. "If we helped people get some new experience and skill," Dan told us, "that would put us in a better position for getting the work done, and also make it easier in future years too."

This approach increased everyone's ownership in the project. It meant that the subgroups had to coordinate their efforts in order for the project to be successful. Everyone needed to take ownership of the section of the float they signed up for so that the whole project would come together in the end and look like a coherent construction. By organizing the project in this way, the students would be dependent on each other to get the final project done. This approach also demanded that the quality of each section be consistent so the groups had to coordinate to meet one another's standards. All together, the students' work on the float was done in a way that built their confidence, and encouraged ownership; more people were fully engaged in the project than ever before. And there was another payoff: the float took first place in the judging competition.

Leaders like Dan know how important it is to turn tasks, assignments, and projects into opportunities to increase people's knowledge and skills and build ownership. In order to make people feel like owners, they need to be able to understand what is going on to the extent that any "owner" would expect. You need to ensure that the people you are working with know the answers to such questions as: Who are the folks we serve or exist for? How do they perceive us? How do we know if we're doing what we should be doing for them? How have we done recently? What can we do that is new and better in the next six months? Your team needs to be able to answer these questions in order to effectively work together.

Encourage Self-Confidence

The reason people don't always do what they know needs to be done, even if they know how to do it, is because they lack confidence. Without sufficient self-confidence, people lack the commitment required for taking on tough challenges. The lack of self-confidence shows up in feelings of helplessness, powerlessness, and self-doubt, as when you hear people say, "This can't be done" or "This is too hard to do." Generating self-confidence means building people's inner strength to push ahead into unknown territories, to make tough choices, and to persevere. They have to believe in their own skills and decision-making abilities, as well as yours.[5]

Encouraging self-confidence is what Francis Appeadu-Mensah did when he provided people the opportunity to participate in various parts of the Drama Club's activities, and what Dan Samuels did in letting people work on any part of the homecoming float they wanted to. This is exactly what Mykell Bates was doing when he started spreading around the soccer team tasks and responsibilities that traditionally had belonged to the team captain. "When Mykell asked me to do something, it instilled confidence in my abilities," teammate Brandon Zimmerman told us.

> When he would ask me to take on some of his day-to-day responsibilities, it gave me the confidence and competence to perform those tasks. All Mykell did was give me the

authority to use the skills that he believed I already had, but maybe I wasn't acknowledging in myself. The more he did this the more it worked to the advantage of the group as a whole, because each of us became stronger.

Having confidence and believing in your ability to handle the job, no matter how difficult, is essential in promoting and sustaining consistent efforts. By communicating to your group that you believe that they can be successful, you help people to push themselves beyond their own self-limiting boundaries.[6]

Mentor and Coach

Although it's true that exemplary leaders communicate their confidence in others, you can't just tell people they can do something if they really can't. There's a direct connection between self-confidence and competence. You need to mentor people because no one ever got to be the best at anything without the benefit of constructive feedback, probing questions, and thoughtful coaching. In strengthening others you not only have to have high expectations for them, but you also have to gently guide them by expressing your confidence in their ability to make good choices, backing them up when they make mistakes, and supporting their decisions. Often this is incremental, in the fashion of small wins, so that people don't feel overwhelmed and stressed out by the gap between their abilities and skills and their initial performance.

Anthony Gochenour worked throughout his college career as one of the building managers of the student union at his midwestern college, eventually becoming the senior building manager and leader of the student employment team. His greatest challenge, he told us, was getting the three different teams of student employees to appreciate how important their work was, and to be motivated to develop their ability to do their jobs better.

Anthony saw their day-to-day attitudes and their lack of commitment to the job as a major problem because the student union was probably the most used building on campus. He began to think about the routine work the staff had to do and looked at these tasks from the perspective of how important they were in serving students who used the building. From there, he began to guide different members of the teams in focusing on particular tasks so that the many things they had to do wouldn't seem so overwhelming. After breaking the whole job down and connecting the student workers to responsibilities that appealed to them more, Anthony coached them one by one, working alongside them to give pointers and feedback on how they were doing. Over time, team members were able to see how progress in their smaller assignments contributed to the bigger picture, and they could see the impact each of them actually had on what happened in the building. With Anthony's support the student teams came to appreciate that their jobs were not just to keep the building running but that their work shaped the experience of everyone who used the building.

Leaders like Anthony never take control away from others. They leave it to their group members to make choices and to take responsibility for them. When leaders enhance self-determination, and otherwise share power, they're demonstrating profound trust in and respect for others' abilities. And, in turn, making people feel strong, capable, and valued is at the heart of trust, which is why people are willing to take the risks that can drive extraordinary results. When leaders help others to grow and develop, that help is reciprocated. People who feel capable of influencing their leaders are more strongly attached to those leaders and more committed to effectively carrying out their responsibilities.[7]

Strengthening others involves paying attention and believing that people are smart enough to figure it out for themselves, if given the opportunity and provided support and coaching. Coaching stretches people to grow and develop their capabilities, and frames the situation so that people can both hone and enhance their skills in challenging assignments.

Good coaching as a leader involves asking good questions. The benefits of asking questions are numerous. For one, you give the other person or group the chance to think and the time to develop responses and see issues from their own perspective. Second, asking questions connotes your underlying trust in people's abilities by shifting accountability, and it has the benefit of almost immediate buy-in for the solution. After all, it is their idea. Asking good questions also positions you into a coaching role, more of a guiding than telling role which frees you up to think more freely and strategically.

The success of every group or undertaking is a shared responsibility. As we said in Chapter 8, you can't do it alone. You need a competent and confident team, and the team needs a competent and confident leader. Mentoring and coaching is an essential part of exemplary leadership. And while you're at it, think about getting someone to mentor or coach you. There's no better way to model the behavior you expect from others than by doing it yourself.

TAKE ACTION: STRENGTHEN OTHERS

Strengthening others is essentially the process of turning everyone into leaders—making people capable of acting on their own initiative. Leaders need to bring others along *as* leaders. Leaders strengthen others when they make it possible for them to exercise choice, when they design options and alternatives to the ways that things get done, and when they encourage accountability and responsibility that leads to action.

Leaders develop in others the competence, as well as the confidence, to act and to succeed. They make certain that people have the information they need to understand how the group operates and what is going on. They help build people's skills, and they coach people on how to put what they know into practice, stretching and supporting them to do more than they might have imagined possible. Exemplary leaders use questions to help people think on their own and coach them on how to be at their best.

Enabling Others to Act requires *strengthening others by increasing their self-determination and developing competence*. This means you need to:

- Let people make choices about how they do their work.
- Structure tasks so that people have opportunities to use their judgment. Provide the necessary resources whenever possible to help get the job done. Be responsive and creative when people identify additional resource requirements.
- Find a balance between people's skills and the work you are asking them to do that stretches but doesn't break them.
- Keep learning yourself and share what you learn with your team.
- Promote an "ownership" perspective by making sure that people understand the big picture about how the group operates.
- Take stock of where people are in their work and make sure they understand how the smaller parts and progress (successes) play into accomplishing the bigger picture, goal, or dream.
- Demonstrate in visible and concrete ways that you believe in the abilities of the people in your group.
- Set aside the time necessary to coach, which begins by learning enough about the skills, interests, and aspirations of the people you are working with to determine how you can enable them to make the most of their talents.
- Ask more questions; give fewer answers.
- Help people to think for themselves, and to think like leaders, to take a big-picture perspective.
- Share your organizational power, such as decision-making authority, with others through delegation; share your personal power by delegating, which demonstrates the trust and faith you have in others to be successful.

NOTES

1. See, for example, L. Wiseman, *Multipliers: How the Best Leaders Make Everyone Smarter* (New York: Harper Collins, 2010), 20.
2. A. Bandura, *Self-Efficacy: The Exercise of Control* (New York: Freeman, 1997); K. A. Karl, A. M. Leary-Kelly, and J. J. Martocchio, "The Impact of Feedback and Self-Efficacy on Performance in Training," *Journal of Organizational Behavior* 14, no. 4 (1993): 379–394; C. M. Shea and J. M. Howell, "Charismatic Leadership and Task Feedback: A Laboratory Study of Their Effects on Self-Efficacy and Task Performance," *Leadership Quarterly* 10, no. 3 (1999): 375–396; and A. Bandura, "Social Cognitive Theory: An Agentic Perspective," *Annual Review of Psychology* 52 (2001): 1–26.
3. A. Wrzeniewski and J. Dutton. "Crafting a Job: Revising Employees as Active Crafters of Their Work," *Academy of Management Review* 26, no. 2 (2001): 179–201; and, M. S. Christian, A. S. Garza, and J. E. Slaugher, "Work Engagement: A Quantitative Review and Test of Its Relations with Task and Conceptual Performance," *Personnel Psychology* 64 (2011): 89–136.
4. Evolutionary psychology demonstrates that in ecosystems, collaboration is what assists species to survive rather than become extinct; the group ends up eradicating bad or inefficient behavior. See R. Wright, *The Moral Animal: Why We Are the Way We Are: The New Science of Evolutionary Psychology* (New York: Vintage, 1995). For another interesting look at the origins of social cooperation, see A. Fields, *Altruistically Inclined?: The Behavioral Sciences, Evolutionary Theory, and the Origins of Reciprocity* (Ann Arbor: University of Michigan Press, 2004).
5. Psychologists often refer to this as self-efficacy. See, for example, Bandura, *Self-Efficacy;* and R. M. Steers, L.W. Porter, and G. A. Bigley, *Motivation and Leadership at Work*, 6th ed. (New York: McGraw-Hill, 1996).
6. Wiseman, *Multipliers*; C. Dweck, *Mindset: The New Psychology of Success* (New York: Ballantine Books, 2007); and, J. Hagel and J. S. Brown, "Do You Have a Growth Mindset?" Harvard Business School Blog (November 23, 2010), http://blogs.hbr.org/bigshift/2010/11/do-you-have-a-growth-mindset.html
7. P. Sweeny, V. Thomson, and H. Blanton, "Trust and Influence in Combat: An Interdependence Model," *Journal of Applied Social Psychology* 39, no. 1 (2009): 235–264.

PRACTICE 5

Encourage the Heart

Making extraordinary things happen is hard work. The climb to the summit is arduous and steep, and leaders need to encourage others to continue the quest. They inspire others with courage, hope, and optimism.

Leaders give heart by visibly recognizing people's contributions to the common vision. With a thank-you note, a smile, and public praise, the leader lets others know how much they mean to the organization.

Leaders express pride in the accomplishments of their teams. They make a point of telling the rest of the organization about what the teams have achieved. They make people feel like heroes.

Hard work can also be fun work. Hoopla is important to a winning team. Everybody loves a parade. Leaders find ways to celebrate accomplishments. They take time out to rejoice in reaching a milestone.

And what sustains the leader? From what source comes the leader's courage? The answer is love. Leaders are in love—in love with the people who do the work, with what their organizations produce, and with the people those organizations serve.

In the next two chapters, we see how leaders:

- **Recognize Contributions by showing appreciation for individual excellence.**
- **Celebrate the Values and Victories by creating a spirit of community.**

10

Commitment #9: Recognize Contributions

Wyatt DeJong was raised on a cattle ranch and has always wanted to stay connected to that heritage in some way. During his first agriculture education class in high school, he had a teacher who focused on the importance of discovering one's potential through doing and encouraged his students to delete the word "can't" from their vocabulary. Wyatt took that advice to heart and became more deeply involved with FFA (Future Farmers of America), an organization that helps young people develop career, leadership, and life skills.

During his senior year in high school, Wyatt attended the FFA national conference, where he encountered another teacher who helped him grow. That teacher's message was that life was too short to be concerned only with making impressions; it should be spent having impact. This idea affected Wyatt deeply, causing him to stop and reflect. "I realized that I had spent most of my life coasting," he told us, "trying to impress people with what I thought they wanted, getting good grades, joining the right clubs. But I was ready to do more; I was ready to have impact."

Wyatt ran for a state office in FFA and became part of a dynamic team of young people with similar hopes and dreams. During one of the state leadership team's meetings the group was talking about the things they could do around the state to make their work helping students be more visible. They were spending a lot of time talking about the challenges they faced, the resources they needed, what they lacked. "At some point," Wyatt said, "we all stopped and said, 'You know, every moment we spend focused on ourselves is a moment we're not focused on others and how we can help them learn and grow.'" This simple truth was so striking to all of them that the team made a pledge to one another that they would choose to focus on others in every interaction, every moment, and every opportunity they saw.

That pledge increased Wyatt's awareness of ways to make his life one of having impact by directing his attention away from himself and toward others. He found himself more aware of the emotions people were exhibiting, more aware of what they needed to feel supported and strong, and more aware of what they were afraid of. By way of example, he told us about the time he was speaking at a local FFA chapter and noticed a young man in the group who was a natural influencer. When people spoke, others would glance over at him to see if he was paying attention. He said very little but he clearly had a lot of influence. Following the FFA pledge to focus on others, Wyatt always engaged in conversations after his speeches to get to know the individuals in the audience. In conversation with this particular young man, Wyatt learned that he had been a sure bet for a college football scholarship and had been counting on football as his path to success. During an FFA field trip he had fallen and lost consciousness, and follow-up tests revealed that he had several blood clots that would be life threatening in any kind of contact sport. His hopes of a college football career were over.

When he got back from his speaking tour, Wyatt wrote to this young man to say that the FFA state officers were all there for him and to remind him that he was part of an organization that valued each and every member for who they were as a person, not just for their success.

Wyatt also shared his perceptions about the young man's immense ability to influence others and urged him to see it as a gift and an opportunity to explore another side of himself. The young man wrote back to tell Wyatt that his letter had arrived at a particularly low point and had brought him to tears. Hearing that he had so much more to give and that people were there to encourage him gave him hope and focus for the future. "This experience showed me that I can have impact by keeping my focus on others," Wyatt said, "It showed me the importance of keeping my eyes open for the unique gifts, lessons, and contributions of each person we meet and acknowledging those whenever I can. Life is too short and too hard not to let people know they matter."

All exemplary leaders make the commitment, as Wyatt did, to Recognize Contributions. They do it because people need encouragement to function at their best and to persist when the work is hard and times are challenging. Getting to the finish line demands energy and commitment. People need emotional fuel to replenish their spirits. They need the will to continue and the courage to do something they have never done before. No one is likely to persist for very long when they feel ignored or taken for granted. It's your job to make sure that people feel that what they do matters and know that they make a difference. Leaders need to recognize others' contributions to success by showing appreciation for their individual excellence.

In order to Recognize Contributions you need to utilize these two essentials:

- **Expect the best**
- **Personalize recognition**

By putting these essentials into practice you uplift people's spirits, helping them reach for higher levels of performance and aspire to be true to the visions and values of the group. You make it possible for people to find the courage to do things that they have never done before.

EXPECT THE BEST

Belief in others' abilities is essential to making extraordinary things happen. The high performance that exemplary leaders elicit is fundamentally because they strongly believe in the abilities of the people who make up the group. They believe in the capacity of others to bring visions to life. Your beliefs about people are broadcast in ways you may not even be aware of. You give off cues that say to people either "I know you can do it" or "There's no way you'll ever be able to do that." The highest levels of performance won't be realized unless you let people know, by what you say and what you do, that you are confident in their abilities.

Social psychologists have referred to this as the "Pygmalion effect," from the Greek myth about Pygmalion, a sculptor who carved a statue of a beautiful woman, fell in love with the statue, and appealed to the goddess Aphrodite to bring her to life. His prayers were granted. Leaders play Pygmalion-like roles in developing others. Ask people to describe the best leaders they've ever had and they consistently talk about individuals who brought out the best in them. They say things like, "She believed in me more than I believed in myself" or "He saw something in me even I didn't see."

Exemplary leaders, figuratively speaking, bring others to life. These leaders dramatically improve others' performance because they care deeply for them and have strong faith in their capacities. People respond positively to these expectations. Research on the phenomenon of self-fulfilling prophecies provides ample evidence that people act in ways that are consistent with others' expectations of them.[1] When you expect people to fail, they probably will. If you expect them to succeed, they probably will. Think about this from a personal perspective. Can you recall a time when you were feeling overwhelmed by something you were being asked to do? Perhaps it was a crucial game your team had to win against a team that hadn't lost all season. Maybe it was being asked to take over a project you knew very little about but would be held accountable for. Chances are good that if you were successful, there was someone who reinforced your own sense of self, someone who said without a doubt, "I believe you can do this." Words like those send a powerful message to people's brains, one that helps them step up to match the image others hold of them.

The best leaders bring out the best in others. If the potential exists within someone, exemplary leaders always find a way to release it. There's solid evidence that leaders who create an affirmative orientation in organizations, foster high standards and ideals, and focus on achieving outcomes beyond the norm, are significantly more successful.[2] There's increasing proof that it pays to be positive.

Show Them You Believe

Tiffany Lee was doing an internship in the vice-mayor's office of a major city in California. As the youngest and most inexperienced person in the office, she was given much of the grunt work, including taking messages for return phone calls, filing, and writing thank-you letters and responses to the routine correspondence sent into the office. She felt out of place in the office where staff members had close relationships based on a history of working together. "I was not seen as a vital part of the staff," she said, "but just an intern who did their leftover work."

At the end of each week, she was required to sit in on staff meetings during which each staff member would share an item that they were currently working on. Each week, as her coworkers stated important issues that they were a part of, such as helping to author legislative bills or working with the health board, Tiffany's response was always the same: "Correspondence." "I would feel almost embarrassed as I hurriedly stated my 'contribution,'" she told us, "and in comparison to my coworkers' responses, I felt insignificant and not a very important part of the team."

A short time later, at one of the meetings, the chief of staff praised the staff members for their contribution to another successful week and then told everyone that due to the way correspondence was being handled, the vice-mayor's office was now receiving thank-you letters because residents felt as if their concerns and welfare were not being ignored, and that the office genuinely cared about them. Knowing that Tiffany was the person responsible for handling this correspondence, her coworkers turned to her and told her what a wonderful job she was doing. The chief of staff went on to say that each member in the office had something valuable to bring to the group, and that their joint efforts were the reason why the office was so highly respected and valued. In telling us about this experience, Tiffany explained how the chief of staff, and her coworkers, demonstrated that they believed in her and made her feel that she was not the most insignificant person on the team, and this, she said, "is something I will take with me forward into every situation."

And that is exactly what she has done, because Tiffany now supervises other interns and makes it a point to expect the best from them, to give them opportunities to make a difference, and watches carefully for the contributions they make to the team, no matter how small or seemingly insignificant. "I make it a rule to help people see how even the small tasks contribute to our collective success," Tiffany says. "People need to know they matter."

As social scientists have documented, leaders' positive expectations aren't trivial feel-good beliefs.[3] They're not just about keeping a positive outlook or getting others psyched up. The expectations that leaders hold provide the framework into which people fit their own realities. They shape how people behave on the task and toward others. Maybe you can't turn a marble statue into a real person, but you can draw out the highest potential of the members of your group. Tiffany's experience, like that of Wyatt's, are clear examples of how showing someone you believe in them, even when they are down, helps them acknowledge that they still have their best to give. Positive expectations of high performance and motivation in others, along with recognizing them for their contributions, easily beats the alternative of the "just do what I tell you" approach. People need to feel they belong, are accepted and valued, and have the skills and inner resources needed to be successful.

If you want people to have a winning attitude, you have to do two things. First, you have to *believe* they are already winners, not someday in the future, but winners right now! If you believe that people are winners, you will treat them that way. Second, if you want people to be winners, you have to behave in ways that communicate to them that they are winners. And it's not just about your words. It's also about tone of voice, posture, gestures, and facial expressions. No yelling, frowning, making fun of people, or putting them down in front of others. Instead, it's about being friendly, positive, supportive, and encouraging. Shaming people to increase their performance simply does not work.[4] Offer positive reinforcement, share lots of information, listen deeply to people's input, provide them with what they need to do their work, give them increasingly challenging assignments, and lend them your support and assistance. The data shows that student leaders who make it a point to let people know about their confidence in their abilities have constituents who report being highly engaged with their organizations, as compared with those whose leaders who are mum on this issue.

It's a very positive cycle: you believe in your group members' abilities, your favorable expectations cause you to be more positive in your actions, and those encouraging behaviors produce better results, reinforcing your belief that people can do it. And what's really powerful about this cycle is that as people see that they are capable of extraordinary things they develop that expectation of themselves. Another positive cycle begins.

Be Clear About the Goals and the Rules

Positive expectations are necessary to generate high performance, but that level of performance isn't sustainable unless people are clear about ground rules and outcomes. When you were a kid you might have read Lewis Carroll's *Alice's Adventures in Wonderland.* Remember the croquet match? The flamingos were the mallets, the playing card soldiers were the wickets, and the hedgehogs were the balls. Everyone kept moving and the rules kept changing all the time. There was no way of knowing how to play the game or what it took to win. You don't have to fall down the rabbit hole to know how Alice felt.

If you want people to give their all, to put their hearts and minds into their work, you have to make certain that they know what they are supposed to be doing and how they are supposed to do it. You need to clarify what the expected outcomes look like and make sure that there is a consistent understanding about how the game is played. Have you ever been involved in a class assignment where the objective wasn't clear? If you have ever found yourself asking "Why are we doing this?" you have experienced the frustration, apathy, fear, and resentment that can surface when you are asked to do something but don't know the reasons why. Doesn't it make sense then as a leader that this is one of the most important things you can provide for people if you want them fully engaged and giving their all?

Liz Eilen was working in the tutoring center at her college when the center's director suggested to her that some kind of encouragement might influence the students' commitment to their study groups, and as a result their academic improvement. Liz decided to come up with ways to recognize active and involved students for their work at the center. She began by challenging the students to involve themselves more fully in the study-group process, setting high expectations for what each of the groups needed to do. What she discovered was that setting the expectations for the groups was just what the individual members needed to feel motivated and enthusiastic about participating and improving their academic standing. "It was as though the high expectations had a way of creating a self-fulfilling prophecy," Liz said. She also noticed students pushing themselves harder to ensure they wouldn't let their group down. "Students started accomplishing so much, showing improvement in new and different areas," Liz told us. "They surprised everyone, including themselves."

As Liz learned, expectations play an important role in developing people and drawing out their highest potential and their desire to achieve the extraordinary. And, as Liz also discovered, expectations can concern goals, including a certain level of group participation, and values, such as the importance of academic achievement.

Goals and values both provide people with a set of standards that concentrates their efforts. Goals imply something shorter term and values (or principles) connote something more enduring. Values serve as the basis for goals. They're your standards of excellence, your highest aspirations, and they define the arena in which goals and metrics must be set. Values mediate the path of action. Goals release the energy.

But what do goals have to do with recognition? They give it context. People should be recognized for achieving something—like coming in first, breaking a record, exceeding the standards, doing something no one else has ever done before. Leaders should absolutely make sure they affirm the effort and worth of every member of the group, as Wyatt DeJong did with the FFA member whose football career and dreams of college had been derailed. But for recognition to reward behaviors that are important to the group's success, you have to have an end in mind. Goals help people keep their eyes on the vision. Goals and intentions keep them on track. They help people put the phone on silent mode—to shut out the noise and schedule their time. Goal setting affirms the person, and, whether you realize it or not, contributes to what people think about themselves.

Give Regular Feedback

People need to know if they're making progress toward the goal or simply marking time. Having goals helps to serve that function, but that's not enough. People's motivation to increase their productivity on a task increases only when they have a challenging goal *and* receive feedback on their progress.[5] Goals without feedback, or feedback without goals, have little effect on people's willingness or motivation to put extra effort into the task.

With clear goals and detailed feedback, people can become self-correcting and can more easily understand their place in the big picture. With regular feedback they can also determine what help they need from others and who might be able to benefit from their assistance. Anyone who has been a part of a fundraising event that has a set goal knows the power of seeing progress toward that target.

Take it from one group of student athletes we talked to that did a "Miles for Kids" event over several months. They got people to sponsor their virtual "trip across the nation" and demonstrated how their journey was going by collecting dollars per miles logged and mapping their progress on a giant map. There was a little friendly competition too, with a bonus incentive for the first person to reach the west coast. They told us that completing the trip, coast to coast, got to be a real focus of pride for them, and everyone's commitment to a daily run or walk went way up.

The Miles for Kids group understood that feedback is at the center of any learning process. For example, consider what happens to your self-confidence without feedback. Think how you might feel in a class when you don't receive timely feedback on assignments or receive a grade on a paper but no explanation for why or what is needed to be more successful in subsequent efforts. We think you'd agree it can be frustrating and demotivating

Saying nothing about a person's performance doesn't help anyone—not the performer, not the leader, and not the group. People want useful feedback. They really do prefer to know how they are doing, and no news generally has the same negative impact as bad news. In fact, people actually would prefer to hear bad news rather than no news at all.

Without feedback there is no learning. Getting feedback about how you are doing is the only way you know whether or not you're getting close to your goal and whether or not you're executing properly. But because it is not always what you expect to hear, feedback can be painful, even embarrassing. Although most people realize intellectually that feedback is a necessary component of self-reflection and growth, they are often reluctant to make themselves open to it. They want to look good more than they want to get good! Researchers consistently point out that the development of expertise or mastery requires receiving constructive, even critical, feedback.[6] Following are some tips you might find useful about getting feedback you can appreciate and use.

Tips on Getting Useful Feedback

1. *Don't be defensive.* People will be reluctant to share feedback if they are afraid of hurting your feelings or having to justify their perceptions.
2. *Listen carefully.* Relax and actively listen to understand what the other person is trying to tell you; be sensitive to how your nonverbal communications is affecting the other person's willingness to share with you.
3. *Suspend judgment.* Listen, don't judge. Don't worry about what you're going to say but rather work to understand what the other person is trying to tell you. Be welcoming and assume that the information is intended to help you be better rather than anything otherwise.
4. *Ask questions and ask for examples.* Make sure you understand what is being said and learn about the context as well as the content.
5. *Say "thank you."* You can't get any better without knowing more about yourself and how your actions affect others, so be sure to let the other person know that you appreciate what he or she has to share.

Feedback should create dialogue. As a leader your goal is to encourage the best in others, to find out what they need to feel more confident and competent to meet the challenges they faces as a member of the group. Giving feedback in a way that encourages dialogue will create a learning opportunity for you both. Following are some tips on giving feedback in ways that make sense.

Tips on Giving Useful Feedback

1. *Don't put people on the defensive.* Present the feedback as a possibility, not a fact. Ask if the idea you put forth rings true for them. Make it a dialogue rather than a monologue.
2. *Listen carefully.* Relax and think about the best way to help the other person hear what you have to say; be sensitive to their nonverbal reactions to what you are saying and be willing to stop and check that they are listening and understanding; make fewer, deeper observations.
3. *Hold your judgment.* There are multiple sides to every story. Explain where your feedback came from and recognize that this may not be the only information that is important. Be willing to hear the other side of things. Stay focused on people's behaviors and not their personalities.
4. *Provide concrete examples and ask for validation of those examples.* Make sure you give specific examples that provide the basis of your feedback, and be open to hearing additional examples and perspectives. Check to ensure that you are being understood.
5. *Say "thank you."* Let the other person know that you appreciate their willingness to receive feedback and what it says about their commitment to personal development and the success of the group. Indicate how you are willing to follow up and help with any changes that make sense.

When leaders provide a clear sense of direction and feedback along the way, they encourage people to reach inside and do their best. Information about goals and about progress toward those goals strongly influences people's abilities to learn and to achieve. Because encouragement is more personal and positive than other forms of feedback, it's more likely to accomplish something that other forms cannot: strengthening trust between a leader and members of the group. Encouragement, in this sense, is the highest form of feedback.[7]

PERSONALIZE RECOGNITION

One of the more common complaints about recognition is that far too often it's highly predictable, routine, and impersonal. A one-size-fits-all approach to recognition feels insincere, forced, and thoughtless. Over time it can even increase cynicism and actually damage credibility.

Recall how Wyatt DeJong took the time to write a note to the young man he had met on an FFA speaking tour. Wyatt spoke to him about the influential quality he had witnessed in him and the potential he saw from that. That sent the message that Wyatt was paying attention. Coming from a State FFA Rep, the message also spoke about the values of the organization to recognize, honor, and support its individual members. Wyatt was able to have an impact on this young man because he had been paying attention. He was able to personalize his encouragement in a way that touched the young man deeply.

When recognition is not personalized, it will quickly be forgotten and discounted. Think of how different the impact of Wyatt's letter would have been had Wyatt not known anything about the young man. It most likely would have come across as a form letter issued by the FAA state office: "We're behind you, get well, good luck, blah blah blah." Recognition needs to come from and be expressed from your heart.

When we've asked people to tell us about the *most meaningful recognition* they've received, they consistently said that it's "personal." They say that it feels special. That's why it's so important for leaders to pay attention to the likes and dislikes of each and every individual in your group. You get a lot more emotional bang for your buck when you make recognition and rewards personal. Step into the shoes of other people and ask yourself, "What do I wish someone would do to celebrate and recognize my contribution?" Let your answer to this question guide your own thinking about how to acknowledge the contributions of others, while also being sensitive to the fact that not everyone is just like you. This means that you have to get close enough to others to know about what would make recognition meaningful to them.

Get Close to People

Think back to Liz Eilen's experience in her school's tutoring center, where she learned that students were more productive when they had a clear understanding of the goals of the program and what was expected of them. That experience also taught her that students were much more motivated and encouraged when they felt someone expected great things from them and was watching to see how they were doing. Liz said she couldn't have helped foster those feelings without making a point of getting to know as many students in the groups as possible: "The time spent connecting with each student, sharing our expectations, helped us motivate each student to succeed, not just for themselves but for the group as well." That time proved to be well spent when Liz wrote a weekly note of appreciation to students who had met or surpassed expectations, occasionally even finding a special little gift that acknowledged their individual progress or their contribution to the group. By getting close to her fellow students, Liz gained insight into the challenges they faced and the efforts they were putting forth, enabling her to recognize their accomplishments in a genuine and significant way.

To make recognition personally meaningful, as Liz did, you first have to get to know people. If you're going to personalize recognition and make it feel genuinely special, you'll have to look past the organizational diagrams and roles people play and see the person inside. You need to get to know who they are, how they feel, and what they think. As a leader this means you need to find a way to get close to people.

Proximity is the single best predictor of whether two people will talk to one another, which means you have to get close to people if you're going to find out what motivates them, what they like and don't like, and the kinds of recognition that they most appreciate. The payoffs are significant. For example, over a five-year period, researchers observed groups of friends and groups of acquaintances (people who knew each other only vaguely) performing motor-skill and decision-making tasks. The results were clear. The groups composed of friends completed, on average, more than three times as many projects as the groups composed merely of acquaintances. In terms of decision-making assignments, groups of friends were over 20 percent more effective than groups of acquaintances.[8]

Another payoff from connecting with team members on a meaningful level is that this will be "reciprocated with loyalty." In other words, paying attention, personalizing recognition, creatively and actively appreciating others increases their trust in you. If others know that you genuinely care about them, they're more likely to care about you. This is one important way to pull people together.

People are just more willing to follow someone they have a relationship with. And relationships are built on trust. An open door is a physical demonstration of a willingness to let others in. So is an open heart. To become fully trusted you must be open to and with others. This means disclosing things about yourself in order to build the basis for a relationship. This means telling others the same things you'd like to know about them—talking about your hopes and dreams, your family and friends, your interests and your pursuits. Certainly, disclosing information about yourself can be risky. You can't be certain that other people will like you, appreciate your candor, agree with your aspirations, buy into your plans, or interpret your words and actions in the way you intend. But by demonstrating the willingness to take such risks, leaders encourage others to take a similar risk—and thereby take the first steps necessary to build *mutual* trust as the foundation for any relationship. When you do, you may also be Modeling the Way or Inspiring a Shared Vision. There are many potential benefits from taking the time to get to know the members of your group.

Be Creative About Incentives

Can you think of something you have been given as an acknowledgment for something you did that makes you smile or feel proud every time you look at it? It may be a picture of your team celebrating after a meaningful victory, a tiny present that was a symbol of what you did or what you love, or a simple handwritten note. Whatever it is, somehow it is attached to a feeling of self-worth and being a part of something. As a leader, you can provide that same meaningful connection with the rewards you give. It is not the size or expense of the token; it's the meaning you associate with it. All it takes is a little thought. If you've done your homework and you know the members of your group, it doesn't take long at all. Let yourself be creative.

Spontaneous, unexpected rewards are often more meaningful than expected, formal ones. Rewards are the most effective when they're highly specific and given in close proximity to when the appropriate behavior happened. One of the most important results of spending time with people on your team and being out and about as a leader is that you can personally observe people doing things right and then reward them either on the spot or at your next public gathering.

People respond to all kinds of recognition and rewards.[9] That's the beauty of being creative and personalizing it. You have lots and lots of options. We've seen people give out stuffed giraffes, rainbow-striped zebra posters, T-shirts, mugs with team photos, crystal apples, rides in a classic car, clocks, pens, plaques, and hundreds of other creative expressions of appreciation. We've seen it done verbally and nonverbally, elaborately and simply. There are no limits to kindness and consideration, as Kara Koser knows. Kara talked to us about how she used what she called "small token surprises" when she was an east coast urban university residence hall adviser. Those "tokens" were all the little things she would do to recognize the students who lived on her floor. "I tried to surprise people with little things, maybe a small handmade gift," she explained. "It doesn't have to be a big expensive deal, it's a simple gesture. I liked to do it when it was least expected. That's what makes it fun."

It's important to understand that genuine recognition does not have to include anything tangible. Exemplary leaders make tremendous use of intrinsic rewards—rewards that are built into the work itself, including such factors as a sense of accomplishment, a chance to be creative, and the challenge of the work—all directly tied to an individual's effort.

Often it's the simple, personal gestures, like Kara's small surprises, that are the most powerful rewards. It's all about being considerate. The techniques that you use are less important than your genuine expression of caring. People appreciate knowing that you care about them and they are more caring about what they are doing as a result. When you genuinely care, even the smallest of gestures reap huge rewards.

Just Say "Thank You"

There are few more basic needs than to be noticed, recognized, and appreciated for one's efforts. It's true for everyone—students, teachers, volunteers, and staff. Extraordinary achievements happen more easily in climates in which performance is nurtured with a higher volume of positive and appreciative comments. Studies show that work teams in which the ratio of positive to negative interactions is greater than three to one are *significantly* more productive than those teams that haven't achieved this ratio.[10]

It is always worth the few extra moments to recognize someone's hard work and contributions. All too often people forget to extend a hand, a smile, or a simple "thank you." People naturally feel a little frustrated and unappreciated when someone takes them for granted. Sometimes this can be overlooked because people are stressed to get something done on time, or have to meet so many competing demands and those overtake expressing gratitude. But it's really important that you stick around for that extra minute to say thanks and include *why* you are grateful. Letting people know why you appreciate them and their efforts reinforces the vision and the values of the group, strengthening everyone.

And, by the way, don't think you have to be the leader in order to provide recognition. We recall talking with Andy Ramans, a student at a small private west coast university, who wondered whether you had to be "the person in charge" in order to really Encourage the Heart. He questioned whether his efforts at saying "good job" or "thank you" would be wasted. Would his classmates value these words from a fellow student? We asked him to think about how he felt when his colleagues thanked or praised him. He smiled, and in so doing came to the self-realization of the power of recognizing and appreciating others: "It made a big difference," he said.

When you take the time to set the bar high, and make it known that you believe people can excel, you will notice extraordinary results. And you will create strong team collaboration and unity. As a leader, it's about creating a winning team through trust, and through a personal connection. This includes extending a simple pat on the back, a handshake, a smile, and saying "Thank you for your hard work. You are helping us achieve our dream."

Making a point of regularly saying "thank you" goes a long way in sustaining high performance. Personalized recognition comes down to being thoughtful. It means knowing enough about another person to answer the question "What could I do to make this a memorable experience so that this person will always remember how important his or her contributions are?"

TAKE ACTION: RECOGNIZE CONTRIBUTIONS

Exemplary leaders have positive expectations of themselves and their group. They expect the best of people and create self-fulfilling prophecies about how ordinary people can produce extraordinary actions and results. Exemplary leaders have clear goals and standards, helping people fully understand what needs to be done. They provide clear feedback and reinforcement. By maintaining a positive outlook and providing motivating feedback you stimulate, rekindle, and focus people's energies and drive.

Exemplary leaders recognize and reward what individuals do to contribute to vision and values. They don't limit their expressions of appreciation to the group, club, team, or school's *formal* events, but look to be both timely and creative in saying thank you. Personalizing recognition requires knowing what's appropriate individually and culturally. Though it may be uncomfortable or embarrassing at first, recognizing someone's efforts is really not all that difficult to do. And it's well worth the effort to make a connection with each person. Learn from many small and often casual acts of appreciation about what works for each person in your group and how best to personalize recognition.

Encouraging the Heart requires *recognizing contributions by showing appreciation for individual excellence*. This means you have to:

- Make sure people know what is expected of them.
- Maintain high expectations about what individuals and teams can accomplish.
- Communicate your positive expectations clearly and regularly.
- Let people know that you believe in them not just verbally, but also through your actions.
- Create an environment that makes it comfortable to receive and give feedback, including feedback given to you.
- Link recognition and rewards with what your group states it wants to achieve so that only those who meet or exceed these goals receive them.
- Find out the types of encouragement that make the most difference to others. Don't assume you know. Ask. Take the time to inquire and observe.
- Connect with people on a personal basis. Stop by and visit them where they are.
- Be creative when it comes to recognition. Be spontaneous. Have fun.
- Make saying "thank you" a natural part of your everyday behavior.
- Don't take anyone for granted.

NOTES

1. Hundreds of research studies have since been conducted to test this notion, and they all clearly demonstrate that people tend to act in ways that are consistent with the expectations they perceive. See, for example, D. Eden, *Pygmalion in Management: Productivity as a Self-Fulfilling Prophecy* (Lexington, MA: Lexington Books, 1990); D. Eden, "Leadership and Expectations: Pygmalion Effects and Other Self-Fulfilling Prophecies in Organizations," *Leadership Quarterly* 3, no. 4 (1992): 271–305; and A. Smith, L. Jussim, J. Eccles, M. Van Noy, S. Madon, and P. Palumbo, "Self-Fulfilling Prophecies, Perceptual Biases, and Accuracy at the Individual and Group Levels," *Journal of Experimental Social Psychology* 34, no. 6 (1998): 530–561.

2. K. S. Cameron, *Positive Leadership: Strategies for Extraordinary Performance* (San Francisco: Berrett-Koehler, 2008). Fostering virtuousness, according to Cameron, is about facilitating the best of the human condition. He argues that an inclination exists in all human systems toward goodness for its own intrinsic value.
3. See, for example: J. E. Dutton, R. E. Quinn, and K. S. Cameron, *Positive Organizational Scholarship: Foundations of a New Discipline* (San Francisco: Berrett-Koehler, 2003); K. S. Cameron, *Positive Leadership: Strategies for Extraordinary Performance* (San Francisco: Berrett-Koehler, 2008); D. Whitney and A. Trosten-Bloom, *The Power of Appreciative Inquiry: A Practical Guide to Positive Change*, 2nd ed. (San Francisco: Berrett-Koehler, 2010); and M. E. Seligman, *Flourish: A Visionary New Understanding of Happiness and Well-Being* (New York: Free Press, 2011).
4. See, for example, B. Brown, *I Thought It Was Just Me (But It Isn't): Making the Journey from "What Will People Think?" to "I Am Enough"* (New York: Gotham, 2007). See also Brown's TED Talk on shame http://www.ted.com/talks/brene_brown_listening_to_shame.html.
5. See, for example, J. E. Sawyer, W. R. Latham, R. D. Pritchard, and W. R. Bennett Jr., "Analysis of Work Group Productivity in an Applied Setting: Application of a Time Series Panel Design," *Personnel Psychology* 52 (1999): 927–967; and A. Gostick and C. Elton, *Managing with Carrots: Using Recognition to Attract and Retain the Best People* (Layton, UT: Gibbs Smith, 2001).
6. K. A. Ericsson, M. J. Prietula, and E. T. Cokely, "The Making of an Expert," *Harvard Business Review* 85, no. 7/8 (2007), 114–121, 193.
7. For more on this topic, see Truth Nine in J. M. Kouzes and B. Z. Posner, *The Truth About Leadership: The No-Fads, Heart-of-the-Matter Facts You Need to Know* (San Francisco: Jossey-Bass, 2010).
8. J. A. Ross, "Does Friendship Improve Job Performance?" *Harvard Business Review* 54, no. 2 (March-April 1977): 8–9. See also K. A. Jehn and P. P. Shah, "Interpersonal Relationships and Task Performance: An Examination of Mediating Processes in Friendship and Acquaintance Groups," *Journal of Personality and Social Psychology* 72, no. 4 (1997): 775–790. There is an important caveat, however. Friends have to be strongly committed to the group's goals. If not, then friends may not do better. This is precisely why we said earlier that it is absolutely necessary for leaders to be clear about standards and to create a condition of shared goals and values. When it comes to performance, commitment to standards and good relations between people go together.

9. Eric Harvey suggests lots and lots of creative ways to recognize people in his handbook *180 Ways to Walk the Recognition Talk* (Dallas: Walk the Talk, 2000). Also see B. Nelson, *1001 Ways to Reward Employees*, 2nd edition (New York: Workman, 2005); L. Yerkes, *Fun Works: Creative Places Where People Love to Work* (San Francisco: Berrett-Koehler, 2001); J. W. Umias, *The Power of Acknowledgment* (New York: International Institute for Learning, 2007); and B. Kaye and S. Jordan-Evans, *Love 'Em or Lose 'Em: Getting Good People to Stay*, 4th ed. (San Francisco: Berrett-Koehler, 2008).
10. B. Fredrickson, *Positivity: Top-Notch Research Reveals the 3-to-1 Ratio That Will Change Your Life* (New York: Random House, 2009).

11

Commitment #10: Celebrate the Values and the Victories

While in college Kevin Straughn and Kaitlyn Morelli spent a summer working as co-head coaches for a swim league team in their local community. With swimmers ranging in age from six to eighteen, and an eight-week season giving them a relatively short time together, they needed to build bonds and a sense of community within the team right from the beginning. They started the season with a get-together where they clarified the goals for the summer: improvement of each individual swimmer of the team and success for the whole team in the Summer Swim League Championship. "The team had won the championship in previous years," Kevin and Kaitlyn told us, "and we wanted to build off of that right from the start, giving swimmers something to set their sights on."

The team's name was the Hurricanes, and the coaches used the name as a metaphor to reinforce its values and the potential victories ahead. At their kick-off get-together, Kevin and Kaitlyn had all the swimmers paint the back wall of the clubhouse with slogans like "Hurricanes—we blow you away" and "Hurricanes—we make waves." All the swimmers signed their names to the wall that day, making a pledge to come to practice and work on their skills to help the team make it all the way to the championship. It was a way to pull the team together on their goals of individual improvement and team success. "Swimming is a sport that makes it easy to feel part of something," Kaitlyn explained. "It has both an individual and a collective component. We could celebrate the success of individual swimmers after each meet and also point to the impact this had on the team's success. We made it a point to help them see that connection, to make them feel part of something bigger than their individual success or loss in each race."

As they worked to create a clear set of goals for each swimmer and for the team, Kevin and Kaitlyn took the time to understand each swimmer's strengths, challenges, and potential for contributing to the team's performance. With this knowledge they could encourage each swimmer individually and celebrate their accomplishments with the rest of the team. "The first practice after each meet was always a game day," the coaches told us.

> We'd talk about the successes of the meet—there were always some, even if we lost the match—and then spend time just having fun in the water, being together and celebrating the hard work they'd all put in to get ready for the meet and the way they'd supported each other. It was fun and pulled the team together.

Celebrations—from swim teams to work teams; across homes, families, communities, and organizations; and around the globe—are an important part of what it takes to make extraordinary things happen. People take time off from classes or work to gather to mark an important occasion. They march in elaborate parades down the city's main street to shower a championship team with cheers of appreciation. They set off fireworks to commemorate great historic victories or the beginning of a new year. They convene impromptu ceremonies to cheer the victories of their colleagues. They attend banquets to show their respect for individuals and groups who've accomplished an extraordinary feat. They get all dressed up in tuxedos and gowns—and sometimes in very silly costumes—to rejoice at the passing of another season. They sit down at elaborate feasts to give thanks for the bountiful harvest. They get together with classmates at the end of a capstone project, give each other high-fives for a job well done, and make plans to get together and celebrate. And in tragic times, people come together in eulogy and song to honor those who showed courage, conviction, and sacrifice.

People take the time to come together, tell stories, and raise their spirits because celebrations are among the most significant ways people all over the world proclaim respect and gratitude, renew a sense of community, and remember shared values and traditions. Celebrations are as important in defining a group as the things that make up their day-to-day existence.

Performance improves when leaders on campus, in communities and corporations, publicly honor those who have excelled and who have been an example to others. That is why exemplary leaders make a commitment to Celebrate the Values and Victories by mastering these essentials:

- Create a spirit of community
- Be personally involved

When leaders bring people together, rejoice in collective successes, and directly display their gratitude, they reinforce the essence of community and commitment. They strengthen in others the courage required to get extraordinary things done.

CREATE A SPIRIT OF COMMUNITY

Human beings are social animals—hardwired to connect with others.[1] We see this all the time on campuses around the world. Students have a desire to connect with other students and the result is student government, fraternities and sororities, honor and service societies, intramural sport teams, and the like. People are meant to do things together and to form communities. When social connections are strong and numerous there's more trust, information flows freely, people help each other out, they work together, and they are happier.

One of the rules Kevin and Kaitlyn lived by was that the Hurricanes team was about more than swimming. It was about a spirit of good health, fun, friendship, and support. They made it a point to create opportunities to do things together outside of practice and meets. "We did outside activities for the whole team, like a car wash fundraiser," they told us. "But we also did things to let the different age groups connect. We did movie night for the seniors and pizza supper for the little guys. It was fun for everyone to be together away from the pool."

Exemplary leaders know that promoting a culture of celebration fuels a sense of unity. Whether they're to honor an individual or group achievement or to encourage team learning and relationship building, celebrations, ceremonies, and similar events offer leaders the perfect opportunity to communicate and reinforce the actions and behaviors that are important in realizing shared values and shared goals. Sometimes celebrations can be elaborate but more often they are about connecting everyday actions and events to the values of the organization and the accomplishments of the team. In the college environment, populated by students eager to have fun and "party down," celebrations can, however, lose their potential for these purposes.

Celebrations are not about having a great party. They often contain the same elements as a great party, but it's the additional ingredient that makes them so important. True celebrations contain a clear articulation of the achievements of the members of the group and say in a loud clear voice, "This is what we stand for, this is what we believe in, and this is what we are proud of." Exemplary leaders seldom let an opportunity pass to make sure that everyone knows why they're all together and how they should act in service of the celebration.

Moreover, recognition and celebrations often are not just about what has already occurred and been accomplished, but are held because leaders are using these occasions to build the foundation for continuing contributions still to come in the future.

Celebrate Accomplishments in Public

Kaitlyn and Kevin took the opportunity to highlight the successes of individual team members after each meet. Swimmers who made personal-best times were recognized on a "Hurricane Heroes" bulletin board for all club members to see. The coaches also took time in the first practice after each meet to highlight the contributions of individual or relay wins and personal bests. "We'd let them know the points each win added to the team's score, and give a round of applause for a personal-best time," Kevin said. "That recognition makes a difference; whether it's for a six-year-old who just beat their very first time or a senior swimmer who hasn't set a personal-best time in a long while, the recognition reinforces that their accomplishment matters." As we noted in the previous chapter, individual recognition increases the recipient's sense of worth and improves performance. Public celebrations have this effect as well, and they add other lasting contributions to the welfare of individuals and organizations that private, individual recognition can't accomplish. It's these added benefits that make celebrating *together* so powerful.

For one thing, public events are an opportunity to showcase real examples of what it means to "do what we say we will do." When the spotlight shines on certain people and stories are told about their actions, those individuals become role models. They represent how the organization would like everyone to behave and demonstrate concretely that it is possible to do so. Public celebrations of accomplishment, if done well, also build commitment, both among the individuals being recognized and to those in the audience. Doing celebrations well requires the ability of the leader to point out the accomplishment of the individual, and effectively reinforces that the entire group wins when people excel in this way. Exemplary leaders understand that celebrations are not about making people feel as though there are favorites in the group, but making them feel proud of what they have accomplished as a result of contributions of particular members. They understand how to instill inspiration, not jealousy; the secret is in the word *we*. Leaders might point to individual accomplishments, but they quickly show how one person's excellence contributes to a "win" for all, pulling the group together and reinforcing the sense of community. The process of creating community helps to ensure that people feel that they belong to something greater than themselves and that they are working together toward a common cause. Public celebrations of accomplishment serve to strengthen the bonds of teamwork and trust.

Some people are reluctant to recognize people in public, fearing that it might cause jealousy or resentment. Put these fears to rest. All winning teams have Most Valuable Players, and usually it's the team that selects them. Public celebrations are important opportunities to reinforce shared values and to recognize individuals for their contributions. They give you the chance to say thanks to specific individuals for their outstanding performance, and they also give you an occasion to remind people of exactly what it is that the organization stands for.

Private recognition is a wonderful thing. It motivates and builds the relationships essential for leading others, but it doesn't have the same impact on the team as public acknowledgment. To generate community-wide energy and commitment for the common cause, you need to celebrate successes in public.

You have most likely attended an awards ceremony or banquet, but there are other ways to celebrate publicly, even when you can't get everyone together in the same room. Kenzie Crane created an online "Brag Room." Responsible for overseeing recruitment for all the sororities at her campus, she worked with a team of twenty recruiters, and the Brag Room was the way she made an opportunity for people to be recognized "publicly" by their peers. Setting it up on the Internet was easy enough but the key was making sure that everyone understood the intention of the space and participated. The Brag Room's message was: "Here's where we want you to share the stories about someone you've seen doing something that made you proud to be associated with that recruiter, and with recruiters in general." Lots of stories, and appreciations, were posted. There was a posting about how someone dealt with a medical emergency in a special way; another acknowledged someone making an important introduction; and others gave examples of people going out of their way to stand up for the sorority system. All those stories, Kenzie said, "really made us all feel great and proud of the work we were doing."

Provide Social Support

Ceremonies and celebrations are opportunities to build healthier groups, to enable members of the organization to know and care about each other, and offer social support. Research across a wide variety of disciplines consistently demonstrates that social support enhances productivity, psychological well-being, and even physical health. Indeed, studies have shown that among undergraduate students, the best predictor of happiness is social support; it is even more important than such factors as GPA, family income, SAT scores, age, gender, or race.[2] Social support not only enhances wellness but also buffers against disease, particularly during times of high stress. This latter finding is true regardless of an individual's age, gender, or ethnic group. In fact, George Vaillant, Harvard professor of psychiatry, who directed the world's longest continuous study of physical and mental health, when asked what he had learned from his forty years of research, said "That the only thing that really matters in life are your relationships to other people."[3]

Take it from Angela Close, who started a school club called Letters to Soldiers when she was a sophomore in high school. One of her teachers suggested that her students write a letter to a US soldier to show appreciation for their service. When Angela wrote her letter she included a few facts about herself plus "some cheesy jokes" and events that were happening around her town and condolences for the loss of friends in the line of duty. It took nearly five months for her to get a response, but that letter was filled with gratitude for her caring and sharing. The reply was from Marine Gunnery Sergeant A. J. Pascuiti, who had graduated from her same high school. He said, "It was the nicest thing anyone has ever done for me. Although they may never physically get to see how they change lives, they are doing something that is helping soldiers who are out on the front lines, it validates what we do." From that moment Angela knew she had to continue sending letters to soldiers abroad. She officially started the letter-writing club and it has been growing ever since. The club members receive very few letters back but that is not the goal. Their purpose is to offer the support and connection they believe the soldiers who are serving the nation deserve. As one student explained, "I feel like it's a small way to change the world."

Social support is not just good for your physical and mental health. It's also vital to outstanding performance. You have probably heard a class valedictorian's presentation, at your own or someone else's graduation. You may not remember the exact message, but if you recall the spirit of the speech it was most likely one of appreciation for the support along the way, gratitude for the friendships and meaningful relationships that led to the speaker's success, and optimism for the future of his or her classmates. These sentiments are quite consistent with what researchers found when analyzing the speeches of baseball players when they were inducted into the National Baseball Hall of Fame. As elite athletes, they had achieved the highest recognition in a field demanding top physical skills. Yet for almost two-thirds of them their words of appreciation were about such factors as emotional support and friendship. And social support was mentioned even more prominently by those elected in their very first year of eligibility.[4]

What's true at home, in the community, and on the playing field is just as true for student organizations. People who have friends at work, or on their team, or in their classes are more productive, and feel informed and comfortable sharing ideas; they report not only being more creative, but they also have more fun in these activities and get more done in less time.[5] Think about how these findings translate to the activities you are involved in as a leader. Isn't it more fun to work side by side on an event with people you know, trust, and can laugh and share with? Doesn't it feel as though you get more done when you are communicating with people you understand and appreciate? Leaders find every opportunity to strengthen the relationships in their groups, not only because it helps get the job done, but also boosts the group's spirits and well-being.

Our files are full of personal-best leadership cases in which strong human connections produced spectacular results. Extraordinary accomplishments are achieved when everyone gets personally involved with the task and with other people. When everyone feels a strong sense of connection to the people in their group they're much more likely to have a higher sense of personal well-being, to feel more committed to the organization, and to perform at higher levels. When they feel distant and detached they're unlikely to get anything done at all.[6]

Leaders understand that what makes people most miserable is being alone. Celebrations provide concrete evidence that individuals aren't alone in their efforts, that other people care about them, and that they can count on others. People are reminded that they need each other, that their work gets done because they're connected and caught up in each other's lives. Kenzie Crane told us about how when sorority rush is completed at her school, everyone meets together in a large open space on campus to welcome their new members. All the recruiters she had worked with came to this event, and had the chance to see the results of their hard work. "I looked around and saw all the recruiters, some in tears, some holding hands, all of them smiling,"

Kenzie told us. "We had done good work and so many were benefitting. That event really helped them see that."

Invest in Fun

Every personal-best leadership experience was a combination of hard work *and* fun. In fact, most people agreed that without the enjoyment and the camaraderie that they experienced with others on the team, they wouldn't have been able to sustain the level of intensity and hard work required to do their personal best. People simply feel better about the work they are doing when they enjoy the people they're working with.[7]

Having fun sustains productivity because it lightens the load. And it's not all about parties, games, festivities, and laughter. Leaders who make addressing challenging issues fun are clearly passionate about their purpose, what they believe in, and how they pass this on to others. They understand that the work required to meet the dreams and goals of the group can be difficult and demanding, and that people need a sense of personal well-being in order to go the distance. And leaders set the tone.

John Gray was a resident assistant (RA) in the Honors Program at his southwestern US college, where student-created events were put on throughout the year to help bring members together as a community. John was responsible for creating and supervising one of these events, which was scheduled to take place fairly late in the school year. Because the school calendar was issued early in the year, when the details of many events were not finalized, his event was simply listed on the calendar as "John Gray Day."

As the date approached, John found himself wondering what kind of event to create. Many fun events took place at the beginning of the school year, but they tended to have a more educational focus to get everyone off on the right foot. "I felt like it was time to get together to just have fun," John told us. But he still wasn't clear on what he wanted to plan. Then John noticed that people were getting curious about what was on the calendar, asking one another, "What is John Gray Day?" He decided to build on the mystery and just have fun with it.

The whole point of these events was to bring people together and so John began to hatch plans for an event to be simply called "John Gray Day." Don't think this was a product of arrogance or self-absorption; it was John's way to play on people's curiosity and reward them with a lot of fun. "It didn't hurt that John already had a reputation as a warm, funny, engaging guy," Resident Community Director Michelle Madsen told us. "People were drawn to him. They'd wait outside their rooms when they knew he was doing rounds just to talk with him and laugh. That's the kind of appeal he had and it meant that people anticipated that John Gray Day would be like him—fun—and it was."

John Gray Day was a big hit, offering lots of entertaining ways for students to get involved in the festivities. John assembled a bunch of people's baby pictures, including some of himself, and held a contest to "find the real John Gray." He made copies of black-and-white pictures of himself that people could color in. There was a chocolate fountain, and lots of food from a local restaurant. "Everyone had a good time," Michelle told us, "but what I remember the most is the laughter."

John created a space for people to come together and have fun, being themselves, being part of a community. John Gray Day spoke to the spirit of the Honors community: they work hard, but they want to have fun and enjoy each other too.

John's investment in fun proved to be a powerful one. John Gray Day took on a life of its own and continued for the next three years that John was an RA. Each year, people got more excited about it and the energy grew. Students even created a "Flat John Gray" and took it to different locations, even over the summer, to capture their adventures with John Gray and then post them for their fellow Honors Program classmates to see. John has graduated and gone on to medical school, but as a student leader he has left a legacy: John Gray Day will continue. "I've promised to Skype in," John says. "I hope I can do it for years to come if it keeps the event going."

When leaders openly demonstrate the joy and passion they have for their organizations, team members, and challenges, as John did, it sends a very loud message to others that it's perfectly acceptable for people to engage in PDPs—public displays of playfulness; it is more than okay to show enthusiasm and have fun while you are doing the sometimes hard work of getting extraordinary things done.

GET PERSONALLY INVOLVED

People are much more likely to join groups and commit themselves to projects that are led by those with whom they feel a personal attachment. Model the Way was the starting point for our discussion of what students are doing when they are at their personal bests as leaders; we've now come full circle. If you want others to believe in something and behave according to those beliefs, you have to Encourage the Heart by being personally involved.

While enrolled in college, Kyle Harvey was coaching a local high school basketball team. At the end of the first season he got some feedback from the team and their families that he had been focusing more on the negatives than the positives during games and practices, and it was affecting the players' enthusiasm and commitment. In his second year of coaching Kyle was determined to be more upbeat and focus on developing his players, not only on the basketball court but also as individuals.

On the first day of practice, Kyle told the team that he intended to be positive and said that he hoped that the team would do the same, keeping an eye out for the things that their fellow players did that were helping the team. As a result Kyle got much more personally involved with the athletes and this helped him discover even more positive qualities in his players. He began recognizing them much more for what they were doing well rather than pointing out what they were doing wrong—and he did it out loud, for the whole team to hear.

Over time Kyle observed the team working harder and holding *each other* to higher standards. He told us, "I could tell that when I was celebrating positive contributions, whether or not the individual played in the game, it boosted that player's confidence and gave us extremely positive results." Kyle saw this change in the many members of the team. One example was a kid who had really been struggling with the game. Kyle spent time getting to know this player better, made it a point to be patient, and concentrated on applauding the improvements in his game and the successes he was having. As a result, the young athlete's performance improved dramatically and subsequently had a huge impact on the success of the team. This experience proved to Kyle that getting more engaged with his players and recognizing their individual contributions to the entire team resulted in stronger relationships with each player and greater individual development, and thus advancement of the team as a whole.

If you want to build and maintain a culture of excellence and distinction, then you have to do as Kyle did: recognize, reward, reinforce, and celebrate exceptional efforts and successes. And you have to get personally involved in celebrating the actions that contribute to and sustain the culture. If you want people to have the courage to push through the tough times, you have to encourage them yourself.

Getting personally involved puts the spotlight on connecting what you preach with what you celebrate. If they are not one and the same, your celebrations will come off as insincere and phony—and your credibility will suffer. Recognition events and celebrations must be an honest expression of commitment to key values and to the hard work and dedication of the people who have lived the values. Remember, it's not just another chance to party. Treat it that way and you lose one of the best opportunities you have as a leader to pull people together, help them feel great about being part of the group, and inspire them to keep going. Elaborate productions that lack sincerity or do not connect in some clear way to the values of the group are more entertainment than encouragement. It's authenticity that makes conscious celebrations work.

When it comes to sending a message throughout the organization, nothing communicates more clearly than what you do as a leader. By directly and visibly showing others that you're there to cheer them along, you're sending a positive signal. When you set the example that communicates the message that "around here we say thanks, show appreciation, and have fun," others will follow your lead. The group will develop a culture of celebration and recognition. Everyone becomes a leader, everyone sets the example, and everyone takes the time to celebrate the values and the victories. As Kyle learned with his basketball team, when leaders are encouraging, others follow their example, and an organization develops a reputation that is magnetic.

Show You Care

Leaders make sure that people know that they are being paid attention to and not being taken for granted. Take it from David Braverman. Iowa summers can be brutally hot, and before heading off to college, David found himself in an organic tomato field supervising an eclectic group of people—two other college students, a teacher interested in learning about organic farming firsthand, an "aging gentleman" who had dabbled at various careers and thought this one might be interesting, and a local health food store employee who had decided to stray from the air conditioning on this particular day to pick tomatoes. As the day wore on, this crew became demoralized and David sensed that they were about ready to quit. He realized that they needed someone to care about them; they needed encouragement if they were going to continue. With this epiphany, David said:

> First I ran from the tomato fields and got all my coworkers an ice-cold glass of lemonade. Next, I explained to them that I knew the work was tough and that the day was hot but that we needed to finish the tomato harvest so as to eliminate any possibility of tomato rotting. I asked them to stay positive. I then pointed out their strong suits as farm workers. I told them to look and see all of the tomatoes we had already harvested and how close we were to completing our task. We were in this together; we were all sweating as one. I thanked them for their help and explained that we were well capable of completing the task and that the faster we did so the faster we could be by the nearest swimming pool.

They did finish the job that afternoon but David says that the lesson from this experience was profound: "When people are down and demoralized they need to be picked up and encouraged. Every person needs to be valued not just for themselves as a person but for their contribution to the team. Showing that you care about someone is a simple yet overlooked quality to the success of a leader," he told us.

What David says is true enough, but also true is that one of the most significant ways in which leaders show others that they care is to be there with them—as David was. Thank-you notes and e-mails expressing your appreciation are important, but being visible makes you more real, more genuine, more approachable, and more human. You show you care when you spend time in the fields yourself sweating, when you are there helping to set up for an event and cleaning up afterward, and when you are attending meetings, work sessions, and organizational functions even when you're not directly responsible. Being there also helps you stay in touch, quite literally, with what's really going on. And it shows you walk the talk about the values you and others share. Credibility goes up when leaders show they care.

Spread the Stories

Storytelling is how people pass along lessons from person to person, generation to generation, culture to culture. Stories aren't meant to be secret; they're meant to be told. And because they're public, they're tailor-made for celebrations. The stories that leaders tell have much the same impact as the stories that parents tell their children, in the sense that the stories chosen provide a viewpoint about what is important and what matters, or not. The content of the stories underscores what values are important and the actions that matter. They help set a both a moral and practical compass."[8] In fact, you can think of stories as celebrations, and celebrations, in turn, are stories.

Being part of the action by showing that they care and getting personally involved in celebrating the group's achievements gives leaders the opportunity to both create and find stories to share. First-person examples always have more impact than third-party examples. It's that critical difference between "I saw for myself" and "someone told me about." Exemplary leaders are constantly on the lookout for "catching people doing things right," and this is difficult to do if you are not out where the action is. Telling a story quickly translates information about how people are actually supposed to act and make decisions.[9]

Stories by their nature are public forms of communication. When you shine the spotlight on someone who's lived out an organizational value you provide others with an example they can emulate. Well-told stories reach inside people and pull them along. They simulate the actual experience of being there and give people a compelling way of learning what is really important about the experience. Reinforcing them through celebrations deepens the connections.

Make Celebrations Part of Organizational Life

One of the Hurricanes swim team's traditions was the Awards Banquet at the end of the season after the League Championship. The swimmers all looked forward to the slide show of candid shots of the team taken throughout the year. Co-coaches Kaitlyn and Kevin also saw the Awards Banquet as an opportunity to reinforce the messages and values shared throughout the season and a chance to celebrate individual and team excellence. "We made a 'paper plate' award for each swimmer," they told us.

> We handed the award plate out with the final stats for the season on it. It also had a name or title we assigned to each swimmer based on their unique personality and contribution to the team. For example, an eight-year-old boy who was always giggling and making people laugh might get the name "Lucas the LaughMaker." A swimmer who had made huge strides during the season might be called "Bonnie the Buzzsaw." Sometimes I think they looked forward to those plates more than the ribbons and trophies. It was fun for us to get ready for the event and really reinforced what summer swim league is all about.

You need to put celebrations on your calendar, just like the Hurricanes do with their Awards Banquet. You schedule celebrations for birthdays, holidays, and anniversaries and you should do it for the important markers in the life of your student organization. Giving them a date, a time, and place announces to everyone that these milestones matter to you, and they should matter to the group. It also creates a sense of anticipation. Scheduling celebrations doesn't rule out spontaneous events; it just means that certain occasions are of such significance that everyone needs to pay attention to them, and remember why they are special.

That's just what they do at Notre Dame University. For one class-free week, seniors have the opportunity to stay on campus and celebrate their years at Notre Dame with their friends. As many members of the graduating class as possible get together to celebrate four years of friendship, fun, and studying. Some Senior Week traditions are carried over from year to year: the traditional kick-off barbeque, the Commencement Ball put on by the Senior Class Council with an estimated 1,500 students in attendance, and attending a Chicago Cubs game. The 2012 senior class president, Anne Huntington, said Senior Week is a perfect way for seniors to have fun and spend a great week together: "We saw Senior Week as a way for us to try and hit on all the different aspects of our time here together one last time and celebrate."[10]

Previous Class Councils have planned trips off campus to entertainment sites like Cedar Point and the Indiana Dunes, but these trips had not been well attended due to weather and costs, so they were removed from the Senior Week schedule for her year as president, Anne said. "We were trying to cut costs and thinking about what was best for 2,000 people and not the 350 that could go; this week was about all of us celebrating," she explained.

What they did instead was give seniors a behind-the-scenes look at some famous campus landmarks they could not access as undergraduates. "We offer seniors a chance to celebrate their new status together," Anne said, "seeing places on campus . . . like the tunnels, the fourteenth floor of the library, the stadium press box and locker rooms, places traditionally off limits to undergraduates."

The final traditional Senior Week event is the seniors' last visit to the school's Grotto and Basilica. That last Grotto trip can be a very emotional experience for graduating seniors, Anne explained.

> This is always the Thursday night before Commencement. It's time for the class to come together one last time to pray and reflect before Commencement. It's usually the kicker. If you haven't cried yet, you're going to cry there. I cried last year and I wasn't even graduating.

In setting up celebrations, leaders like Anne make it their task to decide which organizational values, events of historical significance, or specific successes are of such importance that they warrant a special ritual, ceremony, or festivity. In planning your own celebrations, perhaps you want to honor the group or team of people who started your organization or created an amazing event; maybe you want to praise those who gave amazing levels of community service, or thank the parents and families of the members of your organization. Whatever you wish to celebrate, formalize it, announce it, and tell people how they become eligible to participate.

You need to have, at a minimum, one celebration that draws attention to the key values of your organization. It could be based upon the calendar, such as the date the organization was founded or reunion times like homecoming. You could celebrate special achievements, such as winning an intramural championship, receiving a student government award, or hosting a community event. Member initiation or graduation, or the installation of officers, can provide other opportunities to celebrate. Perhaps you can link your celebration with other campus events like your school's "big game," parents or alumni weekend, or even national holidays like Martin Luther King Day or The National Day of Service. Data from the Student Leadership Practices Inventory clearly shows that how people feel about their organizations is a direct result of the extent to which they report their leaders finding ways to celebrate accomplishments.

There really is no shortage of opportunities to bring people together to celebrate your group's values and the victories. In good times or bad, gathering together to acknowledge those who've contributed and the actions that have led to success signals to everyone that it is well worth the effort. Their well-being, and yours, will be all the better for it.

TAKE ACTION: CELEBRATE VALUES AND VICTORIES

Celebrating together reinforces the fact that extraordinary performance is the result of many people's efforts. By visibly and publicly celebrating the team's accomplishments, leaders create community and sustain team spirit. By basing celebrations on consistency with key values and milestones achieved, leaders reinforce and sustain people's focus.

Social interaction increases individuals' commitments to the standards of the group and has a profound effect on people's happiness. Intimacy heals; loneliness depresses. When people are asked to go beyond their comfort zones, the support and encouragement of others enhances their resistance to stress and resiliency.

Leaders set the example by getting personally involved in celebration and recognition, demonstrating that encouraging the heart is something everyone should do. Telling stories about individuals who have made exceptional efforts and achieved outstanding successes provides role models for others to emulate. Stories make people's experiences memorable, often even profound in ways that they hadn't envisioned, and serve as a guide for future action. Making personal connections with people in a culture of celebration also builds and sustains credibility. It reinforces the sense of "we" within the group. Leaders make it a point to bring people together to bear testimony about what has been accomplished as a result of their collective efforts.

Here are actions you can start doing to even more effectively *celebrate the values and victories by creating a spirit of community:*

- Find and create occasions to bring people together.
- Make sure to relate the fundamental principles that are being honored when you bring people together to celebrate.
- Think and plan how you can take some time at a future group event or meeting to share a success.
- Find out about people's stories—what they are doing to make the organization successful.
- Keep a journal so that you can capture (and remember) examples of exemplary performance.
- Never pass up any opportunity to publicly relate true stories about how people in your group went above and beyond the call of duty.
- Anywhere you interact with others is an acceptable venue for telling a good story. Err on the side of telling stories in a timely fashion rather than saving them up for some special occasion.
- Make sure that people understand how they are "part of the whole" and that lots of others are working to make them successful, even if they don't know them personally.
- Repeat this phrase at every celebration: "We are in this together."
- Plan a festive celebration for even the smaller milestones that your team reaches or the efforts people put forth. Don't wait until the whole project is completed before you celebrate.
- Have fun when you're celebrating—laugh and enjoy yourself, along with others.
- Set aside at least one day as a distinctive organizational celebration day, and remind people why it is important to remember and mark this day as special.
- End each of your team meetings with a round of public praise, being sure to play around with ways to keep this ritual fresh, meaningful, and genuine.

NOTES

1. D. Brooks, *The Social Animal: The Hidden Sources of Love, Character, and Achievement* (New York: Random House, 2011). Social psychologist Elliot Aronson has written the most widely read and most accessible textbook on the dynamics of human behavior in social settings. See E. Aronson, *The Social Animal*, 11th ed. (New York: Worth Publishers, 2011).
2. S. Achor, *The Happiness Advantage: The Seven Principles of Positive Psychology That Fuel Success and Performance at Work* (New York: Crown Books, 2010), 176.
3. J. W. Shenk, "What Makes Us Happy?" *The Atlantic* (June 2009). Available from http://www.theatlantic.com/magazine/print/2009/06/what-makes-us-happy/7439/
4. R. D. Cotton, Y. Shen, and R. Livne-Tarandach (2011), "On Becoming Extraordinary: The Content and Structure of the Developmental Networks of Major League Baseball Hall of Famers," *Academy of Management Journal* 54, no. 1: 15–46.
5. T. Rath, *Vital Friends: The People You Can't Afford to Live Without* (New York: Gallup Press, 2006), 52. See also T. Rath and J. Harter, *Well Being: The Five Essential Elements* (New York: Gallup Press, 2010), 40–43, for an update on this research. Also see: R. Wagner and J. K. Harter, *12: The Elements of Great Managing* (New York: Simon & Schuster, 2006) for a follow-up report on the Gallup engagement research, including a discussion of the importance of having friends in the workplace.
6. R. F. Baumeister and M. R. Leary, "The Need to Belong: Desire for Interpersonal Attachment as a Fundamental Human Motivation," *Psychological Bulletin* 117 (1995): 497–529; H. W. Perkins, "Religious Commitment, Yuppie Values, and Well-Being in a Post-Collegiate Life," *Review of Religious Research* 32 (1991): 244–251; D. G. Myers, "The Funds, Friends, and Faith of Happy People," *American Psychologist* 55, no. 1 (2000): 56–67; and S. Crabtree, "Getting Personal in the Workplace: Are Negative Relationships Squelching Productivity in Your Company?" *Gallup Management Journal*, (June 10, 2004). Available from www.govleaders.org/gallup_article_getting_personal.htm
7. See, for example, Myers, "The Funds, Friends, and Faith of Happy People"; M. Csikszentmihalyi, "If We Are So Rich, Why Aren't We Happy?" *American Psychologist* 54 (1999): 821–827; D. G. Myers and E. Diener, "The Pursuit of Happiness," *Scientific American* 274 (1996): 54–56; and D. Gilbert, *Stumbling on Happiness* (New York: Knopf, 2006).

8. D. Westen, *The Political Brain: The Role of Emotion in Deciding the Fate of the Nation* (New York: Public Affairs, 2008), 28.
9. For more on the importance of storytelling and decision making see: G. Klein, *The Power of Intuition: How to Use Your Gut Feelings to Make Better Decisions at Work* (New York: Crown Business, 2004). After studying professionals in life-and-death situations, Klein concludes that "The method we found most powerful for eliciting knowledge is to use stories."
10. A. Boarini, "Graduating Students Celebrate Senior Week Traditions," *The Observer* (May 16, 2012). Available from http://www.ndsmcobserver.com/news/graduating-students-celebrate-senior-week-traditions-1.2872336#.Ub9aubTsdJU

12

A Call to Action for Young Leaders

We have shared many stories with you throughout this book that clearly demonstrate the ability of students to lead others, making extraordinary things happen for their schools, their classmates and colleagues, and their communities. We believe each and every one of you is capable of leadership and we hope the stories and examples we have provided help you believe that there isn't anything we've written about that you can't do yourself, if you want to. The Five Practices of Exemplary Leadership gives you the framework to liberate the leader within. But exploring your leadership potential while you are a student is truly just the beginning. Let your time in school be the opportunity to learn about yourself, about how to work with others, and about how to put your heart into doing what you think matters. That's exactly what Tarek Aly did.

Tarek experienced his first leadership opportunity just one week after entering college. His instructor was talking about how serving others was a major part of becoming an effective leader, and Hurricane Katrina had just hit the Gulf Coast. Tarek and a classmate came up with the idea of creating a carnival to raise funds to support the relief effort. In just about a month's time their Emergency Mardi Gras was held and, all told, the students raised nearly $28,000.

This was only the beginning of Tarek's leadership journey. He wanted to do something that could help people in the longer term. The local community was embroiled in a debate about how to feed the homeless in the region, and Tarek saw an opportunity to bring students together to address this issue in ways that hadn't even been imagined previously. With a core group of six students, they targeted Daytona Beach, about an hour away from campus, and every Wednesday they would get together in Tarek's campus apartment and make a bag of peanut butter and jelly sandwiches. Then they would hop into two cars and drive to Daytona in search of anyone they found living on the streets. They didn't just want to feed the homeless. "We wanted to do something that could help transform their lives," Tarek said.

> It wasn't about the sandwiches, it was about relationships. We wanted to have conversations with the people most others ignored. The peanut butter and jelly sandwiches were just the tool to begin these conversations.

This was the beginning of "Hope in Hand" and within just a few months there was a caravan of students driving to Daytona every Wednesday afternoon just to hang out with people on the street and talk to them. Week after week, the students would see the same people and relationships grew. The students got to learn about the experiences and aspirations of homeless people in a way that would not be possible if they were simply working on a soup kitchen line.

Local business owners in the area started coming out into the streets on Wednesdays as well to help out or to just listen to what the students and street people were saying to one another. What had been a relatively invisible population had become people with names and hope. Within two years, other student groups modeled after Hope in Hand sprung up in Gainesville, Jacksonville, Tampa, Orlando, and New York City.

Tarek continued to find other opportunities to make a difference as he moved through college. He became one of the founders of his fraternity and worked in a social services agency as a case manager handling some of their most difficult male teen cases. He became the president of the Multicultural Student Association that served as the campus umbrella group for all of the ethnic student groups. In that role he worked to establish a stronger support system for multicultural students on campus.

Tarek's student leadership career is a wonderful example of the ongoing journey at the heart of exemplary leadership. Leadership is not about a box you check, or a single event. It's an ongoing experience of commitment and service. Like a deep friendship, it gets defined with each interaction and gets richer with time. Tarek summed it up for us this way:

> The key to leadership is being intentional. If you have pure intentions people will rally behind you and everything else will fall into place. I found out that learning goes side by side with knowing who I was as a person and as a leader. I learned what was important to me and how I could use those things to make a difference in others.

YOUR CONTINUING LEADERSHIP JOURNEY

Throughout this book, we've told stories of student leaders, like Tarek and many others, who've made extraordinary things happen. They are from campuses all over the globe. Some were just beginning their academic lives and some had graduated. Chances are you haven't heard of most of them. They're not public figures, celebrities, or megastars. They're people who might live in the room down the hall or in an apartment across the street. They're people just like you.

We've focused on everyday student leaders because leadership is not about position or title. It's not about power or authority. It's not about fame or wealth. It's not about the family you are born into. It's not about being a club president or a team captain. And it's definitely not about being a Superman or Wonder Woman. Leadership is about relationships, and about what you do.

You don't have to look up or out for leadership—you only have to look inward. You have the potential to lead others to places they have never been. But before you can lead others, you have to believe that you can have a positive impact on them. You have to believe that what you do counts. You have to believe that your words can inspire and that your actions can move others. And you have to be able to convince others that the same is true for them.[1]

We're certain that you want to become the best leader you can be, not just for your own sake, but also for the sake of others and for the success of the endeavors you are pursuing. After all, it's unlikely that you'd be reading this book if you didn't. But how can you learn to lead better than you do now? In addition to understanding and utilizing The Five Practices of Exemplary Leadership, here are five more important lessons we've learned from our research that we'd like you to keep in mind as you continue on your leadership journey.

Leadership Requires Deliberate Practice

Nearly every time we give a speech or conduct a workshop, someone asks, "Are leaders born or made?" Whenever we're asked this question our answer, always offered with a smile, is this: "We've never met a leader who wasn't born. We've also never met an accountant, artist, athlete, engineer, lawyer, physician, writer, or zoologist who wasn't born. We're all born. That's a given. It's what you do with what you have before you die that makes the difference."

Let's get something straight. Leadership is not preordained. It is not a gene, and it is not a trait. There is no hard evidence to support the assertion that leadership is imprinted in the DNA of only some individuals, and that everyone else missed out and is doomed to be clueless. There was no way that anyone would have picked out from some catalogue the student leaders we shared with you in this book. None of them got to where they were on the basis of winning any leadership competition.

Exemplary leaders like those profiled in this book know that making extraordinary things happen requires learning. They understand that their learning never stops; it is the fuel that keeps them inspired and enables them to keep going when things don't work out the first time.

Leadership can be learned. It's an *observable pattern of practices and behaviors*, and a definable set of skills and abilities. And any skill can be learned, strengthened, honed, and enhanced, given the motivation and desire, along with practice, feedback, role models, and coaching. When we track the progress of people who participate in leadership development programs, for example, the research demonstrates that they improve over time.[2] They learn to be better leaders. But here's the thing. Although leadership can be learned, not everyone wants to learn it, and not all those who learn about leadership master it. Why? Because becoming the very best requires having a deep desire to excel, a strong belief that new skills and abilities can be learned, and a willing devotion to deliberate practice and continuous learning. No matter how good you are, you have to always want to be better. The truth is that the best leaders are the best learners.

What truly differentiates any expert performer from the merely good ones is hours of practice developing their skills. It doesn't matter whether it's in sports, music, medicine, computer programming, mathematics, leadership, or any other field, you've got to work at becoming the best, and it sure doesn't happen over a weekend or by taking a single class. If you want a rough metric of what it takes to achieve the highest level of expertise, the estimate is on average ten thousand hours of practice over a period of ten years.[3] That's about 2.7 hours a day, every day, for ten years! This may seem overwhelming but the good news is that you can build the practice of leadership into your life right now, inserting it into the activities you already do. Tarek didn't add more hours to his day to deliver those peanut butter and jelly sandwiches. He and his friends had the same twenty-four hours in a day that we all have. They simply chose to use some of those hours in a different way, practicing their leadership skills.

In other words, you have to have a passion for learning in order to become the best leader you can be. You have to be open to new experiences and open to honestly examining how you and others perform, especially when the going gets tough or the future is uncertain. You have to be willing to quickly learn from your failures as well as your successes, and find ways to try out new behaviors without hesitation. You won't always be right or do things perfectly, but you will get the chance to grow.

Leadership Is a Relationship

Leaders never get extraordinary things done all by themselves. As we say in our definition at the beginning of this book, *leaders mobilize others to want to struggle for shared aspirations*, and this means that, fundamentally, leadership is a relationship. Leadership is a relationship between those who want to lead and those who choose to follow. It's the quality of this relationship that matters most when trying to make extraordinary things happen. The leader-follower relationship that's characterized by fear, mistrust, or hurt feelings will never stand the test of time.

When Tarek and his classmate began working on the idea of how to benefit Hurricane Katrina survivors, they were new college students in the first or second week of their first semester. In just about a month's time they had recruited a small core of first-year students to help them, enlisted more classmates to work with them, produced a series of small events leading up to the Emergency Mardi Gras carnival, got local businesses to support them, and attracted other students and community guests to participate in the daylong event. Their fundraising success proved that Tarek and his classmates had come to grips with a key leadership fact: leadership is not possible without a strong relationship with others who will be part of the change effort.

Leadership Development Is Self-Development

Engineers have computers; painters, canvas and brushes; musicians, instruments. Leaders have only themselves and their experiences. The instrument of leadership is the self, and mastery of the art of leadership comes from mastery of the self. Leadership development is self-development, and self-development is not about stuffing in a whole bunch of new information or trying out the latest technique. It's about leading out of what is already in your soul. It's about liberating the leader within you. And it starts with taking a look inside.

Your ability to excel as a leader depends on how well you know yourself. The better you know yourself, the better you can make sense of the often incomprehensible and conflicting messages you receive daily as a student: "Do this, do that, support this, support that, decide this, decide that, change this, change that." You need internal guidance to navigate the turmoil in today's highly uncertain environment. For Tarek it was a summer experience he had in Indonesia that "really changed me. I knew in my heart I would someday find a way to make myself available to help others in times of great need."

There is no shortcut when it comes to knowing yourself and discovering who you are, what drives you, what's important to you, whom you want to serve, and the like. What it takes is self-reflection, and the more you do so the better you come to know who you are, the better your chances of discerning the "pure intentions" that Tarek discovered. When you know who you are then you will find it easier to connect with other people and communicate more effectively about what matters to you. Your leadership becomes authentic—because it is an expression of who you are and not some means to an end. Other students joined Emergency Mardi Gras and Hope in Hand because it gave them, like Tarek, an opportunity to express their best selves, to learn and to grow.

No matter where you are on your leadership journey, you will continually be wrestling with some difficult issues, balancing personal, financial, family, community, political, spiritual, and organizational needs, having to make choices and tradeoffs among mutually compelling values and constituencies. From a leadership perspective here is a sample of questions you need to consider:

- What are the values that should guide my decisions and actions?
- What are my beliefs about how people ought to conduct the affairs of our group?
- What are my leadership strengths and areas for improvement?
- How consistent is my view of my leadership with how others see it?
- What do I need to do to improve my abilities to move the organization forward?
- How clear are others about our shared vision of the future?
- How much do I understand about the group and the place in which it operates?
- What are the challenges we face, and how prepared are we to deal with them?
- How prepared am I to handle the complex problems that now confront my group?

- What gives me the courage to persist in the face of uncertainty and adversity?
- How will I handle disappointments, mistakes, and setbacks?
- What keeps me from giving up?
- How solid are my relationships with those in my group?
- How much do members of my group trust me and each other?
- How can I keep myself motivated and encouraged?
- How am I doing at sharing the credit and saying "thank you"?
- What can I do to keep hope alive—in myself and others?
- Why am I the right one to be leading at this very moment, or not?

Grappling with questions like these is essential to your development as a leader. You can't lead others until you've first led yourself on a journey of self-discovery. If you are to become the leader you aspire to be then you will have to take the time to step back and reflect deeply on your past, your present, and your future.

Leadership Is an Ongoing Process

Learning to be an exemplary leader requires that you build a pattern of practice into your life. You commit to take action, you take action, you reflect on that action, and you start again. This learning loop is available to everyone and the only requirement for making it work is a full heart. It won't always be pretty, but nothing in the research hints that leaders should be perfect. Leaders aren't saints. They're human beings, full of flaws and failings like everyone else. They make mistakes. Perhaps the very best advice for all aspiring leaders is to remain humble and unassuming—to always remain open and full of wonder.

As you move into the next phases of your life there will be ongoing leadership opportunities that are very different from those you are having as a student. You will be able to embrace leadership roles in your professional life, your partnerships, your parenting, and your communities. Tarek built the foundation of his leadership capacity during his collegiate experiences, and they all informed his decision to attend medical school and seize the leadership opportunities he's continued to find there. We suspect that pattern will continue long after med school graduation. The same will be true for you.

Your Leadership Makes a Difference

And here's one final lesson. You may or may not be aware of it, but people are watching you. Right now, whether or not you hold a leadership position in some student organization, or classroom project, or community service group, you are having an impact on the other members of that group, intentionally or not. Leadership comes in many different forms and formats. What you say and do affects others' choice to stay or leave, to be involved or not, to follow through with commitments, to support and celebrate each other, and to share the group's values and vision, or not.

As you continue your journey, if you become a parent, teacher, coach, community or corporate leader, *you* will be the person that's setting the leadership example for a new group of people who will look to you for inspiration. Give up the myth once and for all that leadership is about position and power. It simply is not. Leadership is about the actions you take in a role you embrace, like those described throughout this book, whether or not you hold a position of authority.

Whatever position you hold now or in the future, no matter what role you embrace, we believe in you and all you have to offer the world. Your chances to lead will never stop appearing. They are only limited by your ability to recognize them as opportunities and to choose to accept them. If you can commit to this ongoing learning adventure, if you can keep learning as you lead, and if you can always lead with your heart, you will make a difference.

NOTES

1. For more about how "you make a difference," see J. M. Kouzes and B. Z. Posner, *The Truth About Leadership: The No-Fads, Heart-of-the-Matter Facts You Need to Know* (San Francisco: Jossey-Bass, 2010).
2. B. Z. Posner, "A Longitudinal Study Examining Changes in Students' Leadership Behavior," *Journal of College Student Development* 50, no. 5 (2009): 551–563. See also B. Z. Posner, "The Impact of Gender, Ethnicity, School Year and Experience on Student Leadership: Does It Really Matter?" Western Academy of Management Conference, Santa Fe, NM, March 2013.
3. See K. Anders Ericsson, "The Influence of Experience and Deliberate Practice on the Development of Superior Expert Performance," in *The Cambridge Handbook of Expertise and Expert Performance*, ed. K. A. Ericsson, N. Charness, P. J. Feltovich, and R. R. Hoffman (New York: Cambridge University Press, 2006), 692. Others have also written about this metric, for example: Geoff Colvin, *Talent Is Overrated: What Really Separates World-Class Performers from Everybody Else* (New York: Portfolio, 2008); Daniel Coyle, *The Talent Code: Greatness Isn't Born. It's Grown. Here's How* (New York: Bantam Books, 2009); and, Malcolm Gladwell, *Outliers: The Story of Success* (New York: Little, Brown, 2008).

Acknowledgments

You can't do it alone. It's one of the truths about leading. It's equally true about writing. While the tasks of writing are often lonely and tedious, the pleasures of interacting with our colleagues are always fun and uplifting. One of the great joys of writing a book is the opportunity to work with scores of talented, dedicated, and inspiring people. We are profoundly grateful to them, and we cherish the opportunity go to say "thank you" to all who have joined us on this journey.

Thank you to the thousands of students we've worked with over the years. You inspire us and bring us hope. You give us immense confidence that our future is held in capable hands and generous hearts.

The two people most responsible for the development of this new and expanded edition are Beth High and Gary Morgan. Beth and Gary brought it to life with fresh and exciting cases from the amazing emerging leaders featured in this edition. They also acted as our interpreters, making sure our language spoke to the life experiences of students in today's educational institutions. With her background in instructional design and educational media, and her experience in delivering *The Leadership Challenge* worldwide, Beth added a virtual and a global perspective to the selection of material for this edition. Her passion for creating unique opportunities for young leaders to learn and grow is truly uplifting. Gary has been on the frontlines of educational leadership for the past twenty years, and he's served as a dean, director, and faculty member at campuses with enrollments ranging from twelve hundred to fifty-three thousand. He's directed programs in all areas of campus life. He brought that experience to this edition, and the result is a book that is more relevant and relatable.

As always, we offer our deepest appreciation to our immediate loved ones—to Tae and Nick, and to Jackie and Amanda and Darryl. You bring great joy into our lives. We have witnessed—and experienced—your extraordinary feats of leadership; you have taught us more than we can ever share.

We cannot fully express our appreciation to Leslie Stephen, our developmental editor, our collaborator, our cheerleader, and our "Dream Weaver." Leslie generously and graciously gave us her remarkable talents throughout the project. She pulled our voices together over many long hours, keeping us focused and endlessly offering encouragement and a calm presence. She positioned us all for success and then humbly stepped out of the spotlight. We want to acknowledge her substantial and significant role in this book and offer our deepest gratitude. Leslie, you are a gem!

From the start, Erin Null, editor, Higher and Adult Education, championed this project with her colleagues at Jossey-Bass, an imprint of Wiley. She moved us forward with caring leadership and a gracious guiding hand. Without Erin's passion, persuasiveness, and professionalism this new edition would never have been written. Thank you, Erin, for believing in us and in the value of this project. And when Erin took maternity leave in the final months of production, Alison Knowles, assistant editor, took charge and got us across the finish line with confidence and competence. Other Wiley team members contributed greatly to the success of this edition: Adrian Morgan, cover design; Aneesa Davenport, marketing manager; Cathy Mallon, production editor; Donna Weinson, copy editor; and Paul Foster, publisher.

Thank you also to Karyn Bechtel, Daren Blonski, Amanda Crowell Itliong, Amelia Klawon, David Klawon, Laura Osteen, Jackie Schmidt-Posner, and Lisa Shannon who all provided timely, informative, and challenging feedback on early drafts of the first edition manuscript. On this second edition, Katie Burke, JR McGrath, and Larry Mannolini added their valuable perspectives, enabling important and significant improvements in this new edition. Their sage advice and wise counsel improved both the substance and tone of the final version. We deeply appreciate their insights and nudging.

We want to express our thanks to the community of Certified Facilitators of The Student Leadership Challenge who enthusiastically recommended and endorsed their students and encouraged them to share their stories. We would not have been able to find such a rich wonderful group of young people to profile without their help.

Finally, a special round of applause for all those students whose stories, experiences, lessons, and wisdom make up the centerpieces of *The Student Leadership Challenge*. Thank you for what you've accomplished and for who you are. And many thanks to scores of other students who have shared their experiences with us, even if we couldn't put everyone's stories into this book. We know that the readers of this book will become better leaders as a result of reading about the lessons of your experiences.

We wrote this book, as we have each of our books, in order to liberate the leader that lies within each of us. That's our mission and our passion. Each and every one of us matters. Each and every one of us makes a difference. The real challenge for all of us is to continue to make the difference we intended. Live your life forward.

About the Authors

Jim Kouzes and Barry Posner have been working together for more than thirty years, studying leaders, researching leadership, conducting leadership development seminars, and serving as leaders themselves in various capacities. They are coauthors of the award-winning, best-selling book *The Leadership Challenge*. Since its first edition in 1987, *The Leadership Challenge* has sold more than two million copies worldwide and is available in more than twenty-two languages. It has won numerous awards, including the Critics' Choice Award from the nation's book review editors and the James A. Hamilton Hospital Administrators' Book of the Year Award, and was selected as one of the top ten books on leadership in *The 100 Best Business Books of All Time*. *The Student Leadership Challenge*, in its first edition, has been used in leadership classes and programs in educational institutions and organizations around the globe with college students and youth development organizations.

Jim and Barry have coauthored more than a dozen other award-winning leadership books, including *Finding the Courage to Lead*; *Great Leadership Creates Great Workplaces; Making Extraordinary Things Happen in Asia: Applying The Five Practices of Exemplary Leadership*; *Credibility: How Leaders Gain and Lose It, Why People*

Demand It; The Truth About Leadership: The No-Fads, Heart-of-the-Matter Facts You Need to Know; A Leader's Legacy; Encouraging the Heart: A Leader's Guide to Rewarding and Recognizing Others; and *The Academic Administrator's Guide to Exemplary Leadership*. They also developed the highly acclaimed Leadership Practices Inventory (LPI), a 360-degree questionnaire for assessing leadership behavior, which is one of the most widely used leadership assessment instruments in the world. The student version of the LPI has been used by more than 200,000 students. Over six hundred doctoral dissertations and academic papers have been based on their The Five Practices of Exemplary Leadership® model.

Among the honors and awards that Jim and Barry have received is the American Society for Training and Development's highest award for their Distinguished Contribution to Workplace Learning and Performance. They have been named Management/Leadership Educators of the Year by the International Management Council; ranked by *Leadership Excellence* magazine in the top twenty on its list of the Top 100 Thought Leaders; named among the 50 Top Coaches in the nation (according to *Coaching for Leadership*); included among the Top 100 Thought Leaders in Trustworthy Business Behavior by Trust Across America; and listed among *HR Magazine*'s Most Influential International Thinkers.

Jim and Barry are frequent keynote speakers, and each has conducted leadership development programs for hundreds of organizations, including Alberta Health Services, Amazon, American College of Cardiology, Apple, ARCO, AT&T, Australia Institute of Management, Australia Post, Bank of America, Bose, Camp Fire USA, Central Bank of Barbados, Charles Schwab, Chevron, Cisco Systems, Clorox, Community Leadership Association, Conference Board of Canada, Consumers Energy, Deloitte Touche, Dorothy Wylie Nursing and Health Leaders Institute, Dow Chemical, Egon Zehnder International, Federal Express, Genentech, Google, Gymboree, Jobs DR-Singapore, Johnson & Johnson, Kaiser Foundation Health Plans and Hospitals, Intel, Itau

Unibanco, L. L. Bean, Lawrence Livermore National Labs, Lucile Packard Children's Hospital, Merck, NetApp, Northrop Grumman, Novartis, Oakwood Temporary Housing, Oracle, Petronas, Roche Bioscience, Siemens, 3M, Toyota, United Way, USAA, Verizon, VISA, the Walt Disney Company, and Westpac. They have lectured at over seventy college and university campuses.

Jim Kouzes is the Dean's Executive Fellow of Leadership, Leavey School of Business at Santa Clara University, and lectures on leadership around the world to corporations, governments, and nonprofits. He is a highly regarded leadership scholar and an experienced executive; the *Wall Street Journal* cited him as one of the twelve best executive educators in the United States. In 2010, Jim received the Thought Leadership Award from the Instructional Systems Association, the most prestigious award given by the trade association of training and development industry providers. He was listed as one of *HR Magazine*'s Most Influential International Thinkers for 2010–2012, named one of the 2010–2013 Top 100 Thought Leaders in Trustworthy Business Behavior by *Trust Across America*, and ranked by *Leadership Excellence* magazine as number sixteen on its list of the Top 100 Thought Leaders. In 2006, Jim was presented with the Golden Gavel, the highest honor awarded by Toastmasters International. Jim served as president, CEO, and chairman of the Tom Peters Company from 1988 through 1999, and prior to that led the Executive Development Center at Santa Clara University (1981–1987). Jim founded the Joint Center for Human Services Development at San Jose State University (1972–1980) and was on the staff of the School of Social Work, The University of Texas. His career in training and development began in 1969 when he conducted seminars for Community Action Agency staff and volunteers in the war on poverty. Following graduation from Michigan State University (BA degree with honors in political science), he served as a Peace Corps volunteer (1967–1969). Jim can be reached at jim@kouzes.com.

Barry Posner is the Accolti Endowed Professor of Leadership at the Leavey School of Business, Santa Clara University, where he served as dean of the school for twelve years (1997–2009). He has been a distinguished visiting professor at Hong Kong University of Science and Technology, Sabanci University (Istanbul), and the University of Western Australia. At Santa Clara he has received the President's Distinguished Faculty Award, the School's Extraordinary Faculty Award, and several other teaching and academic honors. An internationally renowned scholar and educator, Barry is author or coauthor of more than a hundred research and practitioner-focused articles. He currently serves on the editorial boards for *Leadership & Organizational Development Journal* and the *International Journal of Servant-Leadership*. In 2011, he received the Outstanding Scholar Award for Career Achievement from the *Journal of Management Inquiry*.

Barry received his BA with honors in political science from the University of California, Santa Barbara; his MA in public administration from The Ohio State University; and his PhD in organizational behavior and administrative theory from the University of Massachusetts, Amherst. Having consulted with a wide variety of public and private sector organizations around the globe, Barry also works at a strategic level with a number of community-based and professional organizations, currently sitting on the board of directors of EMQ FamiliesFirst. He has served previously on the boards of the American Institute of Architects (AIA), Big Brothers/Big Sisters of Santa Clara County, Center for Excellence in Nonprofits, Junior Achievement of Silicon Valley and Monterey Bay, Public Allies, San Jose Repertory Theater, Sigma Phi Epsilon Fraternity, and both publicly traded and start-up companies. Barry can be reached at bposner@scu.edu.

Index

A

Accountability, 196–199
Accosta, Angel, 26–27
Actions: aligning with shared values, 61; disempowering others, 189–190; mobilizing on Facebook, 55–56; supporting team work, 45–46
Affirming shared values, 31–33
African Leadership Academy, 186–188, 193
Alice's Adventures in Wonderland (Carroll), 219
Aligning values with group, 34
Aly, Tarek, 257–259, 262
Animating your vision: making images of future, 101–102; overcoming discomfort in public speaking, 98–99; symbolic language for, 99–100
Appeadu-Mensah, Francis, 186–188, 193, 204–205
Arvita, 3, 5, 6
Axelrod, Robert, 178–179, 185

B

Balanced Man Program, 59–60
Bates, Mykell, 197–198, 200, 204–205
Belge, Christina, 201–202
Blum, Arlene, 124–125
Braverman, David, 247–248
Brown, Brené, 96, 98

C

Cannazzaro, Kara, 47, 48
Carroll, Lewis, 219
Celebrating values: actions for, 254; creating fun events, 244–245; example of, 235–236; finding creative rewards, 227–228; getting involved, 246–247; giving encouragement, 247–248; importance of, 211, 237–238, 253; newsletters for, 239; online brag room for, 240–241; providing social support, 240–243; telling stories, 249, 254; ways of, 253–254
Challenge the Process: actions supporting practice, 132–133, 157; commitments associated with, 15, 133–134; developing skills in, 131–134; leaders who challenge with purpose, 123–125, 130–131; overview, 12–13, 113. *See also* Challenges; Initiative

Challenges: dealing with, 114–116; encouraging initiative in others, 120–123; getting others to join in risk, 138–139; helping others achieve, 203–204; importance of, 113; improving outcome of tasks, 118–119; persistence in face of, 144–145; with purpose, 123–125
Change: encouraging with vision of future, 75; maintaining vision in times of, 84–86
Charisma, 104
Chen, Alvin, 81–82
Clarifying values: actions for, 38; affirming shared values, 31–33; allowing unity to emerge, 36–38; becoming clear on personal values, 24–25; example of, 22–24; finding own voice, 25–27; letting values guide you, 27–28; maintaining community's values, 33–36; sparking commitment by, 30–31
Close, Angela, 240–241
Coaching: developing skills in, 205–207; inspiring confidence with, 199–201; setting aside time for, 208
Coalitions, 30. *See also* Teams
Cole, Kirstyn, 69–70
Collaboration. *See* Fostering collaboration
College for Every Student (CFES), 26
Commitment: driving with values, 30–31; to strengthen others, 189; to teamwork, 166–167; visions that attract, 82–84. *See also* Ten Commitments of Exemplary Leadership
Communications: expressing emotion in, 104–106; genuineness in, 106–108; including images of future in, 101–102; learning power of words, 46–49; methods for celebrating values, 239–240; power of "I Have a Dream" speech, 96–97; practicing positive, 102–104; public speaking, 98–99; sharing knowledge with team, 173–174, 190; speaking in own voice, 28–31; storytelling, 249; using symbolic language, 99–100. *See also* Animating your vision; Storytelling
Community: actions creating, 253–254; building with recognition, 14; creating spirit of, 237–239; involving in celebrations, 247–248; maintaining values of, 33–36; making people feel part of, 90
Competence: building in team, 202–204, 208; coaching to inspire, 199–201; sharing information to raise, 201–202
Competition, 178–179
Confidence: coaching to inspire, 199–201; developing within groups, 35; encouraging, 204–205; sharing information and inspiring, 201–202
Cooperation: choosing competition vs., 179–180; defined, 18; developing cooperative roles, 176–178; involving everyone as leader, 7; projects promoting, 180–181
Crane, Kenzie, 53–54, 70, 239–240, 242–243
Credibility: communicating, 24; establishing, 44; finding own voice, 25–27; leadership founded on, 44
CUBE, 130–131

D

Decision making, 34–35
Defensiveness during feedback, 222, 223
DeJong, Wyatt, 212–214, 222, 226
Delgado, Milko, 4–8
Discouragement, 154–156
Disempowering others, 189–190

E

Eilen, Liz, 221–220, 224–225
Einstein, Albert, 75
Enable Others to Act: actions that, 184, 208–; commitments associated with, 15, 163, 168, 188; overview of, 13–14, 163. *See also* Fostering collaboration; Strengthening others
Encourage the Heart: actions that, 231, 254; commitments associated with, 15, 211, 214; overview, 14, 211. *See also* Celebrating values; Recognizing others
Enlisting others: actions for, 108–109; aligning core values when, 96–98; animating your vision, 98–108; appealing to common ideals, 92–93; building common ground for, 92; connecting to others' values, 93–94; example of, 89–91; expressing your emotions, 104–106; genuineness in, 106–108; practicing positive communication, 102–104
Envisioning the future. *See* Vision
Estes, Kelly, 120–122, 127, 128
Expecting best in others, 215–224; bringing out their best, 189–192; demonstrating faith in others, 216–218; Pygmalion effect, 215, 231
Experimenting: actions to take, 156–158; developing psychological hardiness for, 144–148; example of taking risks, 136–139; generating small wins, 139–148; learning from experience, 148–156; strengthening resilience, 154–156; taking incremental steps in, 141–144
Extrinsic motivation, 77

F

Facebook, 55–56
Failure: coping with, 155–156; handling, 154; importance of, 148–149; inevitability of, 157; persisting beyond, 12–13
Fear: of feedback, 53; overcoming intimidation by adults, 31; of standing out from peers, 24, 25
Feedback: fear of, 53; getting, 222; giving, 223; importance of, 220–222; learning from, 152; seeking, 51–53
Finding opportunities: actions for, 132–134; dealing with challenges, 114–116; encouraging initiative in others, 120–123; exercising outsight, 125–132; making something happen, 117–120; seizing initiatives, 116–125
Firefleyes, 32
Five Practices of Exemplary Leadership: about, 8–10; Challenge the Process, 12–13, 115; Enable Others to Act, 13–14, 163; Encourage the Heart, 14, 211; Inspire a Shared Vision, 11–12, 65; Model the Way, 10–11, 21; positive effect of, 16–17; ten commitments associated with, 15. *See also* Leaders; Leadership; *and specific practices*
Fixed mindset, 151
Fostering collaboration: actions for, 183–184; building trust, 168–171; climate of trust, 167–174; developing relationships, 174–182; example of, 164–167; with face-to-face interactions, 181–182; importance of, 163, 167; meaning of collaboration, 18; promoting joint efforts, 180–181; reciprocity in relationships, 178–180; sharing knowledge and information, 173–174, 190; showing concern for others, 171–172. *See also* Cooperation

Fristad, Bethany, 31–32, 70
Fun events, 243–245
Future: ability to conceive, 69; communicating view of, 98–99; as encouragement for change, 75; envisioning, 11–12, 66–68, 69–71, 73–76; thinking of trends in, 76
Future Farmers of America, 42, 212

G

Gbwardo, Christian, 71, 72–73, 74
Giagliani, Alyssa, 102–103
Gilbert, Daniel, 69
Global Leadership Program (GLP), 136, 138, 142
Gochenour, Anthony, 205
Goff, Jordan, 169–170
Gray, John, 243–244
Grit, 155, 157
Groups: defined, 18; defining values of, 35; developing confidence within, 34; honoring uniqueness of, 32–33
Growth mindset, 151, 152, 155
Guerrier, Fabrice, 89–91, 93

H

Haenel, Michael, 46
Hall, Logan, 114–116, 125–126
Hamm, Bailey, 106–108
Harvey, Kyle, 131–132, 245–246
Hillestad, Grant, 22–24, 34
Hope in Hand, 258
Huntington, Anne, 251–252

I

"I Have a Dream" speech, 96–97
Imagination: developing initiatives from, 67–68; developing vision of future, 75–78; imagining possibilities, 69–71
Improvements: creating climate for, 157; encouraging initiative for, 120–123; expectations improving performance, 218–220; positive contributions and performance, 246–248; questions about continuous, 50; social support contributing to performance, 242; upgrading outcome of assigned tasks, 118–119
Initiative: encouraging in others, 120–123; leadership and seizing, 116–117; making something happen, 117–120; taking risks to create vision, 138–139
Innovative thinking, 125–132; drawing on other's ideas, 125–126; encouraging, 12; expanding your vision, 126–128; finding good ideas, 128–129; viewing experience as adventure, 129–132
Insight Dubai, 149, 151, 153, 176–177
Inspire a Shared Vision: actions that, 65, 86–87; animating your vision, 98–108; appealing to common ideals, 93–94; building common ground, 93; commitments associated with, 15, 41, 68, 93, 109; developing your vision, 69–71; envisioning the future, 11–12, 70–72, 69–71, 73–76; finding common purpose, 79–86; imagining possibilities, 69–71; noticing present, 72–73; overview, 11–12, 65. *See also* Enlisting others; Vision
Intrinsic motivation, 77
Itliong, Amanda, 139–141, 144

J

Janus Effect, 72
Jones, Marie, 149–151, 153
Jordan, Michael, 149
Judge, Elliese, 3–8

K

King, Jr., Martin Luther, 96–97, 98
Korayem, Rana, 57–58, 177
Koser, Kara, 35–36, 228

L

Leaders: actions disempowering others, 189–190; as adventurers, 129–132; asking good questions, 207; believing in others, 215–218; building trust, 168–171, 226–227; challenging with purpose, 123–125, 133–132; characteristics of best and worst, 191–192; communicating unique qualities of group, 94–95; creating unity, 36–38, 237–238; credibility of, 26; developing leadership skills, 263–265; difference made by, 17, 266; drawing on others' ideas, 125–126; effect of Five Practices on, 16–17; empowering others, 190–191; encouraging others, 36, 120–123, 207–208, 247–248; engaging in learning, 152–153; enlisting others in vision, 94; envisioning future, 11–12, 66–68, 69–71, 73–76; expressing positive communications, 102–104; expressing your emotions, 104–106; feeling your passion, 76–78; finding common purpose, 79–86; focusing on values, 49–50; fostering accountability, 196–199; genuineness expressed by, 106–108; having goal that impacts others, 44; helping others feel valued, 216–218; imagining future, 73–76; influence of, 48; learning from past, 71–72; learning power of words, 48–50; maintaining community's values, 33–36; mobilizing others, 262–263; nurturing relationships, 174–176; offering latitude in work structure, 194–196; ongoing growth for, 265–266; practicing leadership, 260–262; promoting learning environments, 153–154; providing social support, 240; psychological hardiness of, 144–148, 153, 154–156; purposeful questions for, 50; redefining status quo, 119–120; risks taken by, 138–139; setting example as, 36, 45–46, 61; strengthening others, 189; structuring projects as joint effort, 180–181; sustenance for, 211; thanking others, 230–231, 248; trusting others, 167–168; values guiding, 28–29; working with others, 163
Leadership: affirming shared values, 31–33; art of, 28; continuing journey of, 259–260; defined, 2; developing skills for, 263–265; effect of Five Practices on, 16–17; as everyone's business, 6; five practices of, 8–10; founded on credibility, 44; how it begins, 5–6; making difference with, 17, 266; making something happen, 117–120; nurturing relationships, 174–176; ongoing process of, 265–266; practice required for, 260–262; questions to consider on, 264–265; as relationship, 262–263; ten commitments, 15; transforming values with, 6, 17
Leadership exCHANGE, 136
Leadership Lab, The, 71, 72, 74
Leadership Practices Inventory (LPI), 51, 62
Learning: becoming active learner, 152–154; creating environment for, 153–154; from experience, 148–156; how to model values, 54; leadership skills, 261–262; from past, 71–72; power of words, 48–50; questions about, 50; to trust others, 167–168

Lee, Sheri, 98
Lee, Tiffany, 216–217
LEEHG (Leadership, Economic, Environment, Human Rights, and Geopolitics) Institute for Foreign Policy, 90, 91, 93, 94
Lenhart, Stephen, 100
Letters to Soldiers, 240–241
Levy, Jenny, 47
Lewis, Kjerstin, 180–181
Listening: acting as facilitator and, 151–152; to feedback, 222; importance of, 81–82; to others values, 35–36; respecting others by, 172; when giving feedback, 223
Living shared values, 44–53
Loeb, Alec, 117–119, 120, 127, 128

M

Madsen, Michelle, 244
McCarthey, Kerrin, 174–176
McDougall, Heather, 136–138, 139, 144–145
Mentoring and coaching others, 205–207
Mielke, Christine, 75, 78
Miles for Kids, 221
Mistakes. *See* Failure
Model the Way: actions for, 39; commitments for, 15, 21, 24–25; communicating credibility, 25; overview, 10–11, 21. *See also* Clarifying values; Setting examples
Molly's Closet, 40–43
Morelli, Kaitlyn, 234–235, 237, 238, 250
Mullenburg, David, 102
Murphy, Devin, 55–56

N

National Society of Collegiate Scholars, 140

O

Opara, Ike, 171–172, 185
Orth, Jade, 79–81, 82
Outsight: drawing on other's ideas for, 125–126; expanding your vision, 126–128; finding new ideas with, 128–129; viewing experience as adventure, 129–132
Ownership: organizing work to build, 202–204; projects to foster, 194–196; promoting perspective of, 208

P

Pascuiti, A. J., 241
Passion: feeling your, 76–78
"Pay It Forward Tour", 22, 23
Peers: fear of standing out from, 23, 24; standing up to, 29
Performance: boosting with encouragement, 247–248; clear goals and rules for, 218–220; feedback on, 220–223; improving with social support, 242; positive contributions improving, 246–248
Personal-best leadership stories. *See* Storytelling
Positive expectations, 219–220
Power: actions making others feel powerful, 190–191; actions undermining feeling of, 189–190; of words, 48–50
"Power of Vulnerability, The" (Brown), 96
Powerlessness, 189–190
Prisoner's Dilemma study, 185
Productivity, 194–196
Projects: creating ownership in, 202–204; fostering ownership, 194–196; promoting cooperation, 180–181
Psychological hardiness: developing, 144–148, 153; strengthening resilience, 154–156
Public celebrations, 238–240

Putz, Taylor, 28–30, 35, 70
Pygmalion effect, 215, 231

Q

Questions: asking about feedback, 222; asking purposeful, 49–50; leadership development, 264–265

R

Ramans, Andy, 229
Reciprocity in relationships, 178–180
Recognizing others: actions for, 230–231; believing in others, 215–216; celebrating publically, 238–240; demonstrating faith in others, 216–218; encouraging others, 14; example of, 212–214, 220; expectations improving performance, 218–220; expecting best in others, 215–224; finding incentives for, 227–230; getting close to people, 225–227; importance of, 211; personalizing recognition, 224–230; thanking others, 230–231, 248. *See also* Celebrating values
Relationship: challenge of fostering, 183; developing cooperative roles, 176–178; face-to-face interactions for, 181–182; fostering, 174–182; leadership as, 262–263; nurturing, 174–176; standards of reciprocity in, 178–180
Resilience, 154–156
Respect: encouraging others sharing with, 36; treating others with, 7–8
Responsibility, 196
Risks. *See* Experimenting
Rossi, Amanda, 145–146, 149
Rudd, Haley, 40–43

S

Saddiqi, Saima, 164–166
Samuels, Dan, 194–196, 202–203, 204
Sanders, Kelissa, 56
Scholl, Josh, 66–68, 70
Self-determination, 189–199
Setting examples: actions for, 61–62; asking purposeful questions, 49–50; focusing on values, 48–49; leaders and, 36, 45–47, 61; living shared values, 46–50; power of words, 48–50; seeking feedback, 51–53; story of, 40–43; teaching others to model values, 53–60
Sharing information: developing team confidence by, 201–202; fostering collaboration by, 173–174, 190
Sigma Phi Epsilon, 59, 276
Small wins: developing plans for, 140–141; psychological hardiness required for, 144–148, 153; taking incremental steps in, 141–144
Smith, Gregory, 173–174
Social media, 54–56
Social support, 240–243
Storytelling: celebrating values with, 249, 254; reinforcing values with personal,
60; sources of, 18; for teaching others, 57–58
Straughn, Kevin, 234–235, 237, 238
Strengthening others: actions for, 207–208; bringing out best in others, 189–192; building competence in team, 202–204; developing others as leaders, 207–208; encouraging self-confidence, 204–205; enhancing self-determination, 189–199; example of, 186–189; fostering accountability, 196–199; inspiring confidence with coaching, 199–207; making their own choices, 192–194; mentoring and coaching others, 205–207; offering latitude in work, 194–196

Student Alliance for a Green Earth (SAGE), 201
Students: actions disempowering, 189–190; actions empowering, 190–191; fostering accountability for, 196–199; making their own choices, 192–194; offering latitude in work, 194–196; overcoming intimidation by adults, 30
Students Stay Leaders Forever (STLF), 22, 23, 34
Symbolic language, 99–100

T

Teaching others, 53–60; learning to model values, 53–54; modeling values in critical incidents, 54–56; by reinforcing key values, 60–61; telling stories as means, 56–58
Teams: aligning actions to teamwork, 48–50; building competence in, 202–204; building trust within, 167–168; celebrating values together, 237–238; commitment to working as, 167–168; cooperating on projects as, 180–181; cooperative roles within, 176–178; developing common goals with, 48; fostering accountability within, 196–199; mentoring and coaching, 205–207; power of language to lead, 48–50; questions about teamwork, 50; reinforcing values of, 48–49; sharing knowledge with, 173–174, 190
Temptalia, 75
Ten Commitments of Exemplary Leadership: about, 15, 16; Challenge the Process, 15, 133–134; Enable Others to Act, 15, 163, 167, 189; Encourage the Heart, 15, 211, 214, 236; Inspire a Shared Vision, 15, 40, 68, 93, 109; Model the Way, 15, 21, 24
Tepper, Ella, 83–84
Thanking others, 228–231, 247
Treating others with respect, 7–8
Trust: building, 168–171, 225–227; collaborative teamwork built on, 183; creating climate of, 167–168. *See also* Fostering collaboration
Truth, 28–30
Tyler, Taylor, 55

U

Unity: allowing shared values to emerge, 36–38; celebration leading to, 237–238

V

Values: affirming shared, 31–33; appealing to common ideals, 93–94; being guided by, 27–28; connecting to others', 94–98; defining group's, 35; driving commitment with, 30–31; focusing on, 48–49; learning how to model, 54; living shared, 44–53; maintaining community's, 33–36; speaking in own voice, 28–30; standing up for agreed upon, 21; teaching others to model, 53–60; ways of reinforcing, 60–61. *See also* Celebrating values
Victories. *See* Celebrating values
Vision: actions that inspire, 86–87; appealing to common ideals, 93–94; attracting people's commitment to, 82–84; basing on past, 71–72; developing your, 69–71; envisioning the future, 11–12, 66–68, 69–71, 73–76; expanding with innovative thinking, 126–128; finding common purpose, 79–86; finding shared, 79–81; imagining possibilities, 69–71; maintaining in times of change, 84–86; noticing present, 72–73; taking action to share, 86–87; taking

risks to create, 138–139. *See also* Animating your vision
Voice: finding own, 25–27; helping others find their, 32

W

Warren, Brian, 59
Wei, David Chan Tar, 95
West, James E., 148–149

Y

Yang, Geoff, 84–85

Z

Zimmerman, Brandon, 197, 200, 204

PRAISE FOR THE SECOND EDITION OF THE STUDENT LEADERSHIP CHALLENGE

"Within the academy, we are constantly seeking additional tools to assist us in teaching the valuable lesson of leadership development for students. *The Student Leadership Challenge* is an excellent resource to assist in the important goal of helping students to become better leaders and, ultimately, stellar citizens in the communities of the world."

—Victor K. Wilson, vice president for student affairs, The University of Georgia

"Student leadership challenges are quite similar to adult challenges, and yet they differ as well—in scale and in the power of peer perspective. Kouzes and Posner have constructed a wide and sturdy bridge across these worlds. My college students will find relevant lessons and great inspiration in the diverse and compelling stories that are retold. We'd have a lot less adult leadership problems if more teachers and students used this great book."

—Dan Mulhern, Distinguished Practitioner of Law and Business, University of California, Berkeley, and author, *Everyday Leadership: Getting Results in Business, Politics, and Life*

"Kouzes and Posner provide a comprehensive, research-based, and values-driven resource that is packed with real-life examples. This book makes leadership highly accessible to college students and is sure to empower the next generation to tap into their potential as leaders and social change agents."

—Jennifer R. Keup, director, National Resource Center for The First-Year Experience and Students in Transition

"The Five Practices has provided a framework for students to reflect on their leadership experience and restructure their philosophy and theories relating to leadership as they challenge themselves through these five practices."

—Amy Kuo Somchanhmavong, associate director, Service-Learning, Public Service Center, Cornell University